THE SECRET HISTORY OF
POLTERGEISTS
AND
HAUNTED HOUSES

THE SECRET HISTORY OF
POLTERGEISTS
AND
HAUNTED HOUSES

From Pagan Folklore
to Modern Manifestations

CLAUDE LECOUTEUX

Translated by Jon E. Graham

Inner Traditions
Rochester, Vermont • Toronto, Canada

Inner Traditions
One Park Street
Rochester, Vermont 05767
www.InnerTraditions.com

Text stock is SFI certified

Copyright © 2007 by Éditions Imago
English translation copyright © 2012 by Inner Traditions International

Originally published in French under the title *La maison hantée: Histoire des Poltergeists* by
    Éditions Imago, 7 rue Suger, 75006, Paris
First U.S. edition published in 2012 by Inner Traditions

Library of Congress Cataloging-in-Publication Data

Lecouteux, Claude.
  [Maison hantée. English]
  The secret history of poltergeists and haunted houses : from pagan folklore to modern
manifestations / Claude Lecouteux ; translated by Jon E. Graham. — 1st U.S. ed.
      p. cm.
  Includes bibliographical references (p.   ) and index.
  ISBN 978-1-59477-465-2 (pbk.) — ISBN 978-1-59477-693-9 (e-book)
  1. Poltergeists—History. I. Title.
  BF1483.L4313 2012
  133.1'42—dc23

                                                                    2011043133

Printed and bound in the United States by Lake Book Manufacturing, Inc.
The text stock is SFI certified. The Sustainable Forestry Initiative® program promotes
sustainable forest management.

10 9 8 7 6 5 4 3 2 1

Text design by Virginia Scott Bowman and layout by Priscilla Baker
This book was typeset in Garamond Premier Pro with Tiepolo and Frutiger used as display
typefaces

Inner Traditions wishes to express its appreciation for assistance given by the government
of France through the National Book Office of the Ministère de la Culture in the
preparation of this translation.

Nous tenons à exprimer nos plus vifs remerciements au gouvernement de la France et au
ministère de la Culture, Centre National du Livre, pour leur concours dans la préparation
de la traduction de cet ouvrage.

Contents

Acknowledgments

Dealing with a subject of this nature would not have been possible without my discussions with various specialists in folk beliefs and popular traditions, as well as experts on the psychic sciences. Their constructive criticism made it possible for me to bring this work to a successful conclusion.

I would like to thank Ronald Grambo (Kongsvinger, Norway), who kept an eye on every step of my progress and was an endless source of encouragement and case histories. With his customary generosity, Philippe Gontier (Graulhet, France) fed me with a constant supply of texts drawn from his plentiful library. Philippe Wallon, a psychiatric doctor, shared his insights with me on a subject that fuels his passion, and Emmanuela Timotin (Bucharest) opened a door to the Romanian domain.

A big thank-you is due as well to my son Benoît for his computer expertise—without his help, how many files might I have lost!

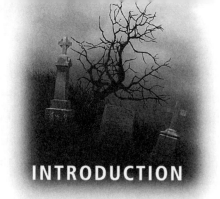

Things That Go Bump in the Night

There are more things in heaven and earth . . . than are dreamt of in your philosophy.

SHAKESPEARE, *HAMLET*, ACT 1, SCENE 5

If we take the time to scrutinize the accounts from popular tradition and even those from literature, we shall find that our world is haunted in thousands of ways! Newspaper headlines regularly feature alleged paranormal phenomena, and television has tirelessly exploited this vein without coming close to exhausting it, simply due to the fact that irrational subject matter has a proven track record. Don't these kinds of things resonate with many people? Haven't divination and predicting the future become acceptable practices over the past few decades and now even commonplace? The devil has made a resurgence, witchcraft remains a vital presence in the rural areas, and talismans and amulets sell as well today as they ever did. In short, humans have hardly evolved at all in this domain, even though Cartesian and Enlightenment rationality has dominated the recent historical landscape. In an irony of fate these rational tendencies have failed to undermine an ancient body of beliefs that merely awaits the opportunity to spring back into life. Recent studies conducted in the 1990s have brought to light the astonishing survival of mentalities thought to have long since been buried in the fog of a medieval obscurantism. Alas, studies of this sort, diligently conducted by ethnologists in the field, do not hold the same appeal for the public at large as do sensational stories.

Because of the ambiguous nature of many people's mental attitudes, everything touching on the "supernatural" and "paranormal" has acquired legitimacy today, and the reasonable voices of objective observers are drowned out by the din created by opportunists and pseudo-experts. In short, readers who approach the subject without any preconceived notions, who are simply seeking to expand their knowledge, are bound to be disappointed because so many of the books dealing with this theme exhibit some combination of naïveté and charlatanism, and the accounts—especially when stirred up by the mainstream media—tend to go overboard in their desire to meet the public's expectations. An event must be sensational if it expects to enjoy any life, even of the most fleeting kind.

The case file on haunted houses is one that deserves to be reexamined and purged of its successive embellishments. It is in fact an extraordinary testament to the different mental attitudes embraced by human beings throughout history. It has the advantage of being a condensation of human hopes and fears, a veritable crucible of beliefs going back to the dawn of time, and an attestation of the relentless quest to provide explanations for anything that is alarming and strange. Mankind's need to explain the world in which we live began very early with simple questions such as "Why is the sea salty?" and "Why are crows black?" and so forth. Each question has often prompted not one but several answers. The same holds true for haunted houses. Confronted by unusual, eerie, or terrifying manifestations, people have sought to name them and determine their cause—the only sure means for reducing the horror felt in the face of the unknown. Identifying the source of the problem is a step toward making it more tolerable, because it can then be countered or eliminated by turning to the man or woman who knows the appropriate rituals, words, and gestures, as well as the objects or plants, capable of bringing an end to the anomalous situation that has been encountered. Depending on the era, these "specialists" were known as magicians, witches, exorcists, or spirits—names that all indicate uncommon knowledge, that is, knowledge regarded as magical by the profane.

Knocking spirits, or poltergeists, represent one of the forms of domestic haunting. Many studies speak of them in passing when they are looking at hauntings in general. This is the case with the book *Haunted Houses* by Richard Winer and Nancy Osborn (New York: Bantam, 1979), centered on the United States and *Haunted Britain: A Guide to Supernatural Sites Frequented by Ghosts, Witches, Poltergeists, and Other Mysterious Beings* by Antony D. Hippisley Coxe (London: Hutchinson, 1973). Older and more precise works include B. Otto's *Die Sprache der Verstorbenen oder das Geisterklopfen* (The Language of the Dead or the Knockings of the Spirits, ca. 1860–1870) and F. W. Rechenberg's *Geheimnisse des Tages: Geschichte und Wesen der klopfenden Geister und tanzenden Tische* (Mysteries of the Day: The History and Nature of Spirit Knockers and Spinning Tables, Leipzig: Otto Spammer, 1853) as well as Robert Papst's interesting study about ghosts in legends and poetry published in 1867. In 1916 Heinrich Ohlhaver studied the life of the dead and their manifestations; in 1920 Felix Schloeny offered the public his book on ghosts titled *Livre des fantômes;* and in 1927 Max Kemmerich investigated ghosts, poltergeists, the double, and the astral body in his book *Die Brücke zum Jenseits.* In 1950 the parapsychologist Fanny Moser devoted a book to the study of these subjects (*Spuk. Irrglaube oder Wahrglaube? Eine Frage der Menschheit**), and Mary Ottinger tackled the ghosts of the British Isles in a 1978 work. These are only a few of the titles that reveal how the English and Germans, more than any other nationalities, have a predilection for all subjects touching on the paranormal.

Among the works that make scientific claims I would point out the studies in French by Camille Flammarion, especially his *Maisons hantées,*[1]

---

*[Phantom: Delusional or Real Belief? A Question of Mankind —*Trans.*]

and in those in Italian by Ernesto Bozzano, who relied on metaphysical journals for a wealth of case studies. Bozzano studied 532 cases of haunting, 158 of which involved knocking spirits. In 105 of these cases various noises were a factor. In the German-speaking countries local poltergeist phenomena are the subject of small monographs, often anonymous, which describe the facts in detail, such as those occurring in Resau in 1889 or in Grosserlach in 1916.

Prominent among the vast number of books devoted to these rapping spirits is the one by the Jesuit priest Henry Thurston. It is distinguished by being based upon rare documentation including old English newspapers, several texts from the Middle Ages, and memoirs. The study extends beyond Europe and into the former British colonies. There is only one flaw, in that it lacks precise bibliographical references that would allow us to verify his sources. Finally, just a short time ago, Philippe Wallon, a doctor of psychiatry and research director of INSERM [National Institute of Health and Medical Research], has provided us with an excellent summation of the whole question.[2]

All of the aforementioned analyses primarily examine events occurring in the period from the nineteenth to the end of the twentieth century. The nineteenth century, the grand era of magnetism, mesmerism, and spiritism, is particularly rich, with a strong concentration of occurrences in the English-speaking world. When it comes to more distant times, the information is scattered through a multitude of texts from which it must be flushed out: lives of the saints, chronicles, clerical literature, dissertations of the sixteenth and seventeenth centuries, and newspapers are a veritable gold mine. Collections of oral accounts, legends, and "folk superstitions" form another avenue of transmission. Novels and literature generally offer only pale echoes that significantly lack the power of the firsthand accounts, which are often collected on the spot by spontaneous witnesses. Thanks to this set of sources it is possible to achieve a phenomenological study of knocking spirits.

The investigator then confronts an annoying problem when assessing this subject diachronically over the course of history. First, the transmission of the accounts is quite uneven depending on the time period, and certain eras are entirely lacking in them. The gaps may be due to my own examination of the data, which I cannot claim to have been exhaustive—one lifetime is far too short a time for such a task!—but may also be due to changes in how the facts are interpreted, which then means their classifications will fall under different headings.

As we will see, the phenomenon of knocking spirits—which were explained in a different manner from how they are today—was formerly attributed to three great agents. It will be necessary to elucidate the relationships between these three players in order to discover the origin of acoustic and other forms of hauntings, as well as the transformations of the belief. For in olden times it was truly a belief—in other words, an act of adherence to the interpretations in which an individual placed his faith. This was rooted in an anthropological basis whose durability is mystifying. The belief may be shared collectively or by a single social or human group. By and large it escapes reason and, when this is not the case, it employs the methods of reason to justify itself a posteriori. It feeds on all that can give it solid standing and legitimacy, constituting itself as a living tradition that ceaselessly discovers new avenues of propagation. And because it is an ancestral tradition, it wields a certain authority: Is it possible for such a large number of people to be deceived or mistaken? The person who asks this question may be overlooking the phenomena of contagion and autosuggestion.

During the course of my investigation I ran in to an unexpected problem. I thought everyone knew what a poltergeist was. Reality taught me otherwise and inspired me to launch an inquiry among my friends, colleagues, and students. I gave the following question to about one hundred people: "What does *poltergeist* mean to you?" Here are the most significant responses:

"I associate the word *poltergeist* with an evil spirit. If I remember rightly there was a role-playing game called this about a dozen years ago. I don't remember too much about the game itself, but I know it revolved around ghosts. I cannot tell you anymore about it!"

J. P., STUDENT

"To me, this word designates a haunted house, in which the haunting manifests not with the appearance of ghosts but by supernatural manifestations (objects moved around, noises, etc.). But I could be wrong!"

T. M., WRITER

"I would say knocking spirits, like in Agobard of Lyon and his ilk!"

J. B., RESEARCH HEAD AT CNRS

"I think a poltergeist is a spirit that manifests through the movement of objects or other physical phenomena. It is generally connected with a particular house. It is traditionally identified as the unhappy or wicked ghost of a former inhabitant, but modern parapsychology tends to establish a connection between these manifestations and the presence of a disturbed adolescent."

L. G., PROFESSOR AND WRITER

"Isn't it a knocking spirit?"

J. P. D., BOOKSELLER

"Right off the bat like this at seven thirty in the morning, without thinking about it, this word brings to mind a rapping spirit who lives in a house and manifests through noises but is not visible. I can say nothing as to its motivations, and I would tend to include it among the local place spirits, displaying its unhappiness with humans who are showing little respect for it or its territory this way."

F. B., LECTURER

"Yes, the term *poltergeist* is very well known among us. In fact, it is inseparable from horror films . . . It can then involve a spirit that makes noises in a house, casts stones, moves furniture, causes accidents or starts fires, and so on. This obviously brings to mind 'haunted houses,' which have been recorded since antiquity."

K. W., PROFESSOR IN TOKYO

"Poltergeist . . . I am mainly thinking of the film by the same name, but to give a definition, that's hard, hard . . . The first thought that springs to mind is the rapping spirit, and that is certainly wrong! In practical terms, I'm in fact thinking of a kind of spirit that haunts a home and makes life impossible for the people unfortunate enough to live there. There is one in *Harry Potter,* by the way, Peeves, who only plays pranks!"

S. H., PH.D. STUDENT

The present study proposes to analyze the evolution and interpretation of poltergeists over the long term, in contrast to the scholars who have, until now, essentially dealt with the subject synchronically by focusing on a particular era. This is the final leg of the investigation I began in 1985 on supernatural beings, one which led me to extensively study elves and dwarves, place spirits, and household spirits.[3] The discovery of the links connecting these creatures quite naturally led to rapping spirits, who, as we shall see, also form a bridge to another field of my research, death and the dead. A certain number of inexplicable facts, which old traditions explained in their own way, led to other approaches at the end of the nineteenth century, notably those of spiritism and parapsychology.

Without forbidding myself any reference to those more recent movements of thought, I am centering this study on popular traditions—traditions that span the centuries and endure despite Cartesian logic or the knowledge of other kinds of beliefs or explanations.

As is my custom, I am going to let the texts speak for themselves and then, with the requisite distance, I will offer an objective analysis of them—an analysis that does not seek to impose any particular point of view. Everyone is free to form their own opinions based on the facts.

1

What Is a Poltergeist?

If we were to look for a definition of *poltergeist* in the standard contemporary French dictionaries, we may be surprised to find that there isn't one. The word is missing from the *Grand Robert* and the *Larousse,* and the *Encyclopaedia universalis* mentions it only once—in a filmography. In France, to find a definition we must refer back to the *Livre des superstitions* by Éloïse Mozzani, who refers to Luther's testimony.[1] On the other hand, we can find knocking spirits under the entry for "spirit" in the *Grand Robert* of 1974, with the following definition: "Souls of the dead who manifest their presence by rapping on the furniture, etc. Spirit, are you there?"[2] This reveals a strong spiritist influence, which was already detectable in 1891 in the *Nouveau Dictionnaire encyclopédie illustré* by Jules Trousset.[3] There, under the entry for "spiritism," we even find the story of the phenomena that struck the Fox family in 1852 (see pages 19–20) and launched the name *poltergeist*. Claude Augé's *Dictionnaire universal encyclopédique,* published in 1897, defines the term as:

> Knocking spirits: souls of the dead who manifest their presence by knocking against the walls, the furniture, or who express their thoughts by knocking a number of times equivalent to the position of the letter of the alphabet they wish to designate.[4]

It must be acknowledged that the notion of dead souls who manifest by making noise is predominant in this definition.

The term *poltergeist* is very well known in the English-speaking world, mainly thanks to a film by Tobe Hooper (*Poltergeist*, 1982) in which a knocking spirit sows terror in the house of a California couple.[5] This film is readily available on DVD. The word *poltergeist* is very well known in Japan and, as my colleague there informs me, "is inseparable from horror films." A television series called *Poltergeist* was aired on the Jimmy Channel in Europe. Currently the novels of James Kahn, the author of the book on which the 1982 film *Poltergeist* was based, are widely available.

According to the *Collins English Dictionary*,[6] *poltergeist* is defined as follows: "a spirit believed to be responsible for noises and acts of mischief, such as throwing objects about." *Longman's Dictionary of the English Language* offers an almost identical definition: "a noisy spirit, generally wicked, believed to be responsible for unexplained noises and physical damage." The *Harrap's New Standard French-English Dictionary*[7] offers "*esprit frappeur*"* as the equivalent for *poltergeist*. *Esprit bruyant* (noisy ghost) is given as a synonym.

To obtain more of a definition, we must refer to books specializing in esoteric studies or spiritism, or else do a search on the Internet. There are countless sites there, some of which—Chaosium and Science et Magie, for example—are quite well informed on the latest theories. The best of the websites is Ouriel, run by psychiatrist Philippe Wallon, a research director at INSERM. The greatest caution is recommended with regard to all other sites. The absence of precise references and means of verification preclude their use in the present study. The same applies to the myriad poltergeist accounts floating around on the Internet, which are totally useless for our purposes as they are completely unverifiable. Separating the wheat from the chaff here is akin to one of the seven labors of Hercules!

---

*[Rapping spirit —*Trans.*]

The "good" Internet sites offer several accepted usages of *poltergeist,* which already infers an interpretation. Some translate the term as "rapping or knocking spirits"—which conforms to customary usage although it is reductive—and conflate our entity with the English knocker and the Welsh *cnocyur,**8* while others translate it as "ghostly spirit," which is too vague or too generalizing.

Multidisciplinary approaches have not truly become accepted in academia, and many scholars do not bother with studying history's auxiliary disciplines, notably linguistics and philology. As a result they handle concepts without defining them and take into account only one meaning out of several, which is a serious methodological error. In all my books I have scrupulously avoided this pitfall, and some have accused me of being more of a philologist than a historian of the way people think, to which I have retorted: "How is it possible to discover mental attitudes without meticulously examining their means of expression?" To not do so would be to deprive myself of a pertinent and effective tool, as the subsequent material in this book will show.

Although they may mention a few accounts of stone-throwing and trouble-making spirits from the remote past, the bulk of the studies on poltergeists concentrate on modern phenomena. However, there are no grounds for assuming that poltergeists somehow spontaneously came into existence during the nineteenth century. There were many such phenomena long before this time, although they may not have necessarily been designated with the term *poltergeist.* Our remote ancestors did not possess our capability for reading facts objectively, but interpreted them subjectively in accordance with their physical and mental environment.

To put together as complete a case file as possible, we must first discover which linguistic terms refer to these phenomena, in order to know where and how to distinguish them in the enormous mass of

---

*More than two hundred years ago, in issue 3 of *Gentleman's Magazine* (1764), it was mentioned that mine workers in Wales were familiar with "Knockers," "a kind of good spirit who were useful but could not be caught. They cannot be seen, but they can be heard at work in the mines."

documents, and then to attempt an interpretation for the reason why such a variety of names exists. As a matter of good heuristics, the linguistic approach is therefore a necessity. I have experimented with it on various occasions, and each time it has opened up new and unsuspected horizons. But in order to grasp how a new word can suddenly emerge as a designation for specific phenomena, it would be helpful to linger for a moment over the cultural context in which it arose.

A SIXTEENTH-CENTURY SPIRIT

The name that designates the knocking spirits of today, *poltergeist,* first appeared in the sixteenth century. To understand how a new concept can suddenly emerge, it is necessary to take a look at the cultural environment surrounding its genesis. A word is created in response to a need to express an idea or fact (*factum*) in some adequate way. When it involves a fact, the latter corresponds to a reality of the times in which those people lived who put the new word into circulation.

It is certainly not by chance that our word appeared in the middle of the sixteenth century, profoundly marked as it was by the Reformation and the polemic that ensued for many long years between Catholics and Protestants. This was a century likewise marked by an extraordinary resurgence of the irrational and superstitious. The people of this era shared a huge passion for spirits, demons, specters, magic and witchcraft, as well as marvels and monstrous births, which were always regarded as signs (*portenta*) heralding catastrophes. A brief survey of the books printed during this time reveals the infatuation with the supernatural.

In 1557 Conrad Lycosthènes published his *Prodigiorum ac ostentorum chronicon* (Chronicle of Portents and Omens), which described a wealth of monsters of all kinds, but it was the 1560 work *Histoires prodigieuses** by Pierre Boaistuau, Lord of Lancy (ca. 1517–1566), that ushered in the vogue of extraordinary narratives. Boaistuau speaks of

*[Miraculous Stories —*Trans.*]

Title page of the 1598 edition of Pierre Boaistuau's Histoire prodigieuses, *a work first published in 1560.*

monsters and devotes his twenty-seventh chapter to "miraculous visions with several memorable stories of specters, ghosts, figures, and illusions that appear at night or day, when waking or when sleeping."

In 1564 Johann Weyer completed his *De praestigiis daemonum* (On the Illusions of Demons), which Jacques Grévin translated in 1567 under the title of *Cinq livres de l'imposture des diables, des enchatements et sorcellerie.** Still in 1564, Jean de Marconville gave the public his *Recueil memorable d'aucuns cas merveilleux advenuz de noz ans,* whose preface forewarns the reader that therein he will find "*monstres hydeux & espouvantables en nature, par lesquelz exemples lon pourra cognoistre qu'il n'y a siècle ny aage qui n'ayt ses merveilles.*"†

---

*[Five Books on the Deceptions of Devils, Enchantments, and Witchcraft —*Trans.*]

†Memorable Anthology of Many Marvels Occurring in Our Time. The preface says: "monsters hideous and frightful by nature, whose examples let it be known that there is no century or age that does not have its own marvels."

In 1569 the Zurich author Ludwig Lavater (1527–1586) published his book on ghosts and other spirits,[9] which was soon translated into French in 1571 and appeared in English in 1572 under the vivid title *Of Ghosts and Spirits Walking by Night and Great and Unaccustomed Noises and Various Presages.*[10] That same year, the theologian Pierre Nodé brought out his *Declamation contre l'erreur execrable des maleficiers, sorciers, enchanteurs, magiciens, devins & semblables observateurs des superstitions,** followed one year later by *De l'imposture et tromperie des diables, devins . . . noueurs d'esquillettes, chevilleurs, necromanciens,*† which was the work of the lawyer Pierre Massé, who tapped in to this same vein while giving the devil a predominant role.

In 1570 Claude de Tesserand added several chapters to Boaistuau's *Miraculous Stories,* the eighth and fifteenth of which dealt with specters, and the ninth with demons. Around 1580, François de Belleforest (1530–1583) expanded Boaistuau's book with another fifteen chapters. Among other things he discussed a phantom that pulled the covers off sleeping victims and a procession of ghosts. Sorcery was the subject of a scholarly treatise written by Reginald Scott in 1584[11] and another by the philosopher Jean Bodin in 1587.[12] Pierre Le Loyer (1550–1634), Lord of La Brosse and judge of the presidial court in Angers, completed his *Discourse des spectres ou Visions et apparitions d'esprits*‡ in 1586. The following year the Provencal Dominican monk Jerôme Cardan examined spirits as well as werewolves, and, in 1588, Noël Taillepied published his *Psichologie ou Traité de l'Apparition des Esprits.*§ In 1590 Pierre Crespet, prior of the Parisian Celestines, offered readers *Deux livres de la hargne de Sathan et malin esprits contre l'homme.*¶ Four years later the Englishman Thomas Nash published his *Terrors of the Night*

---

*[Discourse against the Execrable Error of Evil Spellcasters, Witches, Enchanters, Magicians, Seers, and Similar Observers of Superstitions —*Trans.*]

†[On the Imposture and Deceits of Devils, Seers . . . Braid Weavers, Butchers, Necromancers —*Trans.*]

‡[Discourse on Ghosts or Visions and Apparitions of Spirits —*Trans.*]

§[Psychology or Treatise on the Apparition of Spirits —*Trans.*]

¶[Two Books on the Spite of Satan and Evil Spirits against Man —*Trans.*]

or *A Discourse of Apparitions,* in which he criticized certain beliefs he deemed to be "old wives' tales." The year 1596 saw the appearance of Claude Prieur's *Dialogue de lycanthropy** as well as the book by the Jesuit Petrus Thyraeus (1546–1601), *Daemoniaci, hoc est, de obsessis a spiritibus daemoniorum hominibus* (Demon Possession, that is, of Men Possessed by Demonic Spirits),[13] the first part of which dealt with the spirits of the deceased and persecuting demons. In the second part, "The Booklet of Night Terrors," he tackled the omens and "the commotions that customarily herald the deaths of men."

In the last years of the century, King James I of England (1566–1625) finished his *Daemonologie, in Forme of a Dialogue,*[14] the third book of which is devoted to those spirits that manifest themselves and who are devils. In 1597 Simeone Maioli, bishop of Voltura, mentioned a dead father who returned and tore his child to pieces, a ghost who rejoined her friend in his bed, and many other marvels in his *Dies caniculares* (Canicular Days).[15]

The debate continued into the seventeenth century, during which several important books and translations appeared. The treatise by Pierre Le Loyer was translated into English in 1605 by Z. Jones.[16] Boaistuau was translated into Dutch in 1608, and the Italian demonologist Francesco Guazzo published his *Compendium maleficarum* (Compendium of Witches)[17] that same year. This was also the year that the complete edition appeared of the *Disquisitionum magicarum* (Magical Investigations) by Martin Del Rio (1551–1608), a Jesuit with roots in the Spanish nobility.[18]

In the British Isles, I should mention Richard Baxter's (1615–1691)[19] *The Certainty of the World of Spirits,* and George Sinclair (died 1696), a Presbyterian and philosophy professor at Glasgow University who was not averse to investigating poltergeists.[20] Joseph Glanvil (1636–1680), a Catholic theologian and chaplain to Charles II, collected a number of stories about knocking spirits;[21] and Richard Bovet (ca. 1641–1700)

*[Dialogue on Lycanthropy — *Trans.*]

discussed the Tedworth poltergeist in his *Pandaemonium, or the Devil's Cloyster* (ca. 1661),[22] dedicated to Henry More (1614–1687), professor of theology at Cambridge.

In short, it would be an exhausting task to list every text that appeared on spirits from 1550 to around 1700. It is worth noting that their authors were mainly scholars, learned men, and theologians. Each was fully capable of observing that the problem of demons, ghosts, and other unusual manifestations were one of the major concerns of the day, and from this it is easy to understand why a new name emerged, a term that responded to the need to precisely define a phenomenon that had become a topic of great interest.

THE BIRTH OF A NAME

The term *poltergeist** first appeared in the sixteenth century, initially in the dictionary published by Erasmus Alberus in 1540,[23] and then in the *Tischreden* (*Table Talk;* published 1566) of the well-known figure of the Reformation, Martin Luther.[24] It is obvious that when a word enters a dictionary it is because it already has a life and its usage is spreading. But it also means that its use was not "canonized," so to speak, for a long time; or else it was "suspect" and therefore not collected by the authors of these works. We can, therefore, gather that the term already existed at the end of the fifteenth century. It was first written as two words, *polter geyst,* and then as one word once the meaning was established. The term is composed from the root of the verb *poltern,*† "to make noise," "to tap," and *Geist,* "spirit," which can designate both the devil and demons as well as ghosts and other beings from folk belief. In general, *Geist,* "spirit," is used as a default term—in other words, when uncertainty reigns and people are not entirely sure just what it is they are dealing with. This indetermination is the source of the conflations

---

*Bulergeest in Low German.

†The English translate *poltern* with the verbs *jangle, rumble, bluster, clatter, swashbuckle.*

of different entities and opens the door to the imagination. The interpretation is a result of the knowledge, beliefs, and superstitions of the
witnesses, and—first and foremost—of tradition.

For Luther, the term *poltergeist* essentially designated phenomena
attributed to the devil, assaults, and supernatural noises. The great
reformer mentions these manifestations on several occasions. The first
was in response to a priest who had come seeking his advice when he was
harassed by a spirit of this nature that manifested itself by making all
sorts of noises and by throwing and breaking a good number of objects.

**The story of a poltergeist who was bullying a priest, who asked
Doctor Luther for his advice on how to expel it.**

A priest of Süpz, living near Thorgau, sought Luther while complaining that the devil was causing a din (*poltern*), a fracas, in his house
at night, striking him, and throwing objects with such force that all
his plates and wooden containers had been broken, and never giving
him a moment's peace. Indeed, he cast pots and plates at his head,
which, shattering into pieces, caused him distress. What's more he
mocked at him. More than once he had heard the devil laugh but
never caught sight of him. This game and these manifestations had
gone on for a year, and his wife and children no longer wished to
stay home but set up house in the field.[25]

For Luther this was a devilish illusion that could be dispelled by
prayer!

In a chapter of *Table Talk* titled "The Polter Geysts," Luther reacts
to the opinion voiced one day by Nuremberg theologian Andreas
Oisader, when dining together, that knocking spirits did not exist.
Luther refuted this claim with the help of four personal anecdotes.

Polter Geysts. Oisander claims they don't exist, to which Doctor
Luther responds: "They exist! Oisander always wants to have it his
way. I have observed their existence *propria experencia* (through

personal experience), one day when I was weary from reciting my canonical prayers, a loud noise erupted from behind the stove, which terrified me greatly. But when I realized that it was the devil's play (*des Teuffels spiel*) I went to bed and prayed to God, saying, "*Tu omnia subiecisti sub pedibus eius, scilicet Filii tui.*"* If the Devil has any power over me, let him show it! And I went to sleep.

Another time, when I was in the refectory, such a loud din (*geclapper*) of clattering plates erupted, I thought both heaven and earth must be crumbling to pieces, but I soon realized it was the devil at work, at which point I retired and went to sleep.

A third time I glanced into the garden from the window of my cell after leaving Mass. I then saw a large black sow racing about in every direction although it was impossible for any sow to gain entrance to it. She soon vanished; she, too, was the devil.

The fourth time occurred when I was in Wartburg near Eisenach,† and someone was throwing hazelnuts at me from behind the stove. I soon saw this, too, was the work of the devil, so I went to bed. I personally experienced all this. *Haec vera sunt.*‡26

It will be noted that all these manifestations are attributed to the devil, which is strengthened by the provenance of the noises from behind the stove—case 1 and case 4—a place that in Renaissance-era German was called "hell" (*Helle*).

In another account Luther declares his belief in spirits and states: "Whatever the case may be, it must be acknowledged that people are possessed by the devil, and I have personally experienced wandering spirits who terrify people and prevent them from sleeping, causing them to fall ill."27

---

*[Thou hath put all things in subjection beneath his feet, namely your son—the first part of this phrase is similar to both Hebrews 2:8 and Psalms 8:7. —*Trans.*]
†These events took place in 1521 when Luther was held prisoner in Wartburg. Another account adds that the spirit made a terrible noise on the staircase.
‡["This is true," similar to the words of the angel in Revelation 22:6. —*Trans.*]

This is the context of the first attestations of the word *poltergeist*. Etymologically the term has two translations. The first is "noisy haunting," therefore a primarily acoustic phenomenon. We should recall that the verb *geistern,* which is derived from *Geist,* means "to haunt" and leaves the trouble of designating the cause of the manifestation up to the individual. The second translation is "rapping spirit," which adds a supernatural dimension. In this study I will, however, use "knocking spirit," a time-honored term that avoids any tone of academic snobbery.

THE MEANING OF A WORD

Other words that are built upon the etymon *polter* help us to grasp the primary meaning of the term. *Polterkammer* (eighteenth century) is the word for the "garret," the "junk room," but translated literally means "the room of the commotion,"* and it is here where the household spirit generally hides. A *Polterhammer* is the "planishing hammer or mallet" used by boilermakers, and everyone knows that their activity is rather noisy! Finally we have *Polterabend,*[28] which appeared in German between 1517 and 1534 and designates a custom taking place on the eve of a wedding and that is sometimes translated as "charivari" although there is a notable difference between the two concepts. The guests at the festivities throw and break old dishes in front of the windows or the doors of the future newlyweds' homes, which is supposed to bring them luck and happiness, whereas the French or Norwegian charivari is intended as a noisy condemnation of an inappropriate marriage, such as one between an old man and a young woman. German linguists have produced a seductive hypothesis about the term *Polterabend.* According to their theory it is a contraction of *Poltergeistabend,* "the evening of the knocking spirit," and the behavior of the guests was intended to drive away this kind of spirit and misfortune.[29] It is common knowledge, in fact, that a loud racket is a means of supernatural defense. We

---

*This is also true in Norway, where the junk room is called *pulterkammer.*

have multiple examples of this, from ancient Rome when, during the Lemuria—a time when the dead returned—the *Pater familias* would walk through the house banging a bronze vase, to modern times when bells are rung to send the demons of bad weather fleeing. While such contractions were common during the Middle Ages,* this hypothesis seems quite unlikely to me, first, because I know of no other instance when *geist* vanished from a polysyllable and, second, because the term *geist* itself possesses a strong semantic charge. Whatever the case may be, the actions described are characterized by loud noises: a true hubbub.

From 1568 on, the attested occurrences of this word multiplied. It can be found in Fischart's 1591 German translation of Bodin's *De la démonomanie des sorciers,*† in the *Froschmeusler* by G. Rollenhagen published in Magdeburg in 1595, in Stieler's book on the German language published in 1691, and so forth.

In the sixteenth and seventeenth centuries *poltergeist* had another meaning that seems deeply rooted in the popular mind-set. In 1666 Johannes Prätorius spoke about knocking spirits and provided a description that is incredibly reminiscent of dwarves.

> The ancients could only believe that poltergeists had to be veritable human beings, who looked like small children and wore little robes or multicolored garb . . . . Superstitious folk think they are the souls of people murdered in their houses earlier.[30]

While these two senses for the term *poltergeist* were generally accepted during the sixteenth and seventeenth centuries, a further one has been added since the founding of spiritualism in 1852, which was brought about by the famous poltergeist phenomena that took place in Hydesville, New York. The Fox family had been disturbed by rapping

---

*For example, Middle High German *hinte* is a contraction of *hiute naht,* "this evening"; modern German *Sonnabend,* "Saturday," is a contraction of *Sonntagabend,* "Sunday Vigil."

†[On the Demon Worship of the Sorcerers —*Trans.*]

noises and moving furniture, which continued over a period of time. It was discovered that the two daughters of the couple were mediums.*[31] Thus, when this type of manifestation can be attributed to an identifiable living person, parapsychologists classify the *poltergeist* as a phenomenon of psychokinesis, a term designating the action of mind over matter. It is still customary, however, to use the term *poltergeist* whenever the process is triggered in a "wild," spontaneous, and uncontrolled way, and to use the term *psychokinesis* in other cases.[32]

This aspect has received close scrutiny from the researchers at the International Metaphysical Institute (IMI),[33] a foundation recognized as serving the public good and which will be celebrating its ninety-third birthday in 2012, as well as by the Institut für Grenzgebiete der Psychologie und Psychohygiene (IGPP) of Freiburg-im-Breisgau, founded in 1950 by the psychologist and physicist Hans Bender (1907–1991).

A final detail will show that the semantic approach is never a waste of time in this kind of research. The motif index of folk narratives[34]— stories, legends, and descriptions of beliefs—uses the term *poltergeist* as a synonym for *ghost, spirit,* or *household genie.* In other words, it is taken as an imprecise, generic term to designate an entity that is responsible for all manner of household dysfunctions (F 473), thrown objects (F 473 1), the behavior of objects in a way contrary to their nature (F 473 2), the mistreatment of people (F 473 3), and the making of noise (motif F 473 5). The nomenclature alternates between *spirit* and *poltergeist.* Despite this deliberate vagueness, it does give us a good overview of the actions attributed to poltergeists. We shall reveal them in greater detail beginning with the attested occurrences from the Middle Ages.

---

*In 1848 a family named Fox in Hydesville in the state of New York was disturbed over a long period by knockings and the movement of furniture. The Fox family children, two young girls, were pronounced to be mediums. They put certain questions to the spirit and, after matching raps to letters of the alphabet, were able to spell out replies. This became a news sensation, and soon other mediums were being reported in America. Later, one of the Fox girls, now Mrs. Jencken, revealed that the noises in the original Hydesville rappings were caused by her cracking her knees.

A FAMILY OF SPIRITS

Poltergeists did not wait for the nineteenth century to manifest and spread, they were only evaluated differently. This situation presents the major difficulty for the present investigation. What names did they go by? Under what heading should they be classified? The clarification necessary to complete this linguistic investigation depends on focusing all our attention on precise wordings.

Rumpelgeist

Starting in the sixteenth century, writers and scholars, and Luther in particular,* regularly used *Rumpelgeist,* "noisy ghost," as a synonym for *poltergeist,* but while the verb *rumpeln* has almost the same meaning as *poltern,* "to make noise," it has the additional meaning "to fall noisily" and forms part of a saying with another meaning, to wit, "to throw" or "to toss," as in "to toss everything upside down."† This is also one of the characteristic features of knocking spirits. It is very revealing that the root of this word is also used to form the compound word that is the German for the *Tenebrae,*‡ meaning "shadows" or "darkness," which is a religious service celebrated on the evening before or the early morning of Wednesday, Thursday, and Friday of Holy Week.§ It so happens that this Mass (which received its name because by its conclusion all lights have been extinguished) had a great connection with noise.¶

However, noise and shadows are implicitly combined in the com-

---

*For example, Luther writes: "Until now the world has been filled with incorporeal poltergeists (*voller leibloser Poltergeister*) who have passed for human souls; today it is full of *Rumpelgeister* with bodies, who pass for angels."

†*Alles durcheinander rumpeln.*

‡*Rumpelmette, Mette* meaning "the Mass." This compound word designates a noisy procession of Holy Week.

§There is a custom in Norway of extinguishing the lights and candles in the church on Good Friday, the day Christ was crucified.

¶During the mass, burn fifteen candles that are extinguished one after another. After the fourteenth candle is extinguished, the fifteenth candle is hid behind the high altar. Then the choristers make a great noise with rattles or clappers according to the parish.

pound word, which suggests that the darkness is propitious for a certain kind of knocking. All of this will be made clear later.

According to Fischart, this noisy ghost is a devil, but Luther has an interesting observation when discussing poltergeists and Rumpelgeister.

> Until now the world has been filled with incorporeal poltergeists who have passed for human souls; today it is full of *Rumpelgeister* with bodies, who pass for angels.*

Luther seems to be making a distinction between the incorporeal knocking spirits, connected to the dead, and the corporeal, noisy spirits, connected to the angels—fallen angels, of course. On several occasions he emphasizes the connection between the dead and poltergeists.

> For a long time, under the reign of the Papacy, we have suffered manifestations of knocking spirits or noisy ghosts, who we believed were the souls of deceased men, condemned to wander.†

Gespenst

The knocking spirit to Martin Luther and his contemporaries is a *Gepenst*. This term with an extremely wide semantic field was commonly translated into French as *spectre* (and the English "specter") during the sixteenth century. It in fact covers the following meanings: phantom, ghost, revenant, apparition, spirit, demon, illusion, and phantasmagoria. We should note incidentally that the etymological basis of the word "specter" has a certain relationship to the Latin word *species:* "sight, appearance, apparition, phantom, night vision." "Specter" implies something that can be seen. The original importance of the term is not

---

*Bisher ist die welt voll leibloser poltergeister gewesen, die sich für der menschen seelen ausgaben; itzt ist sie voll leibhafftiger rumpelgeister worden, die sich alle für lebendige engel ausgeben.

†Wir haben bisher lange zeit unter dem bepstlichen regiment manche grausame verfügunge erlidden von den rumpelgeistern oder poltergeistern, welche wir gegleubt und gehalten haben für menschen seelen, die verstorben sind, und in pein umbher gehen sollten.

the spectacular (!) apparition in itself but the conscious awareness of having the vision of something strange and unusual.

"Specter," which I will sometimes use for the sake of convenience and to avoid any anachronism, is the term used by the archdeacon Enoch Zobel, whose household was disturbed by a poltergeist from August 2 to September 26, 1691. This spirit hid objects, threw stones and other things, and, as a finishing touch, set fire to the woodshed.

In his account of the facts, Zobel alluded to popular interpretations that, he said, distinguished between "phantom, satanic knocking spirit, kobold, and Gütel," with this latter term describing one of the domestic spirits.[35] The archdeacon specified that for him, however, "the poltergeist is a devil like any other, except that it allows its wickedness to be seen more clearly and exercises it with more evidence."[36]

In sixteenth-century texts, the poltergeist is essentially a "devil" or a "specter," but these opinions are marred by bias because they fall into the polemic between Protestants and Catholics. The recurring argument is quite simple: many of these facts are "papist" mystifications that permit the Catholic clergy to cement its authority through the use of exorcisms and sacraments, and which bring money into the coffers of the papacy![37]

Kobold

Another name, which may come as a surprise as it describes elf-like beings and household spirits, also appears during the seventeenth and eighteenth centuries. This is the kobold, "the steward" or "manager." In other words, the kobold is the master of a place, as the word is derived from a verb meaning "to rule" and from the noun *Kobe,* meaning "room." The use of the term is the same as in binary expressions in which the poltergeist is given as a synonym for "devil" (*Theufel*) or "noisy ghost" (*Rumpelgeist*). Now, when we learn that the kobold is a tease and a practical joker who sows disorder in the household, especially when he is disgruntled, when we know he produces all kinds of noises and often resides in a corner of the dwelling—attic, cellar, or garret, and this offers us a link to the junk room (*Polterkammer*) mentioned earlier—it is perfectly logical to make this connection.

Here is what the pastor Jeremias Heinisch reported about what took place in his parish in Gröben, south of Berlin, from June 17 to September 8, 1718, "a memorable story that should not be taken at first glance as a fallacious fable and insane invention." It concerned a kobold who threw stones, broke windows, and tossed pots and pans into the air. Quite the skeptic, Heinisch was at first under the impression that these were malicious pranks committed by young smart alecks, but when he was unable to find any cause for the incidents he eventually attributed the manifestations "to an invisible entity that we call a spirit."[38] In support he cited popular opinion: "If some people wish, in accordance with general habit, to call these kinds of evil spirits 'kobolds' or 'spirit familiars' (*Spiritus familiaris*), it does not concern me in the slightest. They should be included among the evil spirits," because, he soon added, he has read nothing in books of theology that obliges him to believe in kobolds.

We should note that in 1737 kobolds were regarded as evil spirits by Johann Jacob Bräuner[39] and that in 1747 Georg Wilhelm Wegner proposed natural causes as an explanation for these phenomena, thinking "that men playact as kobolds . . . and these hoaxers took advantage to play kobolds in a house."[40] The notion of deception even appears in the *Großes Universal-Lexikon* (Great Universal Lexicon) published by Johann Heinrich Zedler from 1732–1754. Under the entry "kobolt" it is written:

> Practically speaking, kobolt means deceiver and flatterer; it is a so-called evil spirit that men claim lingers in stables, barns, and houses . . . and performs useful services or plays all manner of annoying tricks.[41]

This definition describes a being who is half domestic genie and half evil spirit. It is foolhardy to confuse the one for the other under pain of vexing and irritating them, as shown by the reaction of the protean Hinzelmann, the brownie of Hudemühlen Castle in Hanover. He was questioned in 1704 to learn whether he knew kobolds and poltergeists. "I have nothing to do with them," he responded. "They are only diabolical phantasmagoria (*Teuffels-Gespenst*)."[42]

All these accounts let us see that the connections of the kobold and the poltergeist were taking place on the basis of a body of beliefs attributing certain events to supernatural beings. Once again, the interpretation is different for the same set of events and provides new paths of research.

And lastly it should be noted that the large dictionary published by Meyer[43] in 1909 defines poltergeist as "kobold" and "household spirit."

What are the results of the linguistic inquiry?

First, the nature of the poltergeist: it can be a knocking spirit, a household spirit, a devil, a dead person, a hoax.

Next are its essential actions: noise and thrown objects, sometimes setting fires.

Finally, the places and the times for its manifestations: the house and its adjoining area, with a predilection for junk rooms. Everything takes place in particular at night, when shadows have entirely supplanted the day.

These results are not insignificant, and they provide an initial descriptive portrait of the entity. What now needs to be verified with the help of the texts is whether the names exhibit a clear correspondence and if the fundamental elements that have been discerned here should be in some way amended or further supplemented.

2

A Smidgeon of
Objectivity

Spirits have indeed been heard walking up and down the corridors, turning over the leaves of books, seemingly the great elephant folios in the library, counting over money that rattled and chinked, moving tables and furniture about as if dusting the rooms. Not unseldom in houses great noises like sudden claps of thunder or the roar of distant artillery are heard . . .

FATHER NOËL TAILLEPIED, *PSICHOLOGIE.*

TRAITÉ DE L'APPARITION DES ESPRITS

For want of knowledge and appropriate tools of analysis, these incidents astounded and terrified those who witnessed them. The psychological shock caused by these phenomena and ignorance necessarily brought about deviations and distortions, strange mixtures and interpolations. How reliable are the accounts of these incidents? In earlier times they were written down by clerics, and the latter would have altered the accounts to allow an orthodox exegesis. This appropriation, together with changes made to the base narrative, would have naturally enlisted these stories into the battle against deviltry.

One key to understanding the working methods of the clergy is their absolute desire to channel and contextualize a dangerous irrationality they deemed to be a fertile source of deviations and heresies. The proof for such appropriations was already apparent in the fate of tales concerning journeys into the beyond. These gradually became the sole privilege of the clergy, whereas up until the eleventh century this was a voyage even simple peasants could take. The same approach can be seen at work with regard to miracles and popular forms of worship. We must not allow ourselves to be taken in by narrators who have little objectivity and are pursuing objectives dictated to them by their faith and by the mother to all, the holy Church.

To a large extent knocking spirits are still greatly misunderstood, and it is necessary to provide readers with the means they will need to follow this investigation. In order to provide a general overview and before introducing the medieval texts, it seems wise to me to offer a few accounts that will enable readers to plunge into this irrational and astonishing world. I have singled out a few "objective" texts, meaning accounts that do not include any interpretation on the part of the witnesses. Following this analysis it will be much easier to understand how events like this could excite the imagination and produce one or another explanation.

TYPOLOGY OF POLTERGEISTS

In order to permit an easier deciphering of the accounts and to determine the role played by belief in what the researchers have suggested, here is a typology of poltergeists that was drawn up by Ernesto Bozzano, Benjamin B. Wolman, and later by William G. Roll in 1982.[1] It was revised by Charles Hardy in 1986 and again by Philippe Wallon in 1996.[2] I have added an identifying initial—B for Bozzano, R for Roll, W for Wolman—indicating the source for particular typological characteristics referred to when presenting the texts from the corpus of poltergeist accounts.

R 1. The phenomena are focused on one person.

R 2. They exhibit a certain spatial focus.

R 3. The movement of objects sometimes displays a specific target and an odd trajectory.

R 4. Sometimes the objects pass through walls or physical material without damaging the surface.*

R 5. A large number of cases are combined with paranormal voices and visions, and likewise with raps and other means of intelligible communication.

R 6. Exorcisms and rituals have no effect.

R 7. Generally, the disturbances cease if the central figure, the medium (the individual whom E. Bozzano calls the "sensitive"), or other family members leave the premises.

In 1920 E. Bozzano noted what he believed were the principal characteristics of poltergeists.[3]

B 1. They can manifest either at day or night.

B 2. They almost always appear in direct connection with the presence of a sensitive.

B 3. They exhibit great uniformity in all times and places.

B 4. They are characterized by their brief duration.

B 5. They sometimes materialize as an occult personality capable of establishing a connection with those present and answering their questions by means of knocks.

B 6. It is necessary to include exceptional cases in which the mysterious personality speaks out loud, or speaks like a living person.

I shall finish this list with one element borrowed from B. Wolman,[4] who notes:

---

*Wolman says the same thing.

W 1. The objects [involved in the phenomena] can give off a certain amount of heat sometimes hot enough to burn.

On other points Wolman's conclusions match those already cited. They are based on the analysis of 116 poltergeist cases, the statistics for which reveal some interesting tendencies. In 56 cases a young woman was at the heart of the manifestations, whereas in 36 cases it concerned men. In 32 cases apparitions were involved, and 6 cases involved voices.

THE WESLEY CASE

Let's begin with an intriguing case that leaves the identity of the troublemaker in the shadows and at the same time underscores the psychological solidity of a family confronted by something strange and unusual. The original text basically relates the following:*

At the beginning of the eighteenth century, a spirit was haunting the paternal home of John Wesley, the founder of the Methodist denomination. The house was located in Epworth in Lincoln County. The noise began on December 1, 1716, with *moans* in front of the door to the dining room, and lasted until January 27, 1717. All members of the family were fearless and unbiased. They did all that could be done to expose any possible error or deceit. Samuel Wesley recorded the results of the investigation as he found them in his father's journal, and in the letters of his mother, brothers, and sisters.

When the spirit haunting the Wesley house began its tapping, the parents did not lend credence to their children's stories about it, and

---

*[In the various historical and literary poltergeist accounts that are related throughout the book, the author regularly draws the reader's attention to certain details by setting them in italics. It should also be noted that many of these extracts are not direct quotations but rather paraphrasings of the original sources, which often exhibit a much more archaic style. —*Ed.*]

their mother in particular attributed these noises to mice or rats, which had caused them problems earlier. At that time she had scared them away by blowing a horn. She therefore turned once more to the instrument whose sounds had been so successful previously, but this time they had no effect whatsoever. To the contrary, after that very night *the noises became much louder and more distinct* and the extraordinary nature of the noises convinced her that it could not be the work of any human or animal creature. One of Wesley's daughters said it was evident that the large unknown entity was hurt by the interpretation that had been given to its unknown language and it wished to show the entire household they understood nothing.

The family begged their father to speak to the spirit tormenting them. Thus, one evening around six o'clock he went into the children's room, where he heard *moans and knocking.* He demanded the spirit to speak to him if it could and tell why it was haunting his house this way. *The spirit did not answer but knocked three times as was its custom.* Wesley spoke a name and told the spirit that if it was his, to knock thrice if he was incapable of speech. But the spirit knocked no more for the rest of the night. Wesley repeated this several times later, following the spirit from room to room, by day or night, with or without a light, and speaking to it when he felt it approach. *But he never heard one word uttered.* Only once or twice did he hear two or three very faint sounds, slightly more distinct than the chirping of a bird but quite different from the noises made by rats. Once when he was in the kitchen he struck the floorboards sharply with a staff; the spirit answered by knocking each time just as loudly. Wesley then did what he was accustomed to do when entering a room: he rapped in a regular pattern of knocks: 1–2, 3, 4, 5, 6–7. It was notable that when the family gathered together around Wesley to pray, and when he prayed for the king and his heirs, the spirit would knock quite loudly over their heads and would repeat this noise when the prayer was repeated, whereas nothing could be heard if the prayer was not recited. This behavior prompted the children to say that spirit must be a Jacobite and an enemy to King George.[5]

It is also said that the Wesleys heard footsteps in the house as if a man clad in a long nightgown was walking about. The spirit showed itself to the mother in the shape of a basset hound and to a servant in the likeness of a rabbit, "but smaller, and it turned around five times very swiftly. Its ears lay flat upon its neck, and its little scut stood straight up."

It should be noted that knocks occurring in a regular sequence are a herald of what would later be the "spirit alphabet": one knock for yes and two knocks for no. It so happens that this method of communicating with the spirits already existed in 1526. In Lyon, following the death of a nun named Allis, her eighteen-year-old friend Antoinette heard light knocks coming from the ground beneath her feet that, in response to her questions, "knocked as many times as I asked."[6] While at this point things may not have been so clear, they became so when the Franciscans of Orleans buried the wife of an influential personage of the city in 1534.[7] Loud noises could be heard in the sleeping quarters of the monastery. The monks gathered together and ordered the spirit to identify itself. A brother named Pierre commanded the spirit to knock three times if it had permission to speak, and the knocks rang out, indicating that it would do so not through speech but by knocking. Pierre indicated the number of knocks necessary to say yes, and so forth. It is easy to see how certain practices clearly do not date from the present.

SENSATIONAL NEWS ITEMS

Here, in order to provide a more exact portrait of the invisible entity, are several reported incidents, stripped of any judgments or interpretations—in certain respects, they fall under the heading of sensational news items.

In 1741 Father Duboeuf, parish priest of Saint-Maximin, provided this account:

Between midnight and dawn on January 6, a dreadful noise could be heard coming first from the cellar then from the garret in the house of Constantine. It had played drum drills on the tables better than even the most skilled drummer. It did the same thing on the second night, and there were more than twenty people each evening who heard and saw this little trick. The third night after making its usual noise, this spirit picked up a wooden shoe (*sabot*) and threw it at the shoulder of a man named Beauregard, the local surgeon. The fourth night he struck this same man's shoulder so violently that he would have fallen into the fire if others had not held him back. On the fifth night a schoolmaster named Trepai, who lived in this house and had gone to bed at the urging of those keeping watch, was wrapped up in his sheets by the spirit, who had already drawn back the curtains and would have dragged its victim off if Monsieur Paturel, keeping watch with the others, had not kept ahold of him. On the sixth night, after its ordinary tapping, in front of everyone, it drove a plank of the internal partition in with so much force that eight nails holding it in were broken. Finally after this noise had continued successively until the ninth night, Father Bilas, the parish priest of Villard-Benoît, came to bless the house and performed high mass at the Pontcharra Chapel. Everyone had masses said, and since that time nothing has been heard. Here is something that is beyond imagining and no one knows what it was, and it has converted many scatterbrains and young unbelievers who were present.[8]

In October 1818, in the Austrian district of Obergreiffeneck, the house of the Obergemeiner family fell prey to quite similar phenomena.[9] Stones were thrown at the windows several times in the afternoon, and panes were broken in the evening. The noise ceased with evening prayer and the family went to bed. It started up again the next day. It was believed schoolboys playing rude pranks were responsible, but no one could be found. Then noises began occurring at the front and back doors. Herr Obergemeiner gathered thirty peasants and had them encircle the house. But despite this surveillance the stones continued to rain down, including even the interior of the house. At six o'clock in the evening everything would stop. At eight o'clock in the morning stones ranging in weight from a quarter pound to fifteen pounds would be thrown, traveling in a curve that was contrary to the laws of movement, according to eyewitnesses. Then household utensils—spoons, pots, full or empty plates—were thrown at the people present, some of whom were struck. However, they "scarcely felt the blows, to their great surprise"; only a crucifix was respected. Chaplain Hötzel's presence affected nothing. The chaos stopped around eleven o'clock. Herr Obergemeiner promised a thousand florins to whoever discovered the cause of these phenomena, which lasted until All Saints Day. After a hiatus of five to six weeks, a pot went flying, then nothing else happened, and the mystery remained fully intact. It was one of the primary eyewitnesses who lent the account much of its credibility. This was H. J. Aschauer, professor of mathematical physics, who resorted to a variety of scientific measures before determining that the phenomena were beyond the grasp of science.

Readers of *La Gazette des tribunaux* read the following on February 2, 1846:

One of the most peculiar incidents—an incident that recurred each night over the course of three weeks, without its cause being discovered despite the most active study and the most persistent and thorough surveillance—stirred up the entire working-class quarter of the Montagne Sainte-Geneviève, the Sorbonne, and the Place Saint-Michel. This is what was observed, in accordance with public rumor, by the dual judicial and administrative investigation that was pursued without pause for several days.

Demolition work was undertaken to create a new street intended to connect the Sorbonne to the Pantheon. Here, at the end of an area that once housed a public dance hall, is located the yard of a merchant who sold wood by weight and charcoal. This yard was bordered by a house some distance from the street and separated from the houses being demolished by large excavations of the old fortification wall of Paris, constructed under Philip Augustus, that had been unearthed by the recent construction work. Every night, and all night long, this house is assailed with *a hail of projectiles,* which, as a result of their volume and the violence with which they are cast, have done such destruction that it has been laid open to the light of day, and *the window and door frames are broken* and reduced to splinters as if subjected to a siege employing catapults or grapeshot.

Whence come these projectiles, which are pieces of paving stones, demolition fragments, and entire cinder blocks, which, judging by their weight and the distance they were thrown, obviously could not have been cast by a mortal hand? This is what has been yet deemed *impossible to discover.* Day-and-night surveillance under the personal direction of the police commissioner and skilled agents has proven fruitless, and equally vain have been the persistent visits of the head of security to the premises and the release of guard dogs in the adjoining enclosures. Nothing can explain the phenomenon, which, in their gullibility, the people attribute to something mysterious. The projectiles continue raining down noisily, thrown from a great height above the heads of those who assume observation posts on the roofs of the surrounding houses. These projectiles appear to come from a great distance and reach their target with almost mathematical precision, with not a single one deviating in its *parabolic curve* from its designated target [R 3 in the typology cited on page 28].

We shall not enter into the ample details of these facts, which will, without doubt, receive a speedy explanation thanks to the anxiety that they have awakened. Already the inquiry is reaching in every direction possible in light of the adage *Cui prodest is auctor.** Nevertheless we may note that in somewhat similar circumstances that also created a certain sensation in Paris—such as, for example, a shower of coins of low value that attracted the loafers of Paris every

---

*[He who profits is the author. —*Trans.*]

evening in the Rue de Montesquieu, or when *all the bells in the Rue de Malte were rung by an invisible hand*—it was impossible to discover any remotely tangible cause for the phenomena. Let us hope that this time we shall arrive at a more precise result.

This newspaper then noted on February 4 of the same year:

People are lost in speculations. The doors and windows have been sealed by planks nailed inside to protect the inhabitants from being struck as their furniture and even their beds have been shattered by these projectiles.

In December 1849 a coalburner's house in Hazelbourg in Moselle, France, was bombarded for several days with paving stones, cinder blocks, and bricks that entered through the windows and smashed the furniture. The police were alerted, and, on finding nothing, they accused the owner of breaking his furniture and bombarding his house:[10] a classic reaction although there was not a shred of proof for their allegations.

Under the headline reading "A Witchcraft Scene in the Nineteenth Century," the reputable newspaper *Le Droit* recounted the following narrative in June 1860:

The strangest kind of incident is currently taking place on the Rue des Noyers. Monsieur Lesage, bursar for the Palace of Justice, lives in an apartment on this street. For some time, projectiles, coming from no one knows where, have been breaking his windows and entering his home where they have struck people, wounding them more or less grievously. These projectiles are fairly large chunks of half-burnt logs, extremely heavy pieces of coal, and so forth. Monsieur Lesage's servant was struck on the chest by several of them, which caused severe bruises.

Monsieur Lesage decided to seek help from the police. Agents were placed on surveillance, but it was not long before they, too, became targets for the invisible artillery, and they found it impossible to determine where the blows were coming from.

As it was impossible to live in a house where one had to remain constantly on guard, Monsieur Lesage asked his landlord to cancel his lease. This request was granted, and they invited the bailiff, Monsieur Vailliant, whose name was entirely apt under the circumstances,* to draft the legal document.

In fact, the ministerial official had barely begun drafting this writ when an enormous lump of coal, thrown with extreme force, flew through the window and struck the wall where it shattered into dust. Without missing a beat, Monsieur Vailliant used this powder— just like Junot once did with dirt scattered by a cannonball—to spread over the page he had just covered with fresh ink.

No explanation was found for this bombardment by various objects. It is hoped, however, that the investigation pursued by Monsieur Hubaut, Commissioner of the Sorbonne Quarter, will shed some light on the mystery.

In Switzerland between August 15 and 27, 1862, the home of the national councilor Joller of Niederdorf, near Stans in the canton of Unterwalden, was the stage for some mysterious phenomena. An invisible hand overturned tables and chairs. Rapping was heard on the doors and floorboards, and doors opened and closed of their own volition. Finally the uproar became terrible, latches were torn open, and it was feared the entire house would be demolished. For people in their rooms, the rapping came from the cellar under the floor, while for those on watch in the cellar, the noise seemed to come from above; at the same time blows were struck, as if with a hammer, on the tables and chairs. Despite the most meticulous searching, no one could find any visible cause. This did not stop a Lucerne newspaper, *Der Eidgenoss,* from claiming several days later that the phenomena could be explained by the most palpable evidence: rapping instruments had been found that

---

*[Valiant —*Trans.*]

had been used to make the noise for the purpose of depreciating the value of the house and inducing its owner to auction it off, and so forth.

In the September 28 issue of the *Allgemeine Zeitung,* a correspondent from Bern even declared that the matter was finished and that the cause of the uproar was Monsieur Joller's eighteen-year-old son. He had learned all manner of tricks from his Bohemian friends and had practiced this one to scare his parents for his own amusement.[11] Monsieur Joller was mocked, slandered, discredited, and, as he himself put it:

> Caught in the crossfire between a vulgar and fanatical populace on the one side and an incredulous, slandering, and mocking press on the other, I and my large family were left to our misfortune.

The press is definitely an excellent source of information about this kind of phenomena. *Le Journal de la Vienne* of January 21, 1864, reports:

> For the past five or six days such an extraordinary thing has happened in Poitiers that it has become the topic of the most curious conversations and comments. Every evening after six certain peculiar noises are heard in a house of the Rue Neuve Saint-Paul, inhabited by Mlle. d'O, sister of the Count d'O. These noises, according to our reports, resemble discharges of artillery. *Violent blows seem to rain upon the doors and shutters.* The first idea was that they were caused by some urchins or unfriendly neighbors. A close watch was kept. After the complaint by Mlle. d'O, the police took the most detailed measures, and policemen were stationed both inside and outside the house. The explosions continued all the same, and we are credibly informed that Sir M, a brigadier, was surprised by a commotion the night before, which he has until now been quite unable to explain.
>
> Our entire town is disturbed by this unexplained mystery. *The inquiries made by the police have hitherto had no results.* Everyone is

looking for a solution to the riddle. Some persons initiated into spiritism say that *rapping spirits* are the authors of these manifestations and that a certain famous medium, who, however, no longer lives in the district, has something to do with it. Others say that a cemetery once existed in the Rue Neuve Saint-Paul, and we need not elaborate upon the conjectures they indulge in on that account.

We do not know which to choose as the best of all these explanations. In the meantime this event has aroused much public opinion, and last night such a large crowd assembled under the windows of the d'O house that the authorities had to requisition a picket of the tenth regiment to clear the street. At the time this article goes to press, the police and gendarmes occupy the house.

The first explanation that comes to mind is of course that of trickery. An inquiry was therefore launched, but it yielded nothing, and no trickster has been discovered.

Exorcisms have been tried without any result [R 6], for after stopping for some days the noises recommenced with a certain violence. They are said to resemble the noises made by small bombs.

But where do they come from? It is impossible at present to determine their direction. They do not come from the cellar, because pistols fired there cannot be heard on the first floor.[12]

In December 1892, in an apartment in the village of La Lucerne-d'Outremer in the Manche district of Normandy, pots, shelves, a crucifix, and serving tables all seemed to shake as if seized by a frenzy. One day two lamps sitting on a table were thrown into the middle of the room. The police superintendent who rushed to the scene found nothing.[13] Several decades later, on June 7, 1930, *Le Savoyard de Paris* reported the following:

For some time, the home of Monsieur Rozier in Rochepiquet in the Seyssuel commune, has been the theater for some extraordinary incidents that are the subject of the most bizarre comments. Monsieur and Madame Rozier, who run a small farm, have witnessed *plates, glasses, and household items doing a crazy dance* every day, with first one and then another object moving of its own accord. Why? No one knows yet. The children under the farmers' care have fallen ill. Several citizens of Vienne and Seyssuel have come to Monsieur Rozier's house at his request. He prepared some coffee with milk for them. Imagine his astonishment, and that of his visitors, when the cup of coffee they were served was emptied by some unknown means. It was even more striking when the slab of butter that was on the table fell off, breaking the plate it was on as it hit the ground. A witness went upstairs after hearing a noise. He found a vase in the middle of the room. He put it back in its place; it was found back on the floor a few moments later. As one might expect, these incidents are the main topic of local conversation.

We should also note the cautious, measured reaction of a journalist in 1913. A knocking spirit was at work in a house in Marcinelle, Belgium. The editor of an Antwerp newspaper went to investigate the premises where he interviewed the servant, who "seemed to be no more than fifteen years old. The phenomena seemed connected to her because the projectiles only began appearing when she got up from bed."[14] The investigator believed this manifestation was connected with puberty.

In the 1960s, every evening before bedtime, sounds could be heard in a new house in Pripriac that were "like waves crashing in one mass after another down the stairs, although there weren't any." One night footsteps could be heard going up and down the stairs, and then knocking at the door. Another night resounded with an infernal din. "We moved to come here, the narrator said, and nothing more was heard."[15] In a now demolished house in Pont-Réan, "the gentleman living there heard drums beating, you know? To encircle them."[16] Toward 1956 violent noises could be heard in a house in Renac, and witnesses, including a bailiff, came forward to vouch for the facts.[17]

Reading these reports shows that the elements contained in the

The title page to the 1688 edition of Joseph Glanvil's Saducismus Triumphatus

scholarly typology presented at the beginning of the chapter are practically never all present in a single case, although this may also stem from the nature of the narratives, which are not entirely reliable, especially when they are reports from newspapers. Nevertheless the fact remains that the shower of projectiles and the movement of objects and furniture (in other words, telekinetic phenomena), along with all kinds of knocking, are at the heart of poltergeist manifestations.

Following this exploration of the "objective" phenomenon, we now must go back to the accounts from the Middle Ages, consequently taking note of the prevailing beliefs and learning how to spot them.

3

Mischief-Making Spirits of the Middle Ages

We can only understand life by looking back on it.
SØREN KIERKEGAARD

Ernesto Bozzano draws a distinction between knocking spirits and acoustic hauntings, but this distinction can only apply to modern times. In ancient times there was only one category, which Aristotle discussed in his *Marvelous or Miraculous Noises* (*Thauma akousmata*), a book that I was unfortunately unable to locate during the course of my research. Quite often these unusual manifestations are attributed to an evil spirit (*spiritus malignus*), although the nature of this spirit is rarely explained in any precise detail. "Spirit," like "demon," is one of those polysemous terms that is quite convenient for storytellers but so very vexing for us ten or fifteen centuries later. In his *City of God*, Saint Augustine (354–430) provides a good example.

Hesperius of a tribunitian family, and a neighbor of our own, has a farm called Zubedi in the Fussalian district, and finding that his family, his cattle, and his servants were suffering from the malice of evil spirits, he asked our presbyters, during my absence, that one of them would go with him and banish the spirits by his prayers. One went, offered there the sacrifice of the body of Christ, praying with all his might that this vexation might cease. It did cease forthwith through God's mercy.[1]

It will be noted that the mere intervention of a priest put an end to the phenomenon, which is a rule that suffers few exceptions in clerical literature, since the latter operates according to the principle that God is more powerful than all the demons on earth. Furthermore, during the Middle Ages many ecclesiastics were referred to with a charming expression as "athletes of Christ."

STONE-THROWING SPIRITS AND DEAD WITHOUT TOMBS

During the time of Theodoric the Great (fifth century), Saint Caesarius of Arles (470–543) had to step in to deal with a similar case, as his hagiographer Cyprian (died 516), a monk of Saint-Victor Abbey in Marseille and later the Bishop of Toulon, informs us. The doctor Elpidus sought him out to free his house from a *lithobolos,* in other words, a stone-throwing spirit. Caesarius purified the premises with holy water and everything was restored to order.[2] Caesarius also intervened in the canton of Succentriones, which was under the jurisdiction of his diocese. Here in front of a bathhouse, a voice was challenging passersby, immediately after which large stones would crash to the ground at their feet or just behind them (*ingenta saxa aut ante pedes, aut post se cadentia*). The local inhabitants took the staff Caesarius had left at the church when he performed the service and hung it from the wall. The diabolical manifestations (*insidae diaboli*) ceased, and no more was heard of it again.

In the fifth century an episode from Constantius of Lyon's *Life of Saint Germain of Auxerre* (ca. 475–480) opens some new perspectives.

Once while traveling, Saint Germain was asked by his companions to make a stop for the night at once, as night was falling. Some distance away there stood a dwelling with a half-ruined roof, which had been left uninhabited for a long time. It was a dangerous and horrible place, all the more so as two old men living in the neighborhood had specifically warned them that this house was haunted in a most terrifying manner. When he learned this, Germain headed toward the frightful ruins, settled in with his modest baggage, and he and his several companions took a light meal. Next, as it was already late at night, Germain fell asleep while one of his clerics stayed up to read.

Suddenly a horrifying shade (*umbra terribilis*) appeared in front of the eyes of the man reading [R 5], gradually rising before him while the walls were struck by a hail of stones (*parietes etiam saxorum imbribus conliduntur*). The terrified reader then begged the bishop for his aid. Germain leaped up immediately, regarded the silhouette of this frightful ghost, and, after invoking the name of Christ, commanded it to confess who he was and what he was doing there.[3]

The other answered [B 6] that he and his friend had committed numerous crimes and now lay unburied (*insepultos iacere*). Unable to find rest, they tormented the living. Germain asked to be shown the place where their bodies lay; the phantom guided him and pointed to the place where their bodies had been tossed.

Once day had returned, Germain called together the inhabitants of the area. They cleared away the rubble with mattocks and found the corpses spread out every which way, bound in chains (*ossa ferries adhuc nexibus inligata*). A grave was dug, the bodies freed from their chains and wrapped in shrouds, and then covered with dirt while a prayer of intercession was spoken over them. The dead obtained rest and the living found tranquillity. After that the house was once more happily inhabited with no trace of the terror that had once haunted it.

There are two distinct but related manifestations here: an apparition and a stone-throwing spirit, a means of clearly indicating that the dead man was the cause of the rocks striking the walls. Now, as Germain's companions exhumed two corpses, everything suggests that the deceased individual who did not appear was responsible for the phenomenon: one of the dead appeared and spoke; the other showered the site with stones. In fact, it seems that Constantius of Lyon is trying here to explain things he does not grasp very clearly because solitary dead individuals also know how to trigger a shower of stones. In any case, to the best of my knowledge, this is the first medieval account connecting stone throwing to the unburied dead (*insepulti*).

THE DEVIL'S COMMOTION

A century later the *Life of Saint Romanus of Condat,* written around 520, relates how the devil set upon a disciple of a saint named Etienne.

> Every night the devil tormented him continually with such an outburst of fury that he was granted not a moment's peace. In addition to the repeated shocks against the walls (*praeter crebras parietum inlisiones*), he ripped open his poor roof with a loud shower of stones (*tectillum ipsius lapidum reddebat fragore perfossum*).[4]

Before analyzing this text I would like to look at another one that is quite similar. In his *Life of the Fathers,* Gregory of Tours (died 594) recounts those of the abbé saints Lupicin and Romanus.[5] While living as hermits in the Jura region of France, the two men were subjected to assaults by demons.

> The demons did not let up for even a day from casting stones at them (*nam lapidibus uguere eos daemones per dies singulos non desinebant*). Every time they knelt in prayer to the Lord, a hail of stones (*imber lapidum*) thrown by the demons crashed down upon them, often

causing them wounds and making them suffer severe pains (*ita ut saepe vulnerati immensis dolorum cruciatibus torquerentur*).

We find the same thing later in the *Life of Saint Peter of Alcantara* (1494–1562), the founder of the order of Barefoot Franciscans. At night demons would howl all around him and cast stones so large that the noise woke the other brothers. And one day when the Jesuit Sebastiano del Campo of Sassari in Sardinia was traveling, the demons rained a shower of stones upon him "that caused much pain without wounding him."

Both of these accounts feature minions of Satan whose weapons are stones, but with one notable difference. In Gregory of Tour's book Romanus and Lupicin are wounded by the demons, whereas Etienne, in the anonymously written *Life of Saint Romanus of Condat,* is an indirect victim, as if the blows against the walls and the stones were simply intended to intimidate him. The different treatments given in these accounts can only be explained by the existence of two different traditions. Etienne's story is obviously inspired by popular beliefs concerning stone-throwing spirits. The mention of the devil is simply the standard, everyday explanation in ecclesiastical milieus for any paranormal manifestations.

I find one final detail intriguing. We would expect the word "devil" in the anonymous text and "demon" in Gregory's work, as this latter term encompasses the supernatural beings of so-called folk belief. It is necessary to know, however, that the plural of *diabolus* is rarely used in this kind of narrative, and during the Middle Ages it seems that *daemones* functioned most of the time as the plural form of *diabolus*. If we place our trust in the syntax, we find a distinction between the devil and his acolytes, the demons.

The *Life of Saint Godric*,[6] which Reginald of Durham recorded shortly after the death of this pseudo-saint (he was never canonized) in 1170, contains several elements that seem to clearly reflect the clichés of hagiography. Once retired to his hermitage, Godric was targeted by a shower of stones, and the devil even threw his ciborium at him. He also grabbed the horn holding the wine for mass and upended it over his head, then bombarded him with everything in his cell that was not nailed down. The thrown stones and objects are the characteristic feature of poltergeists, but the diabolical origin of all this is immediately underscored here: the wine for mass and the wafers are attacked. With regard to the wine, this makes sense as long as it has not been consecrated, but who ever saw a devil with the power to pick up a ciborium containing the Corpus Christi and send it flying?

EVIL SPIRITS WHO START FIRES

The seventh-century *Life of Saint Theodore of Sykeon*[7] (St. Theodore lived in Asia Minor and died in 613) mentions the misfortunes of an imperial groom, also named Theodore, who had an evil spirit manifest in his house. When members of the household were seated at the table, it hurled stones at them, terrifying the diners, and it also broke the thread on the looms. As a finishing touch, the house was invaded by an enormous quantity of mice and snakes, making it completely undesirable to live there. Saint Theodore made his way to this house and spent the night there in prayer and song, after which he sprinkled the premises with water he had personally blessed, and everything was restored to order.

Alcuin (735–804), whom the historian François Guizot called "Charlemagne's intellectual prime minister," has left us a version of *The Life of Saint Willibrord* (658–739), the apostle to the Frisians. In this text we learn that a head of a family and his household were afflicted by a terrible visitation of devilish sorcery. The man deduced that his house was haunted by an evil spirit.

For it would suddenly seize food and clothing and other household goods and throw them into the fire. Once, indeed, whilst the parents were asleep, it snatched their little boy as he rested in their arms and hurled him into the fire, and it was only with great difficulty that the parents, roused by the child's screams, rescued him from the flames. Many were the ill turns that the family had to endure at the hands of this execrable spirit, and no priest was able to exorcise it. Eventually the holy man Willibrord, at the father's urgent request, sent them some holy water and directed them to sprinkle it over all the furniture, after it had been taken outdoors, for the man of God foresaw that the whole house would be consumed by fire. When they had done this, conflagration broke out in the very place where the bed had stood, and, quickly enveloping the house, reduced it to ashes. After another house had been built on the site of the old one and blessed with holy water the family suffered no more from their former trial and thenceforth lived in peace, giving thanks to the Lord who had deigned to deliver them through the hands of His servant.[8]

Here is a poltergeist who has the peculiarity of being associated with fire, and this is the first testimony of this type. Even if fire remains a rarity in the ancient texts, it is mentioned here and there, which proves that there is something going on, and much more recent documents indeed show that the poltergeist is also an arsonist—a trait that is not mentioned in the typology I provided earlier.

During the reign of Louis II the Younger, a poltergeist phenomenon occurred in the Mainz diocese, which would have a huge impact on the texts all the way through to the sixteenth century. The *Annals of Fulda,* written between 882 and 887, and then the *Chronicle* by the Benedictine Sigebert of Gembloux (ca. 1030–1112) were the first to discuss what initially occurred in 858.

An evil spirit in the bishopric of Mainz was casting stones, striking the walls of the houses as if with a hammer (*malignus spiritus parietes domorum quasi malleus pulsando*). Next, it began speaking in public (R 5), informing about thefts and sowing discord, causing trouble among several persons. It then aroused many people's wrath against a man in whose house it lived, and which it burned down:

the flames caught the entire house from where it entered (*quocumque intrasset, statim illa domus exuretur*); it even declared that everyone had to suffer because of this man's sins. Eventually he had to seek refuge in the fields. When the priests celebrated the Litanies, the demon hurt several of them by throwing stones. Sometimes it was calm and sometimes excited, but things continued in this vein for three years until all the buildings of the area had been consumed in a fire.[9]

This story can also be found in *The Golden Legend* by Jacobus de Voragine,[10] with some minor variations: the dating, for example, is 856. In the sixteenth century Philipp Camerarius places the action in Canmuz on the banks of the Rhine and calls the spirit "cacodemon," a scholarly term that specifically means "evil spirit."[11]

In addition to the typical manifestations—blows against the walls, thrown stones—this tormenting spirit speaks, but none of what he actually said is reported. We merely learn that he sows ill will and discord by revealing thefts and other things. The novelty here is that this entity starts fires. The duration of the phenomenon is worth noting, as is the impotence of the clergy, some of whom it injures. According to Jacobus de Voragine, however, the spirit reveals that when sprinkled with holy water, he sought refuge beneath the cape of a priest of his friends.

In the tenth century Notker the Stammerer (died 912), a monk at the monastery of Saint Gall in Switzerland, tells an astonishing story in his book on the life of Emperor Charlemagne.[12] A demon bearing several names played tricks on men and teased them; he was in the habit of visiting the house of a blacksmith and spending the night playing with his hammers and anvils. The blacksmith sought to protect himself as well as his property with the sign of the cross, but the spirit offered him a bargain: "If you do not close your forge to me, you will have all the wine you could possibly want." The deal was sealed, but one day the spirit was discovered, arrested, bound, and flogged—which is quite extraordinary in any event! Notker does not seem to have any clear idea about how to deal with this creature. He calls him a *larva,* "mask/

demon, spirit, dead man," and then *pilosus,* meaning "hairy." In other words, he wavers between calling it a devil, a dead man, and a *genius loci* (place spirit). The end of the story points the reader toward the devil. In fact, it is thanks to holy water and the sign of the cross that the thief is paralyzed and thus able to be seized. But how plausible is all this? The text has certainly been adulterated and outfitted with an ending that makes it possible for order to be restored—in this case divine order.

THE HERALD OF AN IMMINENT DEATH

In his *Chronicle* (VII, 68), Thietmar (ca. 975–1108), the Bishop of Merseburg, reported an incident that took place in Sülfeld, a locality next to Fallersleben, on the second week of December.

> A certain woman there had barred herself and her children in her house, because her husband was not home. Behold, just before the cock crowed, she heard a loud noise (*sonitus immensus*). Horrified by this intrusion, she called out to her neighbors, indicating that she needed help. When the neighbors rushed to her aid, they were repeatedly thrown back by some force (*iactatione repulluntur*). Finally, breaking down the doors, they entered with swords drawn and diligently searched the house for whatever had attacked the lady of the house and them as well. Because of its supernatural nature as a "revenant" (*monstrum*), however, the enemy could not be discovered. The searchers went away disheartened, while the woman anxiously awaited daybreak. In the morning she fetched the nearest priest, who purified the entire house with saintly relics and holy water. During the following night, she was assailed by the same terror, but to a much lesser extent. Thanks be to God, repeated visits by the priest freed her from it completely.[13]

This sensational story is told with no embellishments, and Thietmar makes use of some astonishing words. He speaks in this regard of a miracle (*miraculum*), whereas we would expect the incident to be labeled rather as a marvel (*mirabilium*), and he calls the chief actor *monstrum,* meaning "revenant," and "ghost" rather than "demon" or "spirit," a fact that distinguishes him from the majority of medieval authors. We can offer the following hypothesis regarding his choice of words. There is implicit reference to other similar incidents in which there is no doubt concerning the nature of the noisemaker: a dead man. The priest's intervention gradually causes the manifestations to recede, but he has to return frequently, which gives the impression—as is often the case in these accounts from much earlier times—that the narrative does not fully conform to reality and that the narrator inserted a happy Christian ending. One detail speaks volumes in this regard: if the *monstrum* were a dead person, a condemned soul, he would have let this fact be known, and if it were a demon, the sacred relics—which are much more powerful than holy water—would have sent it fleeing immediately. Lastly we should note the absence of the husband and the presence of children (*filii*), who will take on their full importance later.

Thietmar tells of another incident[14] dated December 18, 1012: "a great light streamed from the church at first cock crow, filling the whole cemetery, and a very powerful noise 'like grunting' (*grunencium more*) was heard. My brother Frederick observed this along with my retinue and others who gathered there, and the chaplain who was sleeping next to me heard it." When he heard this, Thietmar questioned the older residents if this had ever happened before, and our author connects this event to the death of his cousin Luitgard, who died December 13. He then adds: "once, while everyone else was asleep, my companion and I clearly heard the dead conversing (*defunctos colloquentes*). From these two signs (*in his duobus signis*), I concluded that a death would occur the following day (*crastino subsecuturum funus intellexi*)." From this account we will retain the interpretation of the noise (whether or not it is connected to the light) as an omen or, to borrow a term commonly used in folk traditions, an "advent" (*avènement*).

When relating the marvels of the year 1122, Guibert de Nogent (ca. 1054–1125) mentions a large din that the monks of Saint Vincent's in Laon heard one night, "caused one might think, by evil spirits" (*tumultus quidam, ut putabatur, malignorum spirituum*).[15] He also mentions a priest who was unworthy of receiving last rites. Those keeping vigil at his deathbed saw "the windows of the house begin banging in the walls, and this noise was often repeated as if many people were coming and going."[16] The presentation of the facts suggests, casually and by virtue of the narrative sequences, that the devils were impatient to take possession of the dying man's soul and were letting him, and those attending to him, know it. It is easy to see the absence of logic in the two clauses of the sentence cited: In what way does the banging of the windows reflect the comings and goings of a crowd of people? The only logical solution is to accept that these individuals are going through the windows. Whatever the case may be, Guibert provides us with an additional element for our poltergeist typology: they can be portents, "foretellings" that herald an imminent death.

A turning point in the history of knocking spirits comes at the second half of the twelfth century and the beginning of the thirteenth century. This is primarily because popular beliefs had made their way into the texts; it is also because the learned authors designated them with more lucid terms. So while up until this time poltergeists had been largely confined to hagiography and historical writing, they now found their way into geography, the encyclopedia, and the novella.

CONDEMNED SOULS

In 1180 Hugues du Mans recounts a memorable incident that occurred in 1135.

> In the house of Nicholas the magistrate there was a fantastic being (*fantasia*), usually called a faun in pagan books, who was terrorizing those of lesser faith . . . along with most of the women and children.

It could often be heard making a noise similar to an enormous commotion of drums without any of the associated dissonance of the drummers themselves.

He often made sport of amazed and incredulous people with pottery shards or some other sort of crude objects.

With repeated casting of stones, which were launched as if by Herculean strength, it often struck the roof and walls of the house, and, invisible to all eyes, it would move paneling, cushions, platters, cups, and jugs from one place to another.

He lit candles from a distance, and when the foods were cooking or placed on the table, he snuck seed pellets, disgusting cinders, or bitter bits of suet into the dishes.

He wrapped the threads that Amica, Nicolas's wife, had taken great pains to prepare for making cloth, around a stool near the hearth, creating thousands of knots and deviations that were impossible to disentangle and which resembled the famous inextricable labyrinth.

When it was light again, the numerous people who saw this were stunned that someone could achieve such a thing, declaring that such intricate tracery could not be the work of a mortal hand.

Hugues provides a description that leaves no doubt as to the nature of the spirit: it was clearly a poltergeist, a sower of disorder, a noisemaker, and stone thrower. The word used to designate this entity in the Latin text, *faunus,* is an approximate transcription of a vernacular term that the lexicons and glossaries of this period inform us means "dwarves" or "spirits." In keeping with custom, the clergy is solicited to put an end to this haunting, and the text takes another twist.

After sprinkling the walls with holy water, with both words and gestures the priests made the sign of the cross of Our Lord, in the faith in the Holy and Indivisible Trinity, on their own foreheads and on those of the inhabitants of the house who spoke, in a truly terrifying tale (*relatu formidabile*), of things about which the century had never heard.

In the night a faint voice could be heard claiming to be Garnier, the late brother of Nicholas, and it reassured everyone: "The power to do evil to anyone has not been given to me." Garnier was not alone, and he explained that he had come from afar and was accompanied by "wicked troops," in other words demons, avid to wreak havoc. It was revealed that Garnier had come from Purgatory and needed masses and alms, therefore suffrages, in order to find redemption.

We see that knocking spirits can be condemned souls. As in the *Life of Saint Germain of Auxerre,* their manifestations seem to reflect their desire to attract attention so that they might be compelled to speak, their sole means of finding the path to redemption. What we have here is a splendid example of the *interpretatio christiana* of facts having no connection with the religion.

POLTERGEISTS AND PORTENTS

One of the most eminent authors of this period was Giraldus Cambrensis, or Gerald of Wales, who was born in Pembroke County circa 1145–1147. After finishing his studies in France he entered the service of Henry II in about 1180 and traveled to Ireland and Wales. He has left a fine account of these travels in his *Topographia Hibernica* (Topography of Ireland) and his *Itinerarium Cambriae* (Journey to Wales). He completed the latter book in 1191, and in it he reports:

In these parts of Pembroke, in our own times, unclean spirits (*spiritus immundos*) have been in close communication with human beings. They are not visible (*visibiliter*), but their presence is felt (*sensibiliter*) all the same. First in the house of Stephen Wiriet, then, at a later date, in the house of William Not, they have been in the habit of manifesting themselves, throwing refuse all over the place, more keen perhaps to be a nuisance than to do any real harm (*illudere potius quam laedere*). In William's house they were a cause of annoyance to both host and guest alike, ripping up their clothes of linen, and their woolen ones, too, and even cutting holes in them. No matter what precautions were taken, there seemed to be no way of protecting these garments, not even if the doors were kept bolted and barred. In Stephen's house things were even more odd (*majori miraculo*), for the spirit there was in the habit of arguing with humans. When they protested, and this they would often do in sport, he would upbraid them in public for every nasty little act they had committed from the day of their birth onward, things that they did not like to hear discussed and which they would have preffered to keep secret.[17]

Gerald saw in these facts the portent of a sudden change (*subitae mutationis*), therefore interpreting them as wondrous things, and, in referring to the sequel to these events—a sequel that he refrains from elaborating on—he says that these poltergeists herald either a transition from wealth to poverty, or the reverse. He finishes his story by revealing his surprise that the holy sacraments have been shown to be ineffective in such cases.

It seems most remarkable to me that these places cannot be cleansed of visitations of this sort by the sprinkling of holy water, which is in general use and could be applied liberally [or by high holy water*], or by performing some other religious ceremony. On the contrary, when priests go in, however devoutly and protected by the crucifix and holy water, they are among the first to suffer the ignominy of

---

*"High holy water" is water whose sacred quality has been increased by relics. The original text here reads: *quod nec aquae benedictae respersione, non tantum communis sed etiam magnae, nec ullius ecclesiastici sacramenti remedio, non illusionibus, tam sacramentalia quam sacramenta tuentur.* There were also folk methods in use until the nineteenth century; plants were employed to strengthen the power of the holy water.

having filth thrown over them. From this it appears that the sacraments and things pertaining to them protect us from actual harm
but not from trifling insults, from attack but not from our own
imaginings.[18]

Finally Gerald introduces two different kinds of poltergeists: The
one pestering William Not was connected with cloth, which he could
not tolerate being intact—he could also pass through walls. Stephen
Wiriet's poltergeist was a chatterbox. Both spirits shared the same habit
of throwing filth and being mischievous.

KNOCKING SPIRITS AS PRACTICAL JOKERS

Another Welshman, Gervase of Tilbury, born around 1152, confirms
the spread of manifestations of knocking spirits. He wrote his *Imperial
Diversions* (*Otia imperialia*) when he was the marshal of the Kingdom
of Arles in the service of Otho IV of Brunswick. Between 1209 and
1214 he compiled the first ethnographical inquiry of the Middle Ages.
In his work he discusses werewolves, spirits, demons, genies, and so
forth. With regard to brownies, "who live in the dwellings of simple
peasants," he notes three interesting details in passing. First, they slip
among the stones, wood, and household implements and make noise;
second, neither holy water nor exorcism will put them to flight (*nec
aqua nec exorcismus arcentur*); finally, they talk like humans.[19]

By patiently following the trail of the knocking spirits, we happen
upon a leading expert: William of Auvergne, who was born in Aurillac
shortly before 1180, was named Bishop of Paris in 1228, and died in
1249. In his treatise *De Universo*,[20] William studied spirits in general
and focused on demons in particular. Some spirits, the *joculares* or *jocu-
latores,* "so named because they play pranks," he said, are nothing more
or less than knocking spirits. William informs us that he had seen (*vidi*)
one of them who kept him from sleeping by throwing stones against the
walls, making noise by knocking containers together (*aut cum tumult*

lapidibus ad parietes allisis, aut vasorum collisione, quietum huiusmodi & somnum impediebat), stealing his sheets and covers off him, and tormenting him in his bed. He also spoke of a knocking spirit who had found his way into a house in the Saint Paul district of Poitiers, where he threw stones and broke windows, information that we also find in the work of the theology professor Petrus Mamoris of Limoges, author of *Flagellum maleficorum* (The Scourge of Evil, ca. 1462).[21] The spirits cast stones, moved furniture, broke windows, and struck people, but lightly so, making it impossible to discover how he was assaulting them. William adds that these spirits make off with objects—for example, "books and similarly light objects that are easy to carry"—removing them right in front of people's eyes and sometimes even directly from their hands, in order to take them elsewhere. What William says about the *joculares* can be compared to what the Scottish pastor of Aberfoyle, the Reverend Robert Kirk (1644–1692), wrote in his treatise on elves, fauns, and so forth.

> The invisible wights that haunt houses seem rather to be of our subterranean inhabitants, which appear often to men of the Second Sight, than [to be] evil spirits or devils. Though they throw great stones, pieces of earth, and wood at the inhabitants, they hurt them not at all [just] as if they acted not maliciously like devils, but in sport like buffoons and drolls.[22]

By grouping together the passages dealing with these particular spirits we can draw up a typology: they hurl stones but cause neither wounds nor injuries (*nec vulnus nec lesionem*);[23] they destroy houses (*eversiones domorum*)[24] and knock the dishware together.[25]

A COUSIN TO THE HOUSEHOLD SPIRIT

When the literature opened up to elements from popular culture, this undoubtedly added to an extremely healthy oral tradition concerning

knocking spirits, which seems to have encouraged this theme's incorpo-
ration into the novella or short story (*maere*). *The Little Crier and the
Polar Bear*[26] appeared around the middle of the thirteenth century; its
plot can be summed up as follows:

> A Norwegian accompanied by a bear stopped one evening at
> the home of a peasant who warned him that a spirit called Crier
> haunted his farm and turned everything upside down, literally jug-
> gling furniture and household tools. The man elected to spend the
> night there all the same. He ate and went to bed while his bear slept
> near the fire. In the middle of the night the Crier popped out of
> his hiding place and approached the hearth to warm himself. He
> saw that the bear had taken his place, punched it to drive it away,
> and a rowdy brawl ensued. In the morning the Crier came to see the
> peasant and asked him if that huge cat was still there. The other
> answered yes and added that the animal even had babies. Disgusted,
> the Crier left the premises for good.[27]

This text plays on the farcical and on folk beliefs. The Crier is
described as a brownie hardly three hand spans in size. He wears
a red cap and has extraordinary strength. An examination of the
names used by the anonymous author is quite telling, however. The
peasant states that "the minion of the devil and his phantoms have
settled in at my farm . . . It has been impossible for me to discover
just what kind of creature it is exactly."[28] It is a being (*kunder*)* who
is "so strong and agile that tables, chairs, and benches are like balls
to it; it throws plates, pots, everything on to the ground; it is ceaselessly making noise (*rumpeln*), throws the stones and boards of the
stove, baskets, and chests and everything else in every direction."[29] It
is alarming or monstrous (*ungehiure*), brutal or vulgar (*ungeslaht*), and
a "wicked kobold" (*boesez tuster*).

---

*A derivative from the Latin *genus,* this word is used to designate something that cannot
be named, a spirit, entity, supernatural creature, or unknown animal.

This Crier is a tormenting, rapping spirit presented by the author as kin to household spirits or dwarves. The name *tuster* is also applied to the latter. The manifestations—stones, boards, furniture, and dishes flying in all directions, and the tapping—are explicitly attributed to a diabolical being, as in the earlier Latin texts, but in contrast to those texts, the individual is partially described. So is this literature or the transcription of a belief? Undoubtedly it is a blend of both.

FINAL MEDIEVAL TESTIMONIES

Although attested at a fairly late date, the story of Vauvert Castle, at the gates of Paris, has its place here. Abandoned after the death of Philip the Fair, it was occupied by an evil spirit called "the devil of Vauvert" who "tormented and afflicted all who chanced to pass that way, for none could get by without being thwarted, insulted, or distressed. It also made loud cries and frightened everyone with these horrible voices."[30] Louis IX gave the castle to the Carthusians in 1257, and the spirits left. The text does not tell how this demon afflicted and struck people, but, by comparison with the other accounts, we have good reason to believe that the verb "afflict" refers to throwing stones and to slapping people.

Oddly enough, I have found only one account from the period that spans from 1270 to around 1500, if we ignore the retelling of Sigebert of Gembloux's text by the Rhineland inquisitors and authors of *The Hammer of the Witches*, Jacob Sprenger and Heinrich Kramer.

This following story can be found in *The Anthill*, by Johannes Nider (ca. 1380–1438), a Dominican monk of Colmar.

As a Dominican monastery was undergoing reformation, a demon attacked the house, breaking its windows, overturning the furniture, and cutting and making off with the bell ropes. At night it would bang the cymbals used to convoke the monks during the day, and it tormented the brethren without respite, driving some of them nearly mad. During the day the demon would lurk in the lower rooms of the monastery, and at night it would haunt the dormitory. It tore apart a novice's habit and ordered him to leave the holy order; it tormented him and threw his robes in the fire. . . . But once the reform was complete, the demon departed.[31]

This case is interesting because it involves a novice, thus an adolescent, just as in modern telekinesis phenomena. Everything is viewed in terms of the demonic, in conformity with monastic culture.

Although only a limited number of texts exist for a period of one thousand years—and it is certain that some did not survive into the present—they do teach us that we are confronting a perennial phenomenon closely linked to human beings. In more remote times the victims were specifically members of the religious community, and this was an invariable feature until the nineteenth century.

The activities of poltergeists cover a broad range:

Casting stones and/or filth

Vague noises: moans, hammer taps, knocking on the walls, dishes and other objects banged together

Banging of windows

Mischievous or malicious acts

Attacks on property: clothing torn, sewing thread tangled, dishes broken

Destruction of houses by fire

Attacks on specific individuals

The places where these incidents take place are essentially dwellings (houses, hermitages) or their immediate surroundings, but sometimes the poltergeist unexpectedly appears in the open. *Le Courrier de l'Isle* of June 3, 1843, mentions two young girls, about fourteen years old, from the village of Clavaux, who were caught in a hail of stones while they were walking along the main road. The manifestations are not confined to the nighttime.

The stone throwing is not always harmless; sometimes it causes injury. This makes it possible to distinguish between malignant spirits and mischievous spirits.

The Christian measures that are implemented—exorcisms, holy water, relics, sign of the cross, prayers—do not always succeed in stopping the phenomena, to the great astonishment of the narrators, who moreover emphasize this fact. This allows us to make another distinction: devils and demons must flee when confronted by sacramental methods, whereas the other "spirits"—place spirits such as fauns and sprites—are able to successfully resist these measures.

Another detail clearly shows that we are dealing with a heterogeneous population: some poltergeists talk and provide revelations, while others do not. Among those we might call the "revealers," there are two categories. The first group is openly evil and harmful, causing tension and discord. The second group consists of condemned souls who have come to seek aid. The noise that appears as a herald or foretelling of death is grafted marginally on this group as a whole, although over time it will come to occupy an important place.

We shall now follow the leads indicated to us by the texts, starting with the rapping and noise-making dead.

4

The Knocking and Noise-Making Dead

*[The seers] also affirm those Creatures that move invisibly
in a House and cast huge great Stones but do not much
Hurt because counter wrought by some more courteous and
charitable Spirits that are everywhere ready to defend Men, to
be Souls that have not attained their Rest.*

ROBERT KIRK, *THE SECRET COMMONWEALTH
OF FAIRIES*, 1691

In the previous chapters, we were able to compare the poltergeists who
are manifestations of the dead, and the medieval accounts allowed us to
bring an important facet of their history to light. The present chapter
will explore this point more deeply by relying primarily on the oral traditions the folklorists have handed down.

NOISES AS PORTENTS

One of the most frequent characteristics of the dead is to manifest through
various noises and actions,[1] as we have seen earlier in Hugues du Mans'

account. In the nineteenth century at Ingersheim Castle (Alsace), there was one called "the specter," *e Gespenst,* a term we saw earlier in Luther's writings, which opened and shut doors. It could also be heard moving through the halls and going up and down the stairs; it broke everything it could find in one of the rooms.[2] In Catalonia creaking sounds and moved objects were the sign that a dead person had returned home.[3] In the Vosges it was said that the dry cracking noises like the blows of a hammer that could be heard in furniture at night were the announcement of an imminent death, that of a friend or relative,[4] an opinion we already encountered in the narrative by Thietmar of Merseberg. This is a belief that can be found almost everywhere in France and throughout Europe. In Bas-Vannetais, Brittany, in Merlevenez, a carpenter sometimes could hear hammering and sawing in his workshop, as if someone were building a coffin, and he knew a death was near.[5]

Sometimes it is at the very moment of death that the deceased announces it to his family and friends.

> A scrawny cellist who was often ill had only two friends. When his health took a turn for the worse he was hospitalized in Rennes. One winter morning around five o'clock his pharmacist friend heard several knocks at the door. He went down, opened the door, and saw no one. Suddenly he heard repeated knocking—but still nobody was there. A short while later the sick man's other friend came by and told him the same thing had just happened to him. Both went to the hospital and learned that the cellist had died that morning at five o'clock: the very same time they had heard knocking.[6]

We should not suppose that this kind of incident is limited to folklore: modern studies have shown that belief in the dead who come to take their leave of those close to them or let it be known, by whatever means available, that they have just died, is widespread throughout the world. One of the most frequent means, when not in the form of an apparition,[7] is noise. Here is a completely unadorned account:

"I had a young child who died in town, a little two-year-old boy I had brought there for treatment. I stayed at my sister's house while I was there taking care of him," a woman recounted. "My husband stayed here [home] by himself. The little one died in my arms at two or three in the morning. I had telephoned to say he was not doing very well. That morning there was a terrible noise in the house, as if chairs were being flung about and as if everything in the kitchen had been sent flying. My husband got up, asking himself: Just what is going on here? He got up at the very moment the little one died. He was all alone and heard a terrible noise like someone sweeping in the kitchen. He got up but saw nothing. When I returned later that morning and told him I was bringing the dead child, he understood: 'That's the time I got up.'"[8]

And to clearly illustrate just how deeply certain beliefs are anchored in the human mind, the following statement leaves not even the shadow of a doubt.

My husband, after he died, appeared several times. He moved the furniture and made a lot of noise. I could hear tapping. But I did not realize what it was right away. Once at night I heard a loud rattling of chains, which woke me up. I quickly went down to the stables and saw all the oxen were up—someone had removed their chains. It was because my husband needed a mass to be said for him in order to find rest. The next day I went to the church to have one said and that put an end to it.[9]

The noise of chains rattling is a recurring motif in the stories of dead people who are in need of help.

A young woman from Bruz drowned in the Vilaine River, and one of her friends was apprised of this in the following manner. First she heard the noise of a pot falling to the ground, then another noise woke her up a moment later; it was like a vase falling and break-ing; finally she heard something like a person breathing. When she learned of the death of her friend, she did not doubt for a second that she had heard her "coming."[10]

In Ille et Vilaine, a terrifying noise one night awoke a young mar-ried couple on the Barre de Cicé farm, who thought they had heard a gigantic log falling into the fireplace. The husband went to see what it was but found nothing. They also heard someone climb-ing up and down the ladder to the attic, and the door to the cellar, although barred, was found open. If it was closed, it would noisily reopen. The wife, who was more and more frightened, had a mass said for the dead to rest in peace and the priest of Broz climbed up to the attic where he said several prayers. Following his visit the sin-ister noises were not heard again.[11]

And because these beliefs are often capable of being made use of by ill-intentioned people, I would like to point out an incident in the London neighborhood of Battersea, where a poltergeist gave two family members the idea to intensify the phenomena in order to induce mortal fear in an aged parent, and they succeeded.[12]

NOISY GHOSTS

One of the oldest accounts of noises caused by a dead individual is from Pliny the Younger (62–113), who, in a letter to his friend Sura, tells us this:

There was at Athens a large and roomy house, which had a bad name, so that no one could live there. In the dead of the night a noise, resembling the *clashing of iron* (*sonus ferri*), was frequently heard, which, if you listened more attentively, sounded like the *rattling of chains* (*strepitus uinculorum*), distant at first, but approaching nearer by degrees: immediately afterward a specter (*idolon*) appeared in the form of an old man, of extremely emaciated and squalid appearance, with a long beard and dishevelled hair, rattling the chains on his feet and hands. The distressed occupants meanwhile passed their wakeful nights under the most dreadful terrors imaginable. This, as it broke their rest, ruined their health and brought on distempers, their terror grew upon them, and death ensued. Even in the daytime, though the spirit did not appear, the impression remained so strong upon their imaginations that it still seemed before their eyes, and kept them in perpetual alarm. Consequently the house was at length deserted, as being deemed absolutely uninhabitable, so that it was now entirely abandoned to the ghost. However, in hopes that some tenant might be found who was ignorant of this very alarming circumstance, a bill was put up, giving notice that it was either to be let or sold.

It happened that Athenodorus the philosopher came to Athens at this time and, reading the bill, inquired the price. The extraordinary cheapness raised his suspicion; nevertheless, when he heard the whole story, he was so far from being discouraged that he was more strongly inclined to rent it and, in short, actually did so. When it grew toward evening, he ordered a couch to be prepared for him in the front part of the house and, after calling for a light, together with his pencil and tablets, directed all his people to retire. But that his mind might not, for want of employment, be open to the vain terrors of imaginary noises and spirits, he applied himself to writing with the utmost attention.

The first part of the night passed in entire silence, as usual; at length *a clanking of iron and rattling of chains was heard* (*concuti ferrum, uincula moueri*): however, he neither lifted up his eyes nor laid down his pen but, in order to keep calm and collected, tried to pass the sounds off to himself as something else.

The *noise increased* and advanced nearer, till it seemed at the door, and at last in the chamber. He looked up, saw, and recognized the ghost exactly as it had been described to him: it stood before him, beckoning with the finger, like a person who calls another. Athenodorus in reply made a sign with his hand that it should wait a little, and threw his eyes again upon his papers; the ghost then rattled its chains over the head of the philosopher, who looked up upon this, and seeing it beckoning as before, immediately arose, and, light in hand, followed it.

The ghost slowly stalked along, as if encumbered with its chains, and, turning to the area of the house, suddenly vanished. Athenodorus, being thus deserted, made a mark with some grass and leaves on the spot where the spirit left him. The next day he gave information to the magistrates and advised them to order that spot to be dug up. This was accordingly done, and the skeleton of a man in chains was found there; for the body, having lain a considerable time in the ground, was putrefied and moldered away from the fetters. The bones, being collected together, were publicly buried, and thus after the ghost was appeased by the proper ceremonies, the house was haunted no more.[13]

The reasons for the noises are clear and are the same as those in the *Life of Saint Germain of Auxerre*. The dead man is seeking to draw attention to his sad fate. Not having received a ritual burial, he cannot find rest. The noise here is therefore a language that expresses a request, an interpretation that has traveled down through the centuries to the present day. This story enjoyed great success and was picked up by Robert du Triez in *Ruses, finesses et impostures des esprits malins** (Cambrai, 1563), by the Capuchin monk Noël Taillepied (died 1589) in his *Traicté de l'apparition des esprits*,† as well as by Béroald de Verville (1558–1612), canon of Saint Gautier of Tours in his *Le Palais des curieux*‡ (Paris, 1612), which ensured it widespread distribution over the sixteenth and seventeenth centuries.

---

*[Tricks, Frauds, and Impostures of Evil Spirits —*Trans.*]
†[Tract on the Apparition of Spirits —*Trans.*]
‡[The Palace of the Curious —*Trans.*]

An account from 1583 clearly shows that a notion had arisen connecting a human death to poltergeist phenomena. An inhabitant of a house in Riga died, and peculiar things began occurring in the house: when the household was at the table, it would suddenly be lifted up; piles of straw were chopped into chaff; the doors to the rooms, although padlocked, were torn from their hinges; enormous stones covered with pitch were cast from on high, seriously wounding a Polish man who was present. The disorders came to an end when a priest blessed the house with water and incense before they even had to resort to an exorcism.[14]

In the Morvan area of Burgundy, observed Alfred Guillaume in 1923, "ghosts haunt houses at night making loud noises; here making dull knocking noises, there turning everything upside down."[15] In the Languedoc region ghosts and revenants are designated by the word *pôus*, the "fears." "They move furniture, turn off lights, pull away covers, and sometimes slap people who are sleeping. . . . Many people believe that the souls of the dead return during the night to ask for prayers and masses."[16] In the Pyrenees, people blame the *paüs* (fears) for creaking noises, the moving of objects, and the banging of doors and windows. In Catalonia these noises are warnings (*avisos*) indicating that a dead member of the household has returned home.[17] In the Ardèche the term *treva* (corresponding to modern French *trêve*) designates strange sounds that echo in the night: knocks on the doors or against the shutters, noises of chains dragging over the roof, thrown stones. It so happens that this word means "ghost," and the verb *trever* means "to wander," "to travel aimlessly."[18]

Toward 1850 there was a farm in the vicinity of Soudans (Lower Loire) whose inhabitants were awakened every night by church songs or unidentifiable noises. The farmer eventually tore down the wall from behind which the noise seemed to be coming and found priestly objects there that had been walled up during the Revolution. Locals said that a churchman had been discovered and slain by the blues.* The

*[The blues were the revolutionary forces in the War in the Vendée, an uprising that took place in 1793 against the French Revolutionary government. The Vendée is a region just south of the Loire River. —*Trans.*]

ornaments were taken to the town church, masses were said over them, and all the noise ceased.[19] In Nantes during the nineteenth century, an extraordinary noise could be heard in a very old house located on Haute-Grande-Rue. The man living there had a wall torn down where a cave was found, which had been walled up and was filled with human remains. Alerted to their presence, the superintendent of the quarter had the bones transported to the cemetery and nothing more was heard since. It was assumed that the bones came from a long-ago crime and that the dead person had been asking for prayers.[20] Around 1900 a school in Languedoc-Roussillon was haunted by a ghost who knocked under the table or at the second story window. Around midnight the bed would be moved to the center of the room and strange noises could be heard in the attic. The instructor discovered that the school had been built on the site of a hanged man's house. The priest came to bless the school, and the dead man rested in peace.[21] During the eighteenth century in Oberdorf (Alsace), knocking and hammering could be heard in a chimney, which the village elders explained was caused by the murder of a man on that site. The pastor's intervention had no effect whatsoever, and the haunting spirit only fled once the entire dwelling was consumed by flames.[22] In a house in Puy-de-Dôme the noise of chains could be heard every evening in the attic and on the grounds. The priest that was consulted on the matter stated it was a soul in torment and prayers should be said on the following night. This was done, and the children witnessed the appearance of their late father in chains. He led them to a boundary marker, vanished, and reappeared at another spot. They realized that the boundary marker had been moved and that he was indicating to them the place where it should be placed. They moved it to its rightful location, and afterward nothing more was heard.[23]

A Jew was murdered on the Willsmatt meadow in eastern France, and his murderer was never discovered. Shortly thereafter, at the same time every night a huge racket could be heard in the *marcairie*.* Saws,

---

*The name given in the Vosges to the hut where cheese is prepared.

axes, and kindling would fly through the air, and in the house dishes, pails, and utensils would start dancing madly about. Every time this happened, an accident would occur shortly afterward.[24] In Poitiers, following the death of François Coudreau on September 30, 1889, noises could be heard in the funeral home that sounded like someone tossing pebbles against the windows. The dead man's daughter asked, "If that is you, father, speak to us." The noises then stopped. Masses were said and the noises did not recur.[25] In Pézanas a man asked people to swear to have a mass said for him once a year in the chapel he helped to build. Time passed, and people eventually forgot to request that this mass be said. One day, when the Angelus was rung, the chapel's shutters began banging violently, and although they were fastened down they would open and shut every day when the Angelus was rung. It was realized that the dead man was unhappy, and a mass was held to soothe his spirit. Everything was restored to order.[26] In Santenac in the Ariège region, persistent strange noises could be heard in the parsonage following the death of Father Peyton. The local folk explained them by saying that the dead man's soul was in torment because he had not had enough time before his death to say all the masses for which he had received honorariums.[27]

Sometimes the narratives take a turn that seems more like something out of legend, or even an old exemplum. Let's look at two Alsatian examples. A revenant was throwing baskets full of stones against the doors and windows of a barn in Braunkopf; a Capuchin monk from Sigolsheim succeeded in imprisoning it inside a bottle, which he buried beneath the drainpipe,[28] a well-known defensive method since the Middle Ages.[29] Every time an adolescent went to bed at the farm of Petit-Ballon, a frightful din would be unleashed. One day a boy met the ghost responsible for these noises who brought him to a place where he told him to dig. The young boy unearthed a treasure.[30] Implied in this story is the theme of the miserly dead man who cannot rest peacefully until his gold has been found. This theme was commonly featured in medieval exempla so it is no surprise to find it in various ghost stories. In a house in Pont-Rousseau, near Nantes, renters heard weeping and moaning, and four women were seen in the attic, each of whom was holding one corner of an outspread sheet. The priest was consulted, and he advised that they ask the women what they wanted. One of the questioned weepers answered, "We have come on behalf of God. An ill-gotten treasure was once hidden here, just where this sheet is that we are holding. It should only belong to honest folk who have experienced misfortune and can make good use of it." Once this was said, they vanished. The treasure was found, and the noises were never heard again. The story had an amusing sequel. The owner filed suit against his tenant and lost because the justice of the peace felt "he had acted badly by not warning them beforehand that his house was haunted, something of which he was fully aware as no previous tenant had been able to stay there."[31]

In 1575 we encounter the inverse scenario. Gilles Bolacre rented a house in Tours. Once he had settled in, he was disturbed at night by knocking spirits. He turned to the proper authorities and asked for his lease to be canceled. The judge eventually acceded to his request.[32]

There are many additional examples, but the foregoing ones shall suffice as they clearly show the bases upon which it was possible to create a comparison between the poltergeists and the dead. Whatever names they may hold—fears, *treva,* ghosts, phantoms, revenants—the dead communicate with the living by virtue of noise, cast stones (as was already the case in the *Life of Saint Germain of Auxerre*), make knocking sounds in the walls, and move objects.

In two nineteenth-century poltergeist cases the interpretations are transparent, moralistic, and didactic:[33] "Mademoiselle de Z died impenitent, and it goes without saying that it was believed she had returned to the castle"; "in the countryside it was rumored that the father's creditors had not received all the money they were due (around 100 pounds sterling) and that the uncle was responsible for this state of affairs." The nephew's last wish had been for the uncle in question to pay off his father's debts, but the dead man's wishes had not been carried out.

On March 14, 2005, the Romanian newspaper *Evenimentul Zilei* ran a story titled "The Woes of the Grecu Family Were Caused by Titina's Ghost." The article began with the following introduction:

> The story of the Grecu family, whose house has experienced a poltergeist phenomenon, is well known in Craiove, in the Romanian province of Oltenia.* There has been widespread notice in the press over the past several weeks about the rain of stones and the lightbulbs that burn without being turned on. Possible explanations for this have been sought. *Someone said that the incidents were caused by a ghost.* Family members have even identified the revenant. Following a request by the Grecu family, the remains of a family member, who has been dead for two decades, *was disinterred. The priests said a mass,* so that Titina Ciorobea, dead at the age of fifteen, could find rest. It was the second time that phenomena of the poltergeist kind led to the exhumation of the remains of the presumed guilty party.†

This little news item easily demonstrates how little the attitudes have evolved on certain points and how it was believed that the agent behind the poltergeist phenomena was a condemned soul.

Those who died prematurely, killed by murder, suicide, or accident, have customarily, since the time of antiquity, returned to haunt the living. This deep-rooted belief has given ideas to ill-intentioned individuals, a good example of which is provided by events occurring in London at the beginning of 1762. A spirit was bothering the inhabitants of a house on Cock Lane, Westsmithfield, London, and especially a young, twelve-year-old girl. These incidents did not come to a halt until 1775. The apparition of a woman was seen that claimed to be Mrs. Kent, a woman who had died several years earlier. The investigation revealed that Parsons, the producer of the manifestations, wished to make others

---

*[Formerly Lesser Wallachia — *Trans.*]

†The newspaper goes on to say: "The first story took place in the Dolj region, in the village of Marotinul de Sus, where the villagers disinterred the dead girl, tore out her heart, and burned it."

believe that she had been murdered by her husband. Although the incidents proved to be fraudulent, and Mr. Parsons, the young girl's father, was condemned to the stocks and a prison term, Londoners took up a donation for him.[34] This reaction clearly indicates that Parson's staged events were strongly propped up by the extremely vital beliefs of his contemporaries, beliefs that made his manipulations of events credible.

A WELL-ORCHESTRATED NARRATIVE

Given the terms used by the recorders—we could even call them reporters!—of poltergeist phenomena, some narratives are almost unclassifiable if we wish to remain objective. We have two different accounts of the story that follows, and in each instance the narrators diverge concerning the name of the entity causing the manifestations. For the Benedictine Dom Calmet (1672–1757) it is a revenant; for J. J. von Görres (1776–1848), a political journalist and later a professor at Munich University, it is a demon.[35] In fact it is up to each individual to form his own opinion! This is what Dom Calmet says, based on what a cleric (who was probably one of the exorcists) had written him on August 8, 1748:

> They write me word from Constance, the 8th of August, 1748, that toward the end of the year 1746 sighs were heard, which seemed to proceed from the corner of the printing office of Sieur Lahart, one of the common council men of the city of Constance. The printers only laughed at it at first, but in the following year, 1747, in the beginning of January, they heard more noise than before. There was a hard knocking near the same corner whence they had at first heard some sighs; things went so far that the printers received slaps, and their hats were thrown on the ground. They had recourse to the Capuchins, who came with the books proper for exorcising the spirit. The exorcism completed, they returned home, and the noise ceased for three days.

At the end of that time the noise recommenced more violently than before; the spirit threw the characters for printing, whether letters or figures, against the windows. They sent for a famous exorcist outside of the city, who exorcised the spirit for a week. One day the spirit boxed the ears of a lad; and again the letters, &c., were thrown against the windowpanes. The foreign exorcist, not having been able to effect anything by his exorcisms, returned to his own home.

The spirit went on as usual, giving slaps in the face to one and throwing stones and other things at another, so that the compositors were obliged to leave that corner of the printing office and place themselves in the middle of the room, but they were not the quieter for that.

They then sent for other exorcists, one of whom had a particle of the true cross, which he placed upon the table. The spirit did not, however, cease disturbing as usual the workmen belonging to the printing office; and the Capuchin brother who accompanied the exorcist received such buffets that they were both obliged to withdraw to their convent. Then came others, who, having mixed a quantity of sand and ashes in a bucket of water, blessed the water, and sprinkled with it every part of the printing office. They also scattered the sand and ashes all over the room upon the paved floor; and being provided with swords, the whole party began to strike at random right and left in every part of the room, to see if they could hit the ghost, and to observe if he left any footprints upon the sand or ashes, which covered the floor. They perceived at last that he had perched himself on the top of the stove or furnace, and they remarked on the angles the marks of his feet and hands impressed on the sand and ashes they had blessed.

They succeeded in ousting him from there, and they very soon perceived that he had slid under the table and left marks of his hands and feet on the pavement. The dust raised by all this movement in the office caused them to disperse, and they discontinued the pursuit. But the principal exorcist, having taken out a screw from the angle where they had first heard the noise, found in a hole in the wall some feathers, three bones wrapped in a dirty piece of linen, some bits of glass, and a hairpin, or bodkin. He blessed a fire, which they lighted, and had all that thrown into it. But this monk had hardly reached his convent when one of the printers came to tell him that the bodkin had come out of the flames three times, and that a boy who was holding a pair of tongs, and who put this bodkin in the fire again, had been violently struck in the face. The rest of the things, which had been found, were brought to the Capuchin convent. They were burnt without further resistance; but the lad who had carried them there saw a naked woman in the public marketplace, and in the following days groans were heard in the marketplace of Constance.

Some days after this the printer's house was again infested in this manner, the ghost giving slaps, throwing stones, and molesting the domestics in diverse ways. Sieur Lahart, the master of the house, received a great wound in his head and two boys who slept in the same bed were thrown on the ground, so that the house was entirely forsaken during the night. One Sunday a servant girl carrying away some linen from the house had stones thrown at her, and another time two boys were thrown down from a ladder.

There was, in the city of Constance, an executioner who passed for a sorcerer. The monk who writes to me suspected him of having some part in this game; he began to exhort those who sat up with him in the house to put their confidence in God and to be strong in faith. He gave them to understand that the executioner was likely to be of the party. They passed the night thus in the house, and about ten o'clock in the evening one of the companions of the exorcist threw himself at his feet in tears and revealed to him that that same night he and one of his companions had been sent to consult the executioner in Turgau* by order of Sieur Lahart, printer, in whose house all this took place.

---

*In other words, "Thurgovia."

This avowal strangely surprised the good father, and he declared that he would not continue to exorcise, if they did not assure him that they had not spoken to the executioners to put an end to the haunting. They protested that they had not spoken to them at all. The Capuchin father had everything picked up that was found about the house, wrapped up in packets, and had them carried to his convent.

The following night two domestics tried to pass the night in the house, but they were thrown out of their beds and constrained to go and sleep elsewhere. After this they sent for a peasant of the village of Annanstorf, who was considered a good exorcist. He passed the night in the haunted house, drinking, singing, and shouting. He received slaps and blows from a stick and was obliged to own that he could not prevail against the spirit.

The widow of an executioner presented herself then to perform the exorcisms; she began by using fumigations in all parts of the dwelling to drive away the evil spirits. But before she had finished these fumigations, seeing that the master was struck in the face and on his body by the spirit, she ran away from the house, without asking for her pay.

They next called in the Curé of Valburg, who passed for a clever exorcist. He came with four other secular curés and continued the exorcisms for three days, without any success. He withdrew to his parish, imputing the inutility of his prayers to the want of faith of those who were present.

During this time, one of the four priests was struck with a knife, then with a fork, but he was not hurt. The son of Sieur Lahart, master of the dwelling, received upon his jaw a blow from a pascal taper, which did him no harm. All that being of no service, they sent for the executioners of the neighborhood. Two of the persons who went to fetch them were well thrashed and pelted with stones. Another had his thigh so tightly pressed that he felt the pain for a long time. The executioners carefully collected all the packets they found wrapped up about the house and put others in their room; but the spirit took them up and threw them into the market-place. After this, the executioners persuaded Sieur Lahart that he might boldly return with his people to the house; he did so, but the first night, when they were at supper, one of his workmen named Solomon was wounded on the foot, and then followed a great effusion of blood. They then sent again for the executioner, who appeared much surprised that the house was not yet entirely freed, but at that moment he was himself attacked by a shower of stones, boxes on the ears, and other blows, which constrained him to run away quickly.

Some heretics in the neighborhood, being informed of all these things, came one day to the bookseller's shop, and upon attempt-ing to read in a Catholic Bible, which was there, were well boxed and beaten; but having taken up a Calvinist Bible, they received no harm. Two men of Constance having entered the bookseller's shop from sheer curiosity, one of them was immediately thrown down upon the ground, and the other ran away as fast as he could. Another person, who had come in the same way from curiosity, was punished for his presumption, by having a quantity of water thrown upon him.

A young girl of Ausburg, a relation of Sieur Lahart, printer, was chased away with violent blows and pursued even to the neighboring house, where she entered.

At last the hauntings ceased, on the eighth of February. On that day the specter opened the shop door, went in, deranged a few arti-cles, went out, shut the door, and from that time nothing more was seen or heard of it.[36]

When one reads a story this complex, because it offers such a wide disparity of manifestations, one cannot help but wonder about the mentalities of those who produced it. It gives the impression that an entire complex of beliefs has been condensed out of a central incident, presented as proven fact, with the incident acting as a catalyst for the individual fantasies belonging to each of the actors in this little drama. Sieur Lahart tries everything to rid himself of this plague: Capuchin friars, executioners, peasant exorcists. The reason he turned to executioners can be explained easily: the men of this profession formerly had a reputation for being somewhat similar to wizards, as was always said about the so-called marginal professions. What is involved here is fighting back against fate using a counter charm. It is normal that the entity manifesting here be called a specter, as the German word used here, *Gespenst,* is a term whose polysemy has been revealed. It will be noted that the ecclesiastical intervention were futile, as often happens in poltergeist stories, and that the entity even clearly seems to mock their efforts.

To appreciate the thin line that separates the narratives of beliefs, called legends or memorates,* from the purely ethnographical accounts, it suffices to compare the preceding text to the letter that a certain Miss Renaudot addressed to Camille Flammarion (1842–1925) in 1912.

We arrived at Cherbourg, M. and Mme. Flammarion, myself, and the cook, on Thursday, April 25. Ever since Doctor Bonnefoy's invitation came I had been wondering how we should be lodged in that house, where we shared the family life more than three years before with charming and most devoted hosts, where we should find ourselves in a very different atmosphere, seeing that the doctor had married again. I had not wished to be given the room and the bed of the departed lady, my old friend, who had shown me so much sympathy, and whom I mourned with a profound sorrow.

It turned out that though I did not get Mme. Suzanne Bonnefoy's

---

*We should not forget that the legend is a story situated in a certain time and place and whose protagonists are named, which distinguishes it from the fairy tale that evolves with anonymous figures and outside time: "Once upon a time." The memorate is a form of legend that records a memorable incident that left its mark on people's minds and was deemed worthy of handing down to posterity.

room, I at all events got her bed, taken from the ground floor, where she died, up to a first-floor room, which had been her room as a girl. It was a great Breton bed, very old, of carved wood, and surmounted by a canopy hung with tapestry. The whole room was furnished with artistic old wooden furniture, bedside table, hat rack, ecclesiastical desk. Opposite the bed was a portrait of Mme. Bonnefoy—a photographic enlargement of a striking likeness.

I was much impressed with it. The memory of the past came upon me constantly. I saw our friend again, as she seemed so happy in her active and harmonious life devoted entirely to good deeds, and I figured to myself how she must have been on this same bed, which for two days and three nights had been her deathbed.

The first night, April 25 to 26, I did not sleep, thinking of her in the past and the present state of her house. I was also rather indisposed.

Next day, April 26 to 27, I promised myself a good night. About 11 p.m. I went to sleep and put away my old memories.

At 4 a.m. on the 27th *a loud noise awakened me.* On the left of the bed, *terrible cracklings were heard in the wall,* then went on to the table and around the room. Then there was a slighter sound, repeated several times, as of a person turning in a bed. The wood of my bed also creaked. Finally, I heard a noise of a light step gliding along to the left of the bed, passing round it, and entering the drawing room on the right, where Mme. Bonnefoy had been in the habit of listening to her husband playing the organ or the piano, he being an excellent musician.

These sounds impressed me so much that my heart nearly choked me with its beating, and my jaw became stiff.

In my emotion I got up, lighted a candle, and sat down on a basket standing on the landing outside the room. There I tried to account for the noises. They continued with still greater force, but nothing was to be seen.

At 5 a.m., a *prey to unreasoned terror* and unable to hold out, I went up to the cook, Marie Thionnet, who slept on the third floor. She came down with me. After her arrival we heard nothing more. It may be useful to remark that the cook's character did not harmonize at all with that of Mme. Bonnefoy.

At 5:45 a.m. the doctor on the second floor got up and went into his dressing room. The noises he made on getting up and walking about did not in the least resemble those I had heard an hour before.

In the course of the day I sought for an explanation of the phenomenon: cats, rats climbing along the walls. I examined the wall to the left of the bed. It was very thick, covered outside with slates, smooth and overlooking a yard. It was a bad run for cats or rats, as it was the front wall on the Rue de la Polle. Besides, the noises were very different from those produced by animals

On Saturday, April 27, I went to bed at 10:45 p.m., disturbed and nervous.

At 11 p.m. the noises started, as in the morning. I at once went upstairs to the cook, in my trepidation. She came down and lay on the bed beside me. We left our candles alight. *For half an hour the noises continued, with loud cracks on the wall on the left. Raps sounded on Mme. Bonnefoy's portrait or behind it,* and the raps were so loud we feared it would fall. At the same time steps glided through the room. The cook heard all this, too, and was much impressed. She is twenty-six years of age.

At 11:30 p.m. the noises ceased. As these manifestations were very disagreeable, especially as being due to an unknown and incomprehensible cause, I composed myself in the course of the next day, and, *supposing that the deceased might be associated with them,* since it happened in her house, I begged her to spare me such painful emotion.

We remained in the house until Saturday, May 4. Having heard nothing more, and having calmed down, I then asked the deceased to manifest herself, and to let me know in some way what she might desire.

But I have not observed anything since then, in spite of my wish (mixed with nervousness) to test the phenomena and to obtain, if possible, an explanation of this strange manifestation.

SIGNED GABRIELLE RENAUDOT,
CHERBOURG, MAY 7, 1918[37]

PLACE MEMORIES

In her *Légendes rustiques* [Rural Legends], George Sand echoes a belief that could be called "place memories." It was once believed that at any spot where violent events occurred "the cries of the victims and various noises accompanying a massacre were imprinted on the walls as if upon a magnetic tape recording."[38]

In the canton of Le Châtre, it is not only animals that return but even furniture. From the times in which Briantes Castle was still inhabited, otherworldly scenes would take place there. A certain peasant manager, who wished to get a deeper understanding of these mysteries and brought a strong mind to the task, was forced to abandon his plan. There was a prison cell in the uppermost room from which emitted at night the most dreadful noises, animal howls, human moans, and huge gusts of wind that would blow out the lights. These were the souls of men and beasts who had been massacred in this domain by pillaging Huguenots and merciless horsemen. But there is more, because the furniture had been smashed and thrown out the windows, and everything laid waste in these calamitous times, the creaking and shuddering of invisible objects could also be heard that seemed to be rolling down the staircases upon you and threatening to crush you.

The above-mentioned manager, having braved these enigmas for some time without incurring any harm, figured he was in the clear, but one night on returning from the marketplace and entering the castle's kitchen to rest and get warm, the chair on which he wished to sit turned over, dumping him upside down. While he was looking for a seat with a friendlier disposition, all the chairs and benches of this same kitchen rushed at him, striking him so severely that he had to turn and flee—especially as the spits and cleavers had joined the party, chasing him out into the center of the courtyard.

The last section of the text is noteworthy because it shows that the belief we just examined had already been adulterated in George Sand's time. Here inanimate objects are endowed with the same properties as human beings. Sand also mentioned the haunting of Briantes Castle in her correspondence, but in more sober fashion.[39]

In contrast to what our author says, the cries and noises were generally heard, so it was believed, on the anniversary date of the massacre. It could be cautiously proposed that this belief intersects with that of the influence of remains, an example of which I gave earlier with the story of the haunted farm in Soudan in 1850. In 1926, E. Bozzano suggested the following explanation.

Inanimate matter has the property of recording and storing in a potential state all manner of physical, mental, and vital emanations and vibrations . . . the telesthetic faculties of the subconscious have the ability to find and interpret these vibrations and emanations, just as the mnemonic faculties have the ability to find and evoke anew the latent vibrations of thought.[40]

THE TREE SPIRIT AND THE DEAD PERSON

In Lourouer-Saint-Laurent, in the canton of La Châtre, a man chopped down a box tree because it was annoying him. Afterward he was awakened at midnight every evening by three violent knocks that threatened to shatter his door, and until first cockcrow "he constantly heard the blows of an ax and the loud *hans** combined with muffled, plaintive

---

*[A muted grunting sound synonymous with a type of noise-making spirit. The *hans* is described in more detail in chapter 6. —*Trans.*]

sighs." The noises lasted six weeks and stopped when he had a mass said.[41]

Here we find a melding and superimposition of various beliefs: the very ancient belief that spirits (dryads, hamadryads, and so on) inhabit trees—in the Middle Ages offerings were made to these spirits before the tree was chopped down; in the words of the penitentials this was called *obligationes ad arbores*—together with a belief in portents. In the subsequent Christianized version of the earlier belief concerning spirits, trees can become the abode of tormented souls. It was believed that the soul of the dead person buried at a certain spot could pass into a tree that was growing there.[42] Thus, interpreted along these lines, the plaintive, muffled sighs would be those of the tree spirit—recall Ronsard's *Ode à la forêt de Gastine**—or those of a condemned soul asking for a mass. A psychological reading would say that the man was gripped with remorse and dreamed each night about cutting down the tree.

Knocking spirits have been closely linked with death in the human mind. In 1849, in Orton (Westmoreland), the Bland family abandoned their house not only because of a poltergeist but also because of how the neighborhood interpreted the situation. According to the local people, it was because the elder Gibson, the former owner, who had been found drowned, had certainly not died by accident. It was therefore thought that the spirit of the unhappy dead man manifested by sowing disorder and making a din.[43] In 1916 the neighbors of an Irish farmer had their own explanation regarding the poltergeist who was knocking at his house. A short time before, a man claiming he had been wronged swore to have revenge on the farmer's wife and child. It was said that all the troubles began when this man died in America.[44] These two examples are characteristic of how poltergeists resort to noises, as as we have described.

It was this mental backdrop that determined the attitude of spiritualists attempting to communicate with the entity responsible for an

---

*[A famous tale by the French poet Pierre de Ronsard (1524–1585) —*Trans.*]

incident in order to find out who it is and why it is manifesting. They think frequently of the deceased, as is the case in folk traditions, which view poltergeists as tormented souls who need someone to do something for them, such as say masses, for example.

We shall now examine another equally prevalent interpretation that views deviltry and sorcery as the source of the manifestations under consideration here.

5

Deviltry, Magic, Sorcery, and Poltergeists

A good means for tracking down the knocking spirits hidden in popular traditions is to list all houses that have experienced singular, inexplicable, and alarming manifestations, and which are often described as the "devil's house." A designation like this is already the product of an interpretation that is based in the religion of both the narrator and those involved, but it cuts short any further consideration of the subject. "That's just how it is," they seem to be telling us. The need to label these incidents has certainly played a predominant role, for it is one way of compartmentalizing things and overcoming fear. It is only one reaction of many, however, but because of its productive nature—one that's been in operation since the Middle Ages, as we have seen—it will be helpful to take a closer look at the actions attributed to the devil.

THE DEVIL'S HOUSE

As our first example, let's take one from the *Chronicle* that Johann of Winterthur began writing in 1340.

In 1307 a woman of Walenstadt died. She arose from her funeral bier and spoke of numerous people that were in the beyond and stated that she had almost been damned because of a sin she had dared not confess, but that Saint Francis had saved her. He had restored her to life so she could confess and then, once purified, find rest. She then lay back down and died. In the dead woman's house an evil spirit manifested because the Franciscans had stolen a soul away from him. It terrified the inhabitants, and its manifestations stopped when the house was given to the Franciscans. From then on the building served to house the lesser brethren who collected alms.[1]

The narrator does not harbor the slightest bit of doubt that the devil is present, but unfortunately he does not inform us about what kind of manifestations the devil used to scare the inhabitants. The readers are therefore left with the task of imagining these. In earlier eras readers would infallibly do this with recourse to their contemporary religious beliefs. Fortunately, other texts are more precise, although they are of more recent vintage.

Philipp Camerarius (1537–1624) reports that in 1553, in the Wurttemberg town of Schildach, an evil spirit (*cacodemon*) had been manifesting for some time in the Gold Star Inn (*Aurea Stella*) located by the marketplace. Howls and extraordinary sounds could be heard there (*clamoribus ac clangoribus mirifice exagitasset*). It was believed that the maid was an accomplice to this evil spirit (*incubus*), and she was dismissed from service. Several days later a devilish fire (*incendium diabolicum*) spread throughout the entire town in two hours. What was so unusual about this is that balls of fire were raining down here and there onto the houses. The priest of Schildach, from whom Camerarius heard this story, provided several singular details on the demon's tricks (*miras artes diabolicas*). He knew how to imitate the voices of birds and charm the ear with the sweetest melodies. The priest bore a crown of gray hair, which had been caused by a circlet the demon had placed on his head when asking him if he also knew the voice of the raven.[2] It will be noted

CAPVT LXXIV.

De cacodæmone Camontino & Schil-
tacenſi.

VENTINVS refert hiſtoriam,quæ in pago Camõtino ad *Lib.4.annal.* Rhenum accidit ſane memorabilem, de mirificis illuſio- *Boior.* nibus diaboli, quæ vt rectius cognoſcatur, eius verba in- ſerere volui. Ibidem, inquit, hiſce diebus deſertor ac per- fuga ſpiritus, multa miracula edidit, circulatorias præſti- gias luſit, incolas infeſtauit. Primo vmbra feralis, à nemine quidem con- ſpecta, lapides in homines iactare, pultare fores cœpit. Mox ſub humana effigie peſtilens ac nequiſſimus ille genius delitefcens, reſponſa reddidit, furta prodidit, criminatus quoſcunq; nota infamiæ afperſit: diſcordias, ſimultates excitaut. Paulatim horrea, caſas omnes ſuccendit atque exuſ- ſit. Sed vni moleſtior extitit, perpetuo eius lateri, quocunque diuerteret, hærens atque domum comburens: Et vbi viciniam vniuerſam in necem innocentis concitaret, ob ſcelera illius hunc locum infamem ac deuotum eſſe, prauus mendaciorum faber iactabat. Coactus eſt homo ſub dio ma- nere. Ab omnibus enim, quaſi lemuribus noſturnis ſacer, tecto arcebatur. Atque vt ille confinibus ſatisfaceret, candens ferrum manibus portauit, ac quum non violaretur, inſontem ſe comprobauit. Nihilominus tamen in agris frumenta eius in aceruos compoſita, idem Lar contaminatus ac perditus combuſſit. Et quum odioſus indies magis atque magis eſſe per- geret, coacti pagani rem ad Pontificem Moguntiauum deferunt. Sacerdo- tes, miſſi agros, villas, ſacris ac comprecationibus, luſtrali aqua, ſaleque
Vu 3   luſtri-

The beginning of the account of the Schildach cacodemon in the 1602 edition
of Operae horarum subcisivarum *by Philipp Camerarius. The work was*
published in English as The Living Librarie *in 1621.*

that yet again the fire was spread by a demonic knocking spirit, like the one in the *Chronicle* of Sigebert of Gembloux, which also turns up in an anonymous treatise published in 1597.[3] Referring to the human- ist Johannes Turmair known as Aventius (died 1534),[4] Camerarius also mentions an evil spirit who was raging in Canmuz near Bingen in the province Rheinland-Pfalz. It began by throwing stones at people (*lapides in homines iactare*) and making tapping noises (*pultare fores*); then it set fire to the lofts and houses. It was fond of appearing in human guise and making revelations. It attacked one resident in particular, excit- ing the neighborhood against him and succeeded in having its victim driven away. An end was put to these misdeeds by the strength of the prayers and benedictions of the priests sent by the Bishop of Mainz.[5]

The sixteenth century is truly the one in which poltergeists acquired their free rein. Not far from Wurttemberg in 1583, all the household implements in a priest's home were violently thrown on the floor and a large number of torches lit in a room were all extinguished in one fell swoop. Pillows and comforters were torn from the beds of the sleeping residents, and the members of the household often felt someone grabbing their throats. The parish priest asked the rector of the Jesuit college to send him a priest and when the latter arrived a plate was tossed forcefully against the wall. The priest put on his stole and went to the room where the knocking was loudest. He then began the standard ceremonies that are called for in such cases. He advised the family to pray and purify themselves through the sacrament of penitence. All this was done and calm was restored to the house.[6]

In 1612–1613 extraordinary events took place in Mâcon, France. A pamphlet was published about them,[7] and the affair is known as the "Devil of Mâcon." It all began when something opened the curtains of Protestant pastor François Perrault's wife's bed, then stripped away her covers. Her husband searched the entire house and found nothing. A loud commotion next broke out in the kitchen, where it was noted that the utensils were being thrown against the walls. Another search was undertaken, but it was equally futile. The pastor went to the royal notary of Mâcon and made a deposition. In September, in the presence of numerous witnesses who had been attracted there by these phenomena, the evil spirit whistled, spoke, sang bawdy songs, and imitated the shouts of the jugglers, merchants of the marketplace, and even the hunters. Long conversations then took place between the spirit and those present, whom he mocked. He recited the Our Father, the Credo, the morning and evening prayers, and even the Ten Commandments, but omitted certain passages—which is what makes him a demon—and he made revelations about past events that proved perfectly exact. The spirit liked to linger in one room in particular, where he systematically tossed all the bedding onto the floor. He joked with a serving maid, whose parents had been accused of witchcraft—which implies that she was more or less a witch—and when the servant quit her post, the spirit took it out on her replacement. He threw stones on the house and at people, without hurting anyone. A witness picked up a stone and found it was burning hot—a detail sometimes noted about "true" poltergeists—and he believed it had come from hell. The entity presented itself as a spirit seeking redemption, but Perrault was of the opinion that it was trying to pass itself off as the soul of a woman who had died in the house a short time before. On another occasion the spirit announced that it wished to draw up its will before going to Chambery, where suit had been filed against it, and it feared it might die while on the way there. Before vanishing it hung bells on a nail above the fireplace.

One cannot help but be astounded by such an accumulation of facts, each more contradictory and irrational than the next. Here is an entity that is a rapping spirit, a soothsayer, a mischief-maker, a stone thrower, a mocker, and a quasi-liar. He even possesses the distinctive sign of the *genus catabuli*[8] and knows the main prayers. This is a lot for just one single entity. As is often the case in these older times, the accounts are composites. Here deviltry and witchcraft are blended together upon a foundation of beliefs that relate to the dead and to household spirits.

In 1654, in the northern Italian area of Valtellina, a young count, priest, and doctor of canon law had been persecuted for two years by demons who threw stones at him every night and raised such a racket that he was unable to remain in his castle or even nearby. One evening two clerics came to spend the night with him in his room, boasting how they had no fear of demons. Shortly before midnight "the noises began, the earth shook, and smoking stones were cast at the three of them." Terrified, one of the clerics collapsed with fever and the other with dysentery; both snuck away the next morning.[9]

That same year a series of incidents took place in Scotland that were so extraordinary that the Bishop of Salisbury, Gilbert Burnet (1643–

1715), included an account of them in *The History of the Reformation of the Church of England*, based on the narrative provided by the son of the principal victim whom the phenomena afflicted. This story has come down to us under the name of "The Devil of Glenluce." During the month of October 1654, the house of the weaver Gilbert Campbell, a resident of the ancient parish of Glenluce in Galloway County, Scotland, fell prey to numerous manifestations that were thought to be diabolical in origin.

An insolent beggar, one Alexander Agnew, later to be hung at Drumfries for the crime of blasphemy, had threatened Gilbert Campbell for not giving what he considered to be sufficient alms. From that time on, misfortune seemed to be bound to the weaver. First of all, all the tools he needed for his trade were broken; then, starting in mid November, stones were cast in force and great number against the windows, doors, and chimneys.* Gilbert advised the local minister and his neighbors of the situation, but everything continued as before. He oftentimes found his warp and thread cut as if by scissors and the apparel of his family suffered from the same fate: coats, bonnets, and shoes even while they were wearing them. However their persons were spared save they were unable to find sleep at night. Chests and trunks were opened and the *objects they contained cut, strewed about, or hidden.* This trouble became so bad that the poor man was obliged to abandon his trade, which was his sole livelihood, and to store all he had in the safety of a neighbor's house. He, meanwhile, remained in his house. He was advised to send his family away, which he did, and calm reigned for four or five days. Following the minister's counsel, he summoned his children to return home, and *the peace continued until one of his sons, Thomas, who had*

---

*About the middle of November; at which time the Devil came with new and extraordinary Assaults, *by throwing of Stones in at Doors and Windows, and down through the Chimney head, which were of great quantity, and thrown with great force, yet by God's good Providence there was not One Person of the Family hurt or suffered damage thereby.*

*been sent the farthest away, returned.** The racket began anew, and on the next day, which was a Sunday, *the house was set on fire.* It was put out though by neighbors returning home from church and thus caused little damage. Fasting and prayers were prescribed for the following day, but despite this, the house was again set on fire at nine o'clock in the morning Tuesday; yet again it was speedily extinguished with little harm done. Campbell, tormented this way both day and night, went to the minister to ask him to let his son Thomas stay at his home for a time. The minister consented but warned him that it would do no good. In fact, *"for notwithstanding that the Child was without the Family, yet were they that remained in it sore troubled, both in the day-time, and in the night season."* They were obliged to stay awake until midnight and often the entire night through, and during this time their clothing was torn, stolen away, and tossed here and there.

Some ministers who had gathered in the township for a feast day persuaded the weaver to bring his son Thomas back home, whatever the consequences. The lad said he heard *a voice* forbidding him to step foot into the house. He went inside nonetheless, but *was mistreated so badly he was obliged to return to the minister's.* On Monday, February 12, the rest of the family began to hear a voice but were unable to tell where it came from. A fairly frivolous conversation took place that evening until midnight. The minister came by the next day accompanied by several other people, and, once the prayer was over, all heard a voice coming from under the bed speaking in proper country dialect: "Would you know the witches of Glenluce, I will give you their names." He then named four or five people of ill repute. Campbell noted that one of these individuals had long been dead. "That true," answered the voice, "but her Spirit is living with us in the World." The minister replied: "May God punish you, Satan, and reduce you to silence! We want no information from you about who are your folk. You seek only to seduce this family, for

---

*No trouble followed, till one of his Sons, called Thomas, that was farthest off, came home.

Satan's kingdom is not divided against itself." After this, all knelt down in prayer again, and during this time the voice was hushed. But once the prayer had ended, *it yelled at the lad who had returned that if he did not leave the house, he would set it on fire.* The minister replied: "God shall preserve the house and this child as well for he belongs to this family and has the right to stay here." The voice said: "He shall not remain here, he was put out once already and cannot stay even if I have to pursue him to the ends of the earth." The minister responded: "The Lord shall protect him from your malice." They then all went to pray again, and the voice said: "Give me shovels and spades; stay away from this house for seven days, and I will dig a grave and lie down in it, and I shall trouble you no more." The weaver answered: "With the help of God, not so much as a straw shall be given you, even if it would obtain rest for us." The minister added: "God shall drive you away in his own good time." The voice replied: "You cannot budge me from here, for Christ gave me the mission to haunt this house." The minister responded: "God shall know in his own time when to withdraw that permission." The voice retorted: "I have a commission that shall perhaps last longer than yours." The minister and the others arose and went over to where the voice seemed to be coming to see if they could find anything. Despite their diligent search, nothing was found. "It seems," one said to the minister, "that the voice comes from the children." Some of the children were in fact in bed. The voice answered: "You are lying and God shall punish you for it; I and my father shall come fetch you down to hell." The voice imposed silence on the other gentlemen, telling them: "Let him that has a commission speak, for he is a minister of God."

They all then sat close to the place from where the voice appeared to be coming. A kind of argument ensued between the Presbyterian and the invisible entity, based in large part on texts from Holy Scripture. When one of the parties countered the other with some disconcerting text, the other would respond in kind. The dispute heated up; finally, when the minister was backing into the room, the voice yelled: "I did not know these passages until my father taught them to me. *I am an evil Spirit, and Satan is my father, and I am come to vex this House.*" Suddenly a hand and arm bare to the elbow appeared. The hand struck the floor so hard that the whole house shook. Then the voice howled out horribly, saying: "Come, Father, come! I want to send my father among you. Don't you see him behind you?" The minister said: "When I heard the blow that was given to the floor, I indeed saw a hand and arm." The voice replied: "Well, that was not my hand; it was that of my father; my hand is blacker on the outside. If you truly wish to see me, put out the light and I will appear in your midst *like Fire-balls.*" During this conversation night had fallen and the visitors prepared to leave. The voice yelled out: "Let not the minister leave, else I shall burn down the house." As he had already stepped out, the weaver begged him to come back. The voice then said: "You have done my bidding." The minister replied: "It was not for you but in obedience to God and to keep company with this poor man in his affliction."

All knelt again in prayer and the minister forbid the family from opening their mouths and speaking with the evil spirit and advised them if he should address them to fall upon their knees and pray to God. The voice shouted: "What, you do not wish to speak with me? Well then, I shall burn down the house and cause you all manner of troubles." No one answered him, and nothing more was heard from him for a long time. But Gilbert was still often vexed and never enjoyed two days free of his torment in any week, and this went on until the month of April.

After this time things went somewhat better until July. But new assaults were made then, and the poor family was soon reduced to the most abject misery, because even what they ate was of no benefit to them. Gilbert therefore turned to the synod, which had planned to again convene in October 1655, to ask whether he should leave his house or stay. The synod sent a commission to Glenluce and commanded there be set aside a day in February for penitence and prayers for this poor family throughout the township. Things went better from that time until April, and from that time until the month of August, nothing was heard at all. But the evil soon reappeared. The foods being prepared for meals *were hidden beneath the threshold; the contents of plates were spilt over the beds or even inside the covers,* or else everything was carried away leaving nothing but bread and water. No one could sleep the night in the house during the entire month of August because of the constant noise. The noise grew even more intense and, to boot, *the spirit began throwing stones and striking them.*[*10] Toward midnight on September 18 a voice was heard shouting: "I am going to burn the house down," and three or four nights later, one of the beds was set on fire. Gilbert continued to be tormented until the day this document was written.

The wealth of information here is extraordinary: the astounding dialogues (R 5; B 6) between the spirit and the churchmen are a good reflection of the beliefs of this time period. The presence of Gilbert's son Thomas seems to be the source of some of the phenomena (R 1),[†] but the persecution to which he is subject shatters this hypothesis, and it is undoubtedly one of the other children who is responsible. The most striking thing is the constant threat of burning the house and the starting of fires. Such threats, although though they are not so frequent, nevertheless recur throughout our corpus.

Around the year 1791, near Miramont-de-Guyenne, France, bordering the old Marmande road, there was an old house that had been long abandoned because of the inexplicable noises that could be heard there with increasing frequency: the clinking of irons, the cracking sounds of beams, and the creaking of the floorboards. The peasants avoided

---

[*]About which time the Devil began with new Assaults, and taking the ready Meat that was in the House, did sometimes hide it in holes by the Door-Posts, and at other times did hide it under the Beds, and sometimes among the Bed-clothes, and under the Linnens, and at last did carry it quite away, till nothing was left there save only Bread and Water to live by.

[†]It could well have been a psychokinesis (PK) subject according to psychic researchers.

going near it, but one of them saw the house one night all illuminated by flames inside, and he could see human shades leaping away from the flames or unsuccessfully trying to escape through the windows. On his return home he told his family that hell would be found not far from Miramont.[11] Rather than the usual notion of a house haunted by the devil, here we see a transposition of hell on earth, an epic exaggeration that is undoubtedly caused by great fright.

During the second half of the eighteenth century, Schupart, a Protestant pastor from the Swabian region of Hohenlohe, was tormented for a period of eight years. Stones were thrown at him both day and night; several thousand were cast without wounding him in the slightest. Ropes were tied around his feet and throat, as well as around his wife, and both were slapped in the presence of witnesses. Ink was spilled on the pages of his Bible, or they were torn. One day the books he needed to prepare his sermon were spirited away, and—in an amusing detail—his wig was found on his wife's head! A lit lamp was knocked onto the ground, where it continued to burn, or else it would be carried elsewhere. The set table and its plates would be tossed about, and he was pricked with needles and bitten. In short, something was making his life a living hell. The Jesuits and Carmelites of Hohenlohe sought "to prove by this that the Lutheran doctrine he had embraced was false," but he was content to continue begging God to deliver him from this plague.[12] To G. P. Verpoorten, who preserved this account, it was obvious that this was the devil's work. It will be noted that Schupart was physically assaulted, which is not a rare occurrence in poltergeist tales: the bites and stings are well attested in modern times.[13]

A Chartres newspaper dated March 14, 1849, tells of a miller named Dolléans, a resident of Guillonville in the Eure-et-Loir region of France, who was victimized by the theft of some bales of hay and the setting of a fire. His maid accused a neighbor, who was arrested and subsequently released for lack of proof. Once this man was arrested, terrifying things began occurring at the Dolléans' home; knocking was heard on the floor, doors were noisily thrown open, the bolts and padlocks disappeared, and the servant fell prey to invisible beings. Ropes, candles, blankets, bread baskets, and bottles full of water would mysteriously find their way onto her back or inside her pockets. Kitchen utensils would cling to her skirt or apron strings. If she entered the stables the horses' harnesses and sacks of oats would attack her. In short, for a solid month the servant was the victim of these vexations, which were blamed on the neighbor alleged to be a vindictive sorcerer. The priest of Cormainville was summoned and exorcised the premises, after which the usual calm was restored.[14]

Around 1879–1880, at a farm in Saugy, a hamlet of Saône-et-Loire, France, two servants were cowering in the hayloft where they slept one winter evening. They had been frightened by the repeated muffled sounds echoing over their heads. They went to awaken their employers, who also became scared. The noises resumed the next night and again on the nights that followed, and they were attributed to the devil. Knocks were also heard on the floorboards and the roof beams as well as the clinking of iron and a tinkling noise on the tiles, but when anyone began looking for their source, the noises all stopped. It soon came turn for the house itself: the table was overturned and all the dishes on it broken, the stew pot was thrown to the ground, and it was as if the handles of the iron tools had been electrified. Anyone entering the stables at night would be struck on the head or back. Every night the servants were tossed to the foot of their beds. Magic was tried—in vain. The investigations by the gendarmes turned up nothing. The manifestations continued but at longer and longer intervals; then it all stopped.[15] This curious tale includes incidents that are known to have happened elsewhere. There are numerous claims, for example, by individuals that they were tossed from their beds throughout the night, even where several people have maintained: "He never knew who the hell threw him on the ground," says a narrator, "people said it was the devil who did it."[16] In other words, when people were confronted by poltergeists in this era, the devil was the first plausible explanation.

In Ampfersbach, in Alsace, there was a house haunted by the devil who had come there to raise hell. A new renter, a freethinker, had recently moved in. In the beginning all was quiet, but one night the renters were woken by the sound of chains and the sound of a very heavy object hitting the door. The iron pots in the kitchen also began clanging together, and this infernal din lasted until one o'clock in the morning. The next day everything was found in its usual place; nothing had been moved. These nightly noises only came to an end when a bread oven was built in the house.[17] While the narrator was convinced it was the devil at work in this house, the end to the manifestations takes on a new perspective when we know that the bread oven is often the home for a household spirit.

Monsignor Barthes speaks meanwhile of another haunted house in Lacrouzette, France, called the *Oustal of the Pooü* (the House of Fear), which is alleged to have been the result of a pact with the devil, but he never tells us anything about the phenomena that inspired this interpretation.[18] In the commune of Saint-Just-de-Claix (Isère, France) the devil had gathered his children in a house where they rapped on the pans and dragged chairs; in Saint-Bueil, France, the house of the devil was identifiable by noises and lights. In Chozeau another house had been the home of a murderer. Unusual noises were heard there, furniture was moved and chairs dragged across the floor.[19] It is worth citing here the observation of the teacher J. B. Bardin, who at the beginning of the twentieth century published accounts of the local beliefs from his region, the Septème (Isère). In the following traditions, the devil is confused with the domestic spirit.

Now it seems that the devil, or rather Mandrin [*sic*], had a larger theater of operations than the house and grounds of Mallissol. The elders of our whole region say that he does not only show himself in lonely valleys but moves into the farms, tangling the manes of the horses and making unusual noises in the stables and haylofts. . . . these strange noises are often heard in the stables, haylofts, and even in the houses, noises that send a shudder up the spine of even the least frightened souls; it is the devil, people say, and they make certain not to investigate what is causing it.[20]

A Czech legend tells how a certain Nebojsa stopped at an inn attached to an old smithy where the devil (*cert*) was living it up. Every night the sound of a chain being shaken could be heard, and loud banging on the anvil. Anyone courageous enough to spend the night there was found dead the next morning. Of course, the hero meets the devil, who suggests he wager his soul in a game of cards.[21] It will be noted that the place this demon appears is a forge, such as we saw in the account by Notker the Stammerer and in the following one from Mülldorf, near Strasbourg.

> On January 23, 1749, hammers, tongs, and other tools, as well as objects never seen before, suddenly started moving violently around the workplace, falling to the ground or on those present, but so gently that they caused no harm. Anne Bayerin, the blacksmith's maid, confessed she had made a pact with the devil and caused these phenomena with his help.[22]

In 1863 Professor Perty of Bern University, in response to public reaction to the poltergeist manifestations occurring at the house of the national counselor Joller, said, "Superficial people, as always, want to provide a mechanistic explanation; the devout see it as the devil's work." And in 1893 an abbé confronted by poltergeists wrote this: "Where could a man be found capable of doing all this? For my part, I know only the devil."[23]

In 1977 the parish priest of Saint-Maur mentioned the village of Planches near Préveranges, France, as being site of a devil's house. It had earned its name because objects moved of their own accord there, the clocks chimed the hour all the time, the drawers and doors on the furniture opened, and bizarre noises rang throughout the place. The local manor owner thought it was knocking spirits. The teacher, who was interested in spiritualism, said:

> "It is a very commonplace phenomenon produced unwittingly by a nervous adolescent living in the house. Send your daughter away; she is thirteen, she is probably causing it." The daughter was sent to live with an old aunt who lived far away but the noises continued. This was when they went to fetch the priest who told this story. He said: "I went to the well-known devil house one day with my stole and holy water. There I did what I thought was necessary: prayers against the apostate angels, sprinklings of holy water, and I spoke some ordinary exorcisms. The phenomena came to a halt almost immediately."[24]

This account easily demonstrates how every individual interprets what happens in accordance with his education and religion. The phenomena persisted after the young girl was sent away. E. Bozzano cites similar cases.[25] But since the Christian methods appear to be effective, the devil's presence is implicitly confirmed.

A story titled "The Devil Shares an Apartment in Tallinn with Two Young Women" recently made the rounds in Estonia.

> Once there were two young ladies sharing a flat in Tallinn. After some time all in the house—the cupboards, beds, sofas, tables, chairs and everything else—began to move around and make a lot of noise. Although the police went around it was to no avail, the things still moved around now and then. At last the two young ladies found a new flat for themselves. They went to the new place with a coachman, but his horses paced and could not move faster. The coachman peeked over his shoulder and saw a young officer sitting between the young ladies. This was how he understood why the horses could not run. But the ladies saw nothing.[26]

In the 1970s the abbé Jean-Claude M., the parish priest of Parigny-sur-Sauldre, France, provided us with a good idea about the "functioning" of people's mind-sets. In a nearby village two old men were complaining of hearing something that sounded like rifle shots against their outside shutters every night, which prevented them from sleeping. The doctor treating them also heard it, as well as something that sounded like a heavy wheelbarrow being wheeled through the attic, and the parish priest concluded: "Oh well, if all these miseries he told me about were brought to an end by the exorcisms and the blessings I gave the houses the following day, then we clearly have to accept the intervention of a diabolical force. Otherwise, we would be foundering in incoherence!"[27]

Sometimes it is only possible to deduce the presence of the devil by virtue of certain details in the text, which I will here italicize. For example, at the home of a young couple in Rennes, France, in 1913, "objects, plates, vases, and candleholders would move from one place to another as if carried by an invisible hand. But sometimes it was as if the hand would open and let these objects fall and break. This happened often, even in the middle of the day. The young couple could hear a dull knocking at the door to their bedroom almost every night after they had gone to sleep. . . . Shouts and voices could be heard." One night, *the Christ on a crucifix hanging on the wall began to bleed.* The young couple turned to the priest of Saint-Étienne, who came to bless their apartment three times, but the phenomena continued. *Another priest came, but he was slapped with a napkin.* A third priest came to perform an exorcism, *but he saw his holy water sprinkler fall from his hands as if someone had torn it from them.* He heard cries resembling those of an injured dog, but there was no dog in the house. While he recited the exorcisms, he saw a vase placed over the fireplace be thrown to the ground and break. "Finally, all these strange noises stopped of their own accord as mysteriously as they had started, and calm was restored to the house."[28] An alternate reading of this account is possible: Because it was not the exorcisms that brought these manifestations to an end, their cause is to be sought elsewhere. The cries and voices suggest the presence of tormented souls. But the text is so ambiguous we cannot take the hypothesis any further.

A STORY OF WITCHES

Sorcery—and, more rarely, magic—is another frequent interpretation of poltergeist phenomena. We have an excellent example of the vacillation of authors between the two explanations in an account titled *The Demon [or Phantom] Drummer of Tedworth*. It was written by Joseph Glanvil, Chaplain of King Charles II of England. Born in Plymouth in 1636, he pursued his education at Oxford and died in 1680, after holding several positions in the church. He enjoyed a reputation for integrity and intelligence and was a contemporary of the incident for which he recorded such a detailed account. I will indicate several important details in italics.

> During Mr. Mompesson's stay in Tedworth in the town of Lugarspal, in Wiltshire, in March of the year 1661, he heard the beating of a drum in the street and asked the bailiff, at whose home he happened to find himself, what it signified. The other responded that over the past several days an itinerant artist, William Drury, who he believed to be in the possession of a fake passport, had been filling their ears with the sound of his drum. Mr. Mompesson had this man brought before him and asked him who had given him the right to stroll the countryside with his drum. The vagrant thereupon showed him his passport and authorization signed by William Cawley and Commander Ayliff of Gretenham. Mompesson, who knew the handwriting of these two gentlemen quite well, was convinced both the permit and the passport were counterfeit. He therefore had the drum seized and ordered the bailiff to bring the vagrant before the next justice of the peace for punishment. The fellow then confessed his imposture and implored only that he be returned his

drum. Mompesson told him that if Commander Ayliff gave him a good account then it would be duly returned, but in the meantime he would keep it. He left this man then in the constable's hands, but it appears that the latter was so scared by his threats, he let him go.

About the middle of the following April, when Mr. Mompesson was preparing to travel to London, the Bailiff of Lugarspal sent him the vagrant's drum. When he returned his wife told him how during his absence she had been in great fear of thieves. He had barely spent three nights in his house before the same things that had terrified his family started up again. *A very loud knocking was heard at the door and on the outside of the house.* He took his pistols, searched every corner, and opened the door on which the knocking was heard. The noise then began at another door. After going back to bed *"the noise was a Thumping and Drumming on top of the House,"* which persisted awhile before fading into the air.

This noise became quite frequent, usually occurring five nights in succession, then stopping for three. It occurred on the outside of the house, which was almost all wood-paneled, and it always began when the family went to bed. A month later it began occurring a little later but no more than a half hour after bedtime and continued five nights out of seven. It lasted two hours in the room where the drum had been stored. This noise was heralded by a wailing in the air above the house and ended with the drumbeat for the changing of the guard. This lasted two months, during which time Mr. Mompesson stayed in the room where the noise occurred in order to see what might be its cause. Mrs. Mompesson had taken to her bed during this time and there was little noise made during the night while she was in Travail, and nothing was heard for about three weeks. But the knocking then began again with greater strength than before, and *tormented the children in particular.* Indeed, *their beds were struck* with such force it seemed they would fall to pieces. No blows were felt when placing a hand upon them, but they could be felt *shaking violently.* For an hour at a time, *well-known military marches could be heard,* then it seemed as if the children's beds were being scratched with iron claws. *The spirit would pick up the children and chase them from room to room,* leaving everyone else alone. They were then sent to bed in the middle of the day in the attic, where no noise had yet been heard, but the spirit soon followed them there.

On November 5, 1661, a terrible noise was heard. One of the servants in the children's room saw *two floorboards start to move* and asked for one of them, upon which the board began moving toward him coming to within a yard of him with no one seeing anyone carrying it. He then shouted: "Place it in my hand," upon which it came closer, then advanced and retreated in similar fashion twenty times until Mr. Mompesson forbid him such familiarities. This happened *in the middle of the day* in a room full of people. A *very strong odor of sulfur* was also smelled at this time. Toward evening the minister, Mr. Cragg, and some of the neighbors came to the house to pray at their bedsides with them in the midst of this racket. *While the prayers lasted, the noise retreated into the attic,* but once over, it returned to the bedroom. *Then all the chairs started dancing around, the children's shoes were cast over their heads,* and everything loose in the room began moving about the room. *A bed beam was thrown at the minister, striking him in the leg, but so gently that it might have been a ball of wool.** Mompesson, seeing that the spirit was primarily persecuting the children, sent them to a neighbor's house, with the exception of his eldest daughter, aged ten, who he had sleep in his own room, where it had not been the month before. *But once she went to bed, the noise began again,* continuing this way for three

---

*"During Prayer-time it withdrew into the Cock-loft, but returned as soon as Prayers were done, and then in sight of the Company, *the Chairs walkt about the Room of themselves, the Childrens shooes were hurled over their Heads, and every loose thing moved about the Chamber.* At the same time *a Bedstaff was thrown at the Minister,* which hit him on the Leg, but so favourably, that a Lock of Wooll could not have fallen more softly, and it was observed, that it stopt just where it lighted, without rolling or moving from the place."

weeks. It was noted that *the spirit responded exactly, by beating the drum,* to any questions asked of it. Because many strangers were lodging in the house to which he had sent his other children, their father summoned them home and set up their beds in the parlor, which had not been disturbed until then. But the spirit followed them here, too, but was content this time to only tug at their hair and nightclothes.

It was noted that *when the noise was loudest, no dog would move around the house,* although it was often so violent that it could be heard in the fields a great distance away, and awakened the neighbors, although no other dwelling was nearby. *The servants were often lifted up with their beds, and gently set back down without incurring any hurt;* they sometimes also felt a great weight upon their feet. Toward the end of December 1661, the noise of the drum became rarer, but a noise as of someone counting money could now be heard in its stead, which was attributed to something that Mompesson's mother had said. The old woman, speaking to the neighbors about fairies and their habit of leaving gold behind them, had added that it would be just if they did the same for them as compensation for all the troubles they had caused. Following this, the noise became less intense and *the spirit contented itself with a few harmless pranks.* A little before dawn on Christmas day one of the younger boys on getting up from bed was struck on the heel with the door latch, whose fastening pin was so tiny, it proved difficult to pull it out. The night after Christmas, Mr. Mompesson's clothing was thrown about his room and *his Bible was hid in the ashes.* Later it was the turn for one of Mompesson's servants, a vigorous and intelligent man named John, *to be fiercely tormented by the spirit.* Several nights in a row *something tried to strip the covers off his bed* while he was sleeping and would half succeed despite how strongly the man held on to them. His shoes would be thrown at his head, and sometimes he felt as if he were bound hand and foot. He had found, however, that when he drew his sword and slashed the air around him, the invisible being clinging to him would tend to leave. A short time later the son of Thomas Bennet visited the house and told Mompesson some things said by the drummer mentioned earlier, who had been a laborer for his father. It appeared this made the spirit quite unhappy, for hardly had they gone to bed when the drum began beating, causing the visitor to get up and rouse his servant, who was sharing John's bedroom. As soon as John found himself alone in his room, he heard a noise there and *saw something coming toward him that appeared clad in silk.* He drew his sword but felt a force holding it back. He had to make an effort to master it, and the ghost then left. He had already observed that it was scared of weapons.

About the beginning of January 1662, *they started hearing something that sang in the chimney and then came down it.* It was also remarked that on one night lights were seen in the house.* One of them entered the room in which Mompesson slept. The flame seemed blue and glimmering and caused those who saw it to stare at it unwaveringly. Afterward *someone was heard climbing the stairs barefoot.* The light appeared four or five times in the children's room, and the servants swore that the door to it was opened and closed at least ten times before their very eyes, and that each time it seemed that five or six men entered, walked around the room, and that one among them rustled as if in silk. During the time the spirit was knocking loudly in the presence of a large number of people, one of those there yelled out: *"Satan, if the one who drums is serving you, knock thrice and no more." The three knocks came and nothing more was heard.*† The men then knocked to see if it would respond

---

*"About the beginning of January 1662, they were wont to *hear a Singing in the Chimney* before it came down. And one night about this time. *Lights were seen in the House."*
†"A Gentleman of the Company said, *Satan,* if the Drummer set thee to work, give three knocks and no more, which it did very distinctly and stopt. Then the Gentleman knockt, to see if it would answer him as it was wont, but it did not. For further trial, he bid it for confirmation, if it were the Drummer, to give five knocks and no more that night, which it did, and lest the House quiet all the night after. This was done in the presence of Sir Thomas Chamberlain of Oxfordshire, and divers others."

as usual, but the spirit kept its silence. For further confirmation he asked the spirit to knock five times if it were the drummer and to keep silent the rest of the night. This is just what happened. This occurred in the presence of Thomas Chamberlain, the Earl of Oxford, and several other witnesses.

On the morning of Saturday, January 10, one hour before daylight, a drum was heard before the door of Mompesson's bedroom. The noise then traveled to the other end of the house, in front of the door of the room where some strangers were sleeping. Four or five military marches were played, after which the noise vanished. One night when the village smith was lying with the servant John, *"they heard a noise in the room, as if one had been shoeing a Horse,"* then it seemed as if someone was trying to snip at the smith's nose with a pair of pincers for the better part of the night. One morning Mompesson heard a great noise in the room below where the children slept. Running down with his pistol drawn, he heard a voice shouting: "A witch, a witch!" Then all became quiet. One night the spirit, after haunting Mompesson's bed, went on to that of his daughter. It went beneath her, passing from side to side, lifting her up each time, and three different noises could be heard coming from the bed. Attempts were made to stab it with a sword, but it avoided the thrusts by hiding under the child. The following night it arrived panting like a dog out of breath. Someone tried to strike it with a bed rod, but this was torn from her hands and thrown to the ground. Several people arrived in the room, and the room filled with *a very unpleasant aroma of flowers,* and quite hot, although it was not heated and this was the middle of winter. The spirit continued panting and scratching for an hour, then went into the adjoining room, where it knocked a little and something that sounded like the rattling of a chain could be heard. This happened two or three nights in a row. *Soon after this, Mrs. Mompesson's Bible was found in the ashes, opened, with its pages down, to the third chapter of Saint Mark, where mention is made of unclean spirits* *prostrating themselves before the Savior and of the power he gave his Apostles to cast out demons.** The following night ashes were spread about the room, and early that morning they found *the imprint of a large claw* in one place, and a smaller one in another, and in a third place some letters meaning nothing and in which nothing could be seen but some inexplicable scratches.

During this time it was the children the spirit attacked, and he began his assault the moment they went to bed. The day of Glanvil's arrival the thing began as usual around 8 o'clock, and a maid went downstairs immediately to let him know. Accompanied by his friend Hill, who had come with him, and Mompesson, he went up to the room. While they were still in the staircase, they heard a strange scratching, and upon entering the room, Glanvil saw the noise was coming from behind the children's pillows and opposite the pillowcase. It sounded like a man scratching with his nails. There were two little girls between seven and eight years old in the bed, who were quite calm. The hands were atop the covers, and the scratching coming out from behind their heads could not have been their doing. They were quite accustomed to this kind of thing and did not seem very scared. Moreover, they always had someone near them. "Standing at the Bed's head," said Glanvil, "I thrust my Hand behind the Bolster, directing it to the place whence the Noise seemed to come, whereupon the Noise ceased there and was heard in another part of the Bed, but when I had taken out my Hand, it returned and was heard in the same place as before. I had been told it would imitate Noises and made trial by scratching several times upon the Sheet as 5 [times] and 7 and 10, which it followed and stopped at my number. I search'd under and behind the bed, turned up the Cloaths

---

*"After this, *the old Gentlewoman's Bible was found in the Ashes,* the Paper side being downward. Mr. Mompesson took it up and observed that it lay open at the third chapter of St. Mark, where there is mention of the unclean Spirits falling down before our Saviour, and of his giving power to the Twelve to cast out Devils, and of the Scribes' Opinion that he cast them out through Beelzebub."

to the Bed-cords, grasped the Bonter, sounded the Wall behind, and made all the search that possibly I could to find if there were any Trick, Contrivance, or Common Cause of it; the like did my Friend, but we could discover nothing. So that I was then verily persuaded, and am so still, that the Noise was made by some *Daemon* or *Spirit*. After it had scratched about half an Hour or more, it went into the midst of the Bed under the Children, and there seemed to pant like a Dog out of Breath very loudly. I put my Hand upon the place, and felt the Bed bearing up against it, as if something within had thrust it up. I grasp'd the Feathers to feel if any living thing were in it. I look'd under and everywhere about, to see if there were any Dog or Cat, or any such Creature in the Room, and so we all did, but found nothing. The motion it caused by this panting was so strong that it shook the Room and Windows very sensibly. It continued thus more than half an Hour while my friend and I stayed in the Room, and as long after, as we were told. During the panting I chanced to see as it had been something (which I thought was a Rat or a Mouse) moving in a Linnen-Bag that hung up against another Bed that was in the Room; I stept and caught it by the upper-end with one Hand, with which I held it, and drew it through the other but found nothing at all. There was nobody near to shake the Bag, or if there had, no one could have made such a Motion, which seemed to come from within, as if a living Creature had moved in it."

Never during this time did Glanvil feel one moment of fear. As he was sleeping with his friend in a room during the night, he was woken shortly before daybreak by someone knocking loudly at the door, and he awoke his companion. He asked the spirit several questions, but it continued knocking without responding. "In the Name of God, who is it," Glanvil asked, "and what would you have?" "Nothing with you," a voice answered. Both thought it was one of the servants of the house and went back to sleep. But when they recounted the incident to the head of the household that morning, he told them no family members slept there or had any business there and that his servants only came when summoned, something he never did before that day. His servants confirmed what he said, swearing they were not responsible for making this noise.

That same morning Glanvil's servant told him that *"one of my Horses (that on which I rode) was all in a sweat and look'd as if he had been rid all Night."* They went out to the stables and found the horse in the condition described. They were assured that this horse, who had always been in sound condition, had been fed and well treated by the stable hand. But after Glanvil rode the horse later for a mile or two on the plain away from Mompesson's house, the horse fell lame, and after making a strong effort to return his master home, fell ill with no one able to determine the nature of the ailment.

One day Mompesson, seeing some pieces of wood moving in the fireplace, fired his pistol at them, after which several drops of blood were found on the hearth and on the stairs. Calm was restored to the house for two or three days, but the spirit then returned and began vexing a small child with such persistence it could not sleep peacefully for two nights in a row. The spirit would not suffer any light in the child's room but would carry them up the chimney or cast them beneath the bed. The poor child was so scared it took hours to recover, and they were a second time forced to send him with his siblings out of the house. Toward midnight the following evening, the spirit climbed the stairs, knocked at Mompesson's door, then sought his servant and appeared at the foot of his bed. He could not clearly make out its shape, but he thought he saw a large figure with two glaring red eyes that stared fixedly at him before slowly disappearing. On another night, when several strangers were present, the spirit began purring like a cat in the children's bed. At the same time the covers and the children themselves were lifted up with such force six men were not enough to hold them down. The children were removed in order to take apart the bed, but they were barely placed in another bed before it was shaken with more intensity than the first. This lasted four hours. The children's legs were pushed so forcefully against the bedposts they were forced to get up and remain standing all night. *The spirit began emptying chamber pots in the beds at night and strewing them with ashes.* He placed a long iron pike in Mr. Mompesson's bed and left a knife with its cutting edge out in the bed of his mother. *He filled the dishes with ashes, threw everything all about,* and made noise all day without interruption. At the beginning of April 1663, a visitor staying at the house had all the money in his pockets turned black. One morning Mompesson found *his horse in the stable stretched out on the ground with one of its back legs stuffed so deeply in its mouth that several men had much difficulty removing it with a lever.* Many other remarkable things also occurred.[29]

With its wealth of detail this story is constructed in such a way that, whether intentionally so or not, the only explanation for the facts can be diabolical. However, there is an appendix of sorts that indicates to the reader that it was witchcraft. William Drury was brought before the court of Salisbury after which he was thrown in Gloucester Prison for theft. A man from Wiltshire went to visit him there. William asked him what news he brought from the area. The visitor answered he knew of nothing.

"Do not you hear of the Drumming at a Gentleman's House at Tedworth?"

"That I do enough," said the other. "I," quoth the Drummer, "I have plagued him (or to that purpose) and he shall never be quiet, till he hath made me satisfaction for taking away my Drum."

He was tried as a witch at Sarum and condemned to exile in the Americas. He embarked but managed to escape, one knows not how, profiting, it is said, from a storm and the sailors' terror. During the time he was in prison and then away, everything was peaceful in the

Mompesson house, but the noise started again once he escaped. This William Drury often spoke of books that he got from an old man who was regarded as a sorcerer. Drury was finally rearrested and boasted of having caused the troubles at the Mompesson home. Glanvil imagined two possible explanations: witchcraft and trickery. He rejected the latter as he could not see how one or more individuals could have been responsible for these phenomena.

If we sort out the elements of this account we shall see they fall into five distinct categories.

1. The intermittent drumming (five nights out of seven), whose causes were attributed to William Drury's witchcraft;

2. Manifestations that are the distinguishing feature of the undead (ghosts seen, apparitions, something climbing and descending, the noise of chains);

3. Diabolical phenomena (sulfurous odor, the Bible in the ashes, the claw marks, the positive answer to the question about Satan, the unpleasant odor, the sudden heating of the room, the spirit that cannot withstand light, the figure with the red, glaring eyes);

4. Psychokinetic phenomena (the persecution of Mompesson's children, as well as the servants, John in particular, while the ten-year-old girl was not affected); and

5. Actions more attributable to kobolds (pranks, covers torn from sleepers, beds knocked on and shaken, horses left all in a sweat, chamber pots emptied, dishes filled with ashes).

In short, Glanvil's account represents a veritable catalog, as is often the case with other highly detailed accounts that have come down to us.

OTHER EVIL SPELLS

Now let us shift horizons and visit Prussia. Jacob Heinrich Zerneke, mayor of the town of Thorn, tells us this:

The Thursday before Lent 1655, a great racket followed by a shower of stones was heard in the house of Hans Goldner, a merchant living on Neustädter Ring. Then, in the middle of the day, the food flew off the table, the plates and glasses in the cupboards broke, the windows were broken by stones, and all manner of evil mischief occurred. Then it was Goldner's thirteen-year-old son's turn to be mistreated. The knocking spirit (poltergeist) appeared to him sometimes in the form of a goat and sometimes a deer, or sometimes that of a bird or some other beast. It would throw him to the ground and pester him in many other ways. After three months, thanks to the intervention of the church and the fervent prayers of the merchant, calm was restored.

A maid was suspected of causing these phenomena by having performed all kinds of incantations (*Gaukelei*) with a swaddling cloth. She was imprisoned but nothing could be proved, even though the manifestations stopped with her incarceration. Even under torture, she confessed nothing and had to be released.[30]

The use of a swaddling cloth or linen to cast evil spells is well attested for back to the thirteenth century, but it is accompanied by the chanting of formulas, no trace of which is provided here. To a person of the nineteenth century it would have been obvious that the medium causing the poltergeists was the maid, but our ancestors vacillated between deviltry—the apparition of a goat and other animals—and witchcraft. It will be noted in passing that our corpus indicates an intensified focus of these phenomena on the female sex. In Mâcon, in the eighteenth century, the "demon" manifested when a maid who was a native of Bresse was present, and this caused her no fear in contrast to all the others involved. In Orton Fell, Scotland, in 1849, everything stopped when the female servant was taken from the scene. Around 1863, in Genoa, Italy, objects began raining down whenever Maddalena Rimassa, aged thirteen, walked in front of a window. In 1874, in Milwaukee, the manifestations only occurred in the presence of Maria Speidel, a neurasthenic fourteen-year-old maid who was also a sleepwalker. In Resau, near Berlin, Germany, in 1888–1889, everything stopped happening when the young Karl Wolter was arrested by the police, which is reminiscent of the Drummer of Tedworth whose story was told by Glanvil. In 1921 in Carinthia, Austria, everything started flying about in an inn where fifteen-year-old Hanni worked. When she went to London, where she had been hired by a marine officer named Kogelnik, who had an interest in the paranormal, the phenomena began to recur, and it was noted that Hanni was peacefully asleep while they were taking place.

For his part, the description Noël Taillepied gives of demons clearly shows the notorious popular association between demons and animals, as demons can take on any form they wish.

> Now no demon is naturally male or female, for demons have no sex, and thus it follows that when they manifest themselves first under one shape and then another, displaying congruent passions and corresponding lusts, the simple substance has invested itself with a number of quirks. Moreover, the bodies they assume are plastic, easy to mold and fashion, and can receive any form or likeness, coloring itself prismatically with as many hues as the chameleon, so that at one time a demon may appear as a man, then as a woman: or again a demon will roar like an enraged lion; bound and leap like a chamois; bark and bay like a dog; meow and mew like a cat; bleat and baa like a sheep; for finally they can, with the utmost facility, assume the image and fanatastical likeness of any animal, or indeed of anything else just as serves their present purpose.[31]

The type of account we just read was not very frequent in older times, and much later modern narratives are more direct and explicit. A little more than a hundred years ago there was a woman in Vauchignon, France, who was a witch. While she was asleep and seized by ominous shudders, her husband could hear strange noises and repeated calls coming from the attic.³² Around 1895, in Hauteville in the Savoy commune of Les Allues, France, a couple and their children were at odds with the local priest. Two of their daughters suffered the consequences of this quarrel. After retiring to bed in the evening they would hear someone coming up the stairs to their room, then an invisible hand would shake them in their bed. This torment only stopped when their parents came to their room or when they lit a candle.

> Worn out by these evil spells, they become seriously ill. Their parents then consulted a person in Allues who was an expert on witchcraft, who advised them to walk backward to the rectory while reciting a rosary, then walk around the cemetery in the same manner. The counter-spell worked, and their children were never again tormented by the priest's actions.³³

It is not uncommon for clerics to be regarded as sorcerers or witches and as the cause of certain phenomena associated with knocking spirits.

Furthermore, in houses where all the objects start dancing around, such as cooking pots, stools, benches, and buckets, as if the place was full of poltergeists, it is said there is "physics,"³⁴ a former name for magic that is still preserved in folk traditions.

Undoubtedly one of the most famous poltergeists of the nineteenth century had the Cideville Presbytery in Seine Maritime, France, for its theater. This was in 1850. The Marquis Jules-Eudes de Mirville (1802–1873) left us a detailed account that was later picked up by many other authors. This is it:

> A man enjoying a *reputation as a sorcerer and a healer* failed in several cases. The priest, Abbé Tinel, scolded him and after a relapse, he was condemned to prison for the illegal practice of medicine. A shepherd named Thorel, convinced that the priest was responsible for the sorcerer's disgrace, decided to avenge him. It so happens that two children were being raised at the presbytery. The shepherd

planned to strike his victim through them. To achieve this, one day when a fair was being held, he approached one of the children and touched him, making him the intermediary that would put the presbytery at the mercy of invisible, wicked forces. First there was a *squall* that shook the building to its very foundations, then knocks could be heard coming from every side, on the ceilings, floors, and panels, and sometimes hammering out certain tunes, it is claimed, that were requested by those present. *The tiles broke and fell in all directions, objects sailed about, the tables turned upside down or toppled over, the chairs moved together and hung in the air, the dogs were thrown pell-mell at the ceiling, the knives, brushes, and prayer books soared out one window and came back in through the one opposite, the shovels and tongs left the hearth and entered the parlor of their own accord, the irons,* which were in front of the fireplace, went backward, and *the flames pursued them to the middle of the floorboards, hammers flew fiercely into the air and then came gently to rest on the floor with all the grace and slowness a child's hand would imprint on a feather. All the toiletries suddenly left the mantelpiece* upon which they had just been placed, and instantaneously returned there of their own accord; *enormous desks crashed together and broke;* what is more, one of them, laden with books, suddenly and violently appeared in front of a witness, where, without anyone touching it, it suddenly abandoned all the laws of gravity and fell at his feet in a perpendicular position.

One day a lady felt the end of her cloak being pulled but could not see the invisible hand responsible; the village mayor was *violently struck* on the thigh, and in response to the howl elicited from him by this attack came a gentle caress that alleviated all the pain in an instant. One witness interrogated the mysterious noise, encouraging it to knock on all the corners of the room and discussed with it the meaning of the knocks. In this way he got the mysterious entity *to confirm the names and ages of his children as well as those of other relatives.* The unknown entity spoke in this way with other individuals, telling one the names of his father, mother, and brother and indicating to another the number of her dog and horses. During this time the child who had been bewitched appeared to be suffering from nerves and complained of feeling a weight on his shoulders and constriction of his chest. He also saw *the shadow of a man* in a smock following him; other witnesses thought they saw a kind of grayish pillar or fluidic vapor. One day the child said he saw a black hand come down the chimney and cried out that it smacked him in the face. No one else saw this hand, but *they could hear the slap* and see that the child's cheek turned red and stayed that way for a long while. The child dashed outside hoping, or saying he hoped, never to see that hand coming out of the chimney again.

As the prayers of the clergy who had come to help their colleague were not enough to bring an end to the *evil spells,* one of them suggested *trying to stab it with swords, which people believed had the power to harm shades. Probes in the direction indicated by the child were eventually met with success as a green flame erupted followed by a noxious cloud of smoke that was so thick all the windows had to be opened to avoid* a swift and total *asphyxiation. After the smoke had dissipated and calm had replaced the terrible emotions that had previously prevailed, this method was reapplied. The sharpened tips were again plunged into the walls, and a low moan could be heard; they continued their efforts and the moaning redoubled* until they could positively make out the word "pardon."

"Pardon!" these gentlemen replied. "Yes, we shall certainly give you pardon, and we shall do better than that, we shall all kneel in prayer for the night asking God to pardon you as well—but on one condition, that you come tomorrow to ask this child for pardon in person."

"You shall pardon all of us?"

"There are more than one of you?"

"There are five of us, including the shepherd."

"We shall give all of you pardon."

Then order was restored to the presbytery, and this terrible night ended in tranquillity and prayer.

The next day Thorel came forth with his face all scorched and asked pardon from the child who recognized him as the man that had been following him for fifteen days. At the priest's request Thorel went to the town hall to repeat his request for forgiveness in front of witnesses. When he was down on his knees he tried to touch the priest, who threatened him with his cane, then when he saw he would not be able to avoid the shepherd's attack, struck him with his stick two or three times. This led to a suit pled in Yerville before the justice of the peace, Floppe. The court dismissed the shepherd's request for damages with interest for the slander and injuries he had suffered because he had boasted of being the author

Title page of the 1627 edition of Demoniaci cum locis infestis *(On Places Infested with Demons) by the German Jesuit author Petrus Thyraeus*

of the disorder in the presbytery and had voluntarily asked for pardon. He had therefore acknowledged his own guilt and had tried to touch the priest in the presence of several witnesses, whose reaction could be described as legitimate self-defense.[35]

The explanation of sorcery is facilitated by Thorel's personality, but if we examine this account closely, we can see that once again adolescents are mixed up with the whole affair. Why seek to attack the priest through children and not strike at him directly? A detail like this suggests that one of the children could be considered a medium— sometimes referred to now as a PK subject (psychokinesis subject)[36]— or one has recourse to the usual explanations. The devil is represented by the apparition of a black hand, the green flame, and the smoke, and the influence of spiritualist theories is perceptible in the mention of a "kind of grayish pillar or fluidic vapor." We should add to all of this the notion of split personality.[37] Thorel is hurt when invisible and when he shows up in flesh and blood his face bears the traces of his injuries. It is odd, however, that Thorel took on the responsibility for this act of revenge and not the sorcerer-healer who was condemned to prison.

As can easily be seen here, it is often public rumor that takes the lead in providing an interpretation of these phenomena, and this is nothing new! In New Hampshire in 1682, the neighborhood believed that the rain of stones and objects in George Walton's house were due to the witchcraft of an old woman whose land he had stolen.[38]

Even if our examples come from a relatively remote time, the mindset they reveal has hardly been extinguished by scientific and technological advances. But judge for yourself! The September 18, 2003, issue of the Romanian newspaper *Ziua* (The Day) offered the following staggering story under the sensational headline "The Haunted Village. Dozens of people of Valea Stanchiului believe they are being haunted by the spirit of a farmer from this village who recently died."

Dozens of people from the Dolj village of Valea Stanchiului have been living a nightmare over the past three days; they maintain they are being haunted by the spirit of a villager they had buried Sunday and *in whose heart they had planted a stake prior to burial,* reports Mediafax [a press agency]. The friends and relatives of fifty-three-year-old Marin Popa swear that *their animals are restless at night, wine barrels spill of their own accord, and objects move from one spot to another.* The people requested the aid of the village priest, Mihai Florea, who, cross and basil in hand, blessed all the haunted houses. Mihai Florea says the villagers should not be scared of an *unclean spirit** and that what is actually involved are *evil spells between enemies.*† The mayor of Valea Stanchiului, Vlad Alexandru, stated that for the next few nights he would also stay with the villagers to oversee the *maisnies.*‡ The mayor's statements did not succeed in calming his citizens, who gathered together every night quaking with fear because of the revenant (*se tremura de frica strigoiului*[39]). The existence of spirits that haunt houses is deeply rooted in folk beliefs; it is said that those destined to transform into the undead are born with a distinctive sign on their heads.

This account establishes, in an extraordinary way, a link between the wicked dead, deviltry, and sorcery. It conforms to the world of popular beliefs in which uncertainty breeds hesitation between interpretations, which end up becoming blended together and superimposed upon one another.

---

*The name used here, *Necurat,* means both "devil" and "unclean."
†*Si ca la mijloc sunt farmece facute intre dusmani. Farmece* corresponds to the Greek *pharmakon* used to designate evil spells.
‡The term designates the house and its grounds, courtyard, and livestock.

6

Brownies and Poltergeists

Majestic Bichester Castle:
Do the brownies and werewolves return to you
Every night to perform their deviltries?[1]

CLAUDE LE PETIT,

LA CHRONIQUE SCANDLEUSE

We have seen that during the Middle Ages many names for knocking spirits were also those of fantastical beings like dwarves or brownies. This confusion persisted into the twentieth century, and we will now see why. For the sake of convenience, and because of their reputation for mischievousness, I am going to use the term "brownie," except when the texts suggest another.

The reader may be surprised to see brownies take the place of devils. In fact, however, this is perfectly logical because in the mentalities of these bygone times, the former were assimilated into the latter. In his *Démonologie,* published in Paris in 1580, Jean Bodin writes, "For Fauns, Satyrs, and other Sylvain creatures are nothing other than these Demons and evil spirits." In 1561, Pierre Viret offers us the fruits of his reflection:

Psellus says that among the six species of demons, the one most wicked is that whose covering is the thickest. Several philosophers name the Demons and those resembling them unreasoning Brutes. The others who the Greeks also name the most gentle, *Coballes,** inasmuch as they are imitators of men, because they laugh with joy, and seem that they do labor much, although they do nothing. Others call them *mountain dwarves*[2] to signify their shape, in which they appear most often like little, elderly *dwarves,* with a height of three palm spans and clad as those who labor in the mines, to wit an old Robon[†] and a leather apron hanging over the bulk of their bodies. They have not the habit of causing harm to the workers but only pester them in the mines and small quarries, and although they do nothing, it seems they are performing the job in every way. They act as if they were digging down in the mines and afterward placing what they had dug in containers, or as if they were handling pickaxes and other tools. And while they may sometimes cast gravel at the workers, they do not hurt them; and they never injure them unless they have been *aggrieved and irritated by insults.* In this they are not so unlike Demons, such as those who often appear to men and perform part of their household chores every day, and serve as stable hands; and because they tenderly perform what they do out of love for us, and seem to be friends of humankind, the Germans call them *Gutels:* like those who are also called *Trulles,*[‡] which disguise themselves as men and women and serve as valets and chambermaids in several lands, primarily in Sweden.

Erika Lindig has compiled a list of the actions performed by brownies in her excellent thesis.[3] They rap and knock and make other noises; they burst out in song or laughter; slam doors; overturn cradles and hit children; tear the covers off sleeping people; overturn candlehold-

---

*In other words, "kobolds."

†[a long smock-frock —*Ed.*]

‡In other words, trolls.

ers, benches, and tables; bombard people with all kinds of objects; make noises of moans and footsteps; aggravate dogs; and live in attics, cellars, and kitchens. People get rid of them by banishing or exorcising them. There are other methods of course, but they smack more of fairy tales than legend. Brownies play a thousand tricks, possess the ability to transform their shape—this is therefore not the devil's prerogative! They are a plague and cause fear. They are invisible and only show themselves when misfortune is imminent. With my own studies I have been able to confirm Erika Lindig's findings.[4] This brief typology repeatedly shows how many points there are that overlap between knocking spirits and brownies.

If we now turn our attention to France and examine popular traditions we shall see the same behaviors. To begin, I will trace the investigations of Charles Joisten (1936–1981)[5] in the region of Isère. Here a *foulaton* throws pebbles at passersby and a *wisp* teases hunters and throws small stones; there a foulaton moves about a junk room and throws stones at a woman, a bizarre noise is blamed on a *familiar spirit;* in another place a *familiar* is bowling in the hallway of a farmhouse. Somewhere else a *sprite* is whistling, singing, and making noise in a barn.[6] And if we consult other sources, the uniform nature of these beliefs is striking. The *drac* disturbs the sleeping household, walking about the attic at night dragging chains and noisily opening doors. The drac of Travet dragged the parish priest's maid out of bed and forced her to indulge in wild capering and dancing but restored everything to order before leaving. In the Languedoc region, the *gripet* makes a huge rapping noise during the night, goes into the chimney, takes the cover off the stew pot, and causes the cats to caterwaul. The *trêve* is always busy at night in the attic or kitchen moving furniture, stopping pendulums, and making noise. In Brittany the *Teuz-skoer* is a knocking spirit: *korrigans* and other Breton brownies (*pilous,* and so on) display their anger by breaking dishes. An eighteenth-century French-Languedoc dictionary mentions the *Drap* and gives this definition: "A flighty spirit, a brownie: a familiar spirit that is assumed to be responsible for nighttime noises and causing disorder in the house, and is foolishly used to threaten children."[7]

In Ireland the clurichaun[8] haunts wine cellars, laughing and causing the bottles to move about noisily; the leprechaun reveals its presence with hammer blows; and the pooka breaks the belongings of the person who does not obey it. In Normandy the goblin of Val-Ferrand, in Gréville, will make knocking noises for fifteen days if people forget to leave out a pancake for him. Jean Fleury also notes:

In certain goblin-infested houses, people are woken in the middle of the night by a dreadful racket; doors are violently opened and closed, heavy bodies can be heard tumbling down the stairs. Copper cauldrons and cruets are violently banged together. The noise of breaking plates and glasses can be heard coming from the kitchen. It will be seen the next morning that everything is in its proper place; nothing has moved.[9]

In 1834, Frédéric Pluquet said almost the same thing about the *hans,* in the Bayeux Quarter.

They are spirits that inhabit certain houses and move furniture, torment the people living there, and make a horrible racket. Noise and disorder appear to be these brownies' natural element. The houses they frequent are difficult to rent out, and they end up being abandoned.[10]

In the Swiss town of Corbeyrier, in the Vaudois Alps, the beating of a drum could be heard under an isolated house near the forest, and it was not until around 1860 that "a very brave man succeeded in evicting the evil spirit and forcing it to leave the land."[11] In Hylton Castle near Sunderland in Great Britain, a brownie called Cauld Lad could be heard every night moving furniture, overturning objects, breaking dishes, and sowing disorder, all while remaining invisible.

But although he wreaked havoc, he would put everything back in order.[12]

When reading the following examples it should be kept in mind that we are trying to discern if the brownies are hiding something else, and vice versa.

TORQUEMADA'S ACCOUNT

As an opening to the festivities, here is what Antonio de Torquemada has to say about our subject in his *Jardín de Flores Curiosas*,[13] published in 1573. This book was translated into French in 1582 by Gabriel Chappuys under the title *Hexameron, ou six journées prodigieuses contenans plusieurs doctes discours* and then into English in 1618 with an addition to the title: *The Spanish Mandeuile of Myracles,** thus presenting the book's content as quasi-fantastical.

> Around ten years ago when I was still at Salamanca University, there was a woman of some importance in this city, a widow of advanced age, who had four or five maids at her home, two of whom were young and well-built. The rumor spread that there was a *trazgo*,† or brownie in the house where they lived who played all manner of tricks. Among other things, from *atop the roof it threw stones* in such quantity that, *although they caused no harm,* the inhabitants of the house found them a great inconvenience. Things reached such a point that the magistrate learned of the matter and wished to get to the bottom of it. He therefore visited the house, accompanied by more than twenty men, and ordered a constable to take four men with torches to carefully examine every corner where a man might hide. They did exactly as commanded and did not even neglect to lift up the floorboards. When not a nook was left unexamined, they

---

*[Translation attributed to L. Lewkwnor or Richard Hawkins. —*Trans.*]

†In modern Spanish in addition to *trasgo*, "brownie, sprite," there is also the term *duende*, "brownie, fairy." The knocking spirit is called an *espíritu inquieto*, a "nervous spirit."

returned afterward to the magistrate and said no one could be hiding in the house. He then tried to convince the widow that she was the victim of a hoax. It was probably her young maids entertaining lovers, and the best means of removing this scourge was to diligently watch everything they did. The good woman was completely flabbergasted and did not know what to say. She nonetheless continued to believe there was something real to these stones being thrown at her constantly, from which no one could protect her despite all precautions. The magistrate and those with him left, continuing to scoff at her, but hardly had they come to the end of the staircase when they heard a loud noise and saw rolling down the stairs toward their feet such a mass of stones that it seemed someone had thrown three or four baskets full. *These stones fell amid their feet, although without hurting anyone.* The magistrate commanded the men he had already sent to go back up the stairs quickly so they could catch in the act the person who dared play this trick on them, but after a thorough search they still found nothing. While they were still searching, a large shower of stones began at the main entrance. After striking the top of the entrance they seemed to bounce off and fall to the ground. As everyone was dazed and astounded, the constable picked up one of the largest stones and threw it over the roof of the facing house, saying: "Whether this is a devil or a trazgo, send this stone back to me." At that very instant, in the sight of everyone, the stone came back over the roof and struck his cap just above his eyes. Everyone finally had to accept that they were not the victims of a hoax. Awhile later one of the clergy whom people call *Torres Menudas** came to Salamanca and spoke several exorcisms in the house, after which all these peculiar phenomena ceased immediately.

Except in the stories collected starting in the nineteenth century, exorcisms never put brownies to flight! There is, however, some appar-

---

*Experts have been unable to determine who this Torres Menuda—whose name translates to "little tricks"—was.

ent hesitation in the constable's statement "Whether this is a devil or a trazgo." It will be noted that there are two conflicting points of view here: that of the magistrate, who has both feet firmly on the ground and who thinks this is an illusion or a hoax and examines all the reasons for it—a hidden individual, the maids' lovers—in order to rule out anything irrational, and that of the widow who persists in believing it is supernatural phenomena.

In 1579, in Bologna, a spritely spirit was active in the home of a bourgeois gentleman who turned to theologians and exorcists. Despite everything they attempted, they could not get the sprite out of the house. As in the story of the "Devil of Mâcon," he was attached to one of the female servants and followed her everywhere, teasing her. If her bosses scolded her, he avenged her by playing some mean tricks in the house. They began feeding the maid excessive amounts of food, and this angered the sprite so much that it left the house once and for all.[14] Girolamo Menghi (1529–1609), who left these notes to us, also mentions a similar incident that occurred a year later, and this allows us to dicipher the fact that poltergeists are hiding behind these stories about brownies.

A sprite in another bourgeois home was constantly pestering a fifteen-year-old girl, sometimes playfully and sometimes maliciously. It broke jugs and threw stones into the master bedroom. All measures taken to halt this annoyance proved fruitless, and calm was only restored to the house when the young girl left.

Another fine account comes from the Jesuit scholar Martin Antonio Del Rio. Born to a large Catalan family on May 17, 1551, in Antwerp, he pursued philosophy studies in Paris, then law in Douai and Leuven. After presenting his thesis in Salamanca, he became legal counselor to Philip II and was named vice chancellor of Brabant in 1578. He died on October 19, 1608, in Leuven. In 1599 he published his *Disquisitionum magicarum* (Magical Investigations), an encyclopedic work dealing with magic, alchemy, sorcery, divinations, and apparitions. In it one can read the following:

There was a *familiar spirit* among the inhabitants of Drepano in 1585 who spoke with the folk of the house and *played tricks on them. It threw stones, but without causing harm and cast household utensils in the air without breaking them.* However, once when a young man was playing a stringed instrument, he accompanied him singing scandalous songs. The spirit accompanied the master of the house when he took his wife to another town, and as they were returning to the house, soaked by the rain, he preceded them with loud shouts, forewarning those there to light the fire and telling them their master was soaked to the bone. But the head of the household viewed this quite poorly and threatened to summon a Jesuit priest to expel the spirit from his house. At this the spirit began making a huge racket and uttering threats, saying it would hide for as long as the Jesuit father was in the house. Despite this, the man sought out a priest and told him about the entire matter, begging him for assistance. The priest thought it best if he did not go to the house personally for fear of the rumors that might inspire, but he urged the man to purify himself and his family through sacraments of penitence and the Eucharist. At the same time he forbid them from conversing with the spirit and asking it to reveal hidden things, telling him they would be better served to regard everything it said as lies. He gave the father an *agnus dei*[15] to hang around his daughter's neck, as [the spirit] was pestering her more than the others. They did as he advised and were freed of this annoyance.[16]

FROM BROWNIES TO SPRITES

In 1622 the Senator of Montfalcon put a house in Rumilly in the Upper Savoy region of France at the disposal of the Reformed Bernardines. They moved in, but the phenomena that took place there, and that were attributed to brownies, caused a commotion.

As this House had not been inhabited for some time, a vast quantity of rubbish had collected on all sides, so much that two Sisters went there every day to remove it. Little accustomed to this labor as they were, they found it provided them a sure field for exercising their Patience and their Humility. "This was," Sister Louise said with much insight, "the first exercise of our Sisters in Rumilly. So must it be, O my Lord, that to render ourselves your worthy servants, our first concern and our first Occupation is to cleanse our Souls of their spiritual stains. Or rather, it is You, O Lord, who should cleanse this inner House with the purity of your precious Blood."

There was not only material Filth to remove from this same Place; there were yet *Unclean Spirits* to drive away to make it habitable for these pure Virgins. A horde of brownies had made themselves its Masters and had almost transformed it into a Hell, by the *confused noises* that they excited both day and night and by the *capricious Ravages* they perpetrated on all sides. Sometimes *they overturned all the Dishes, and sometimes they threw all the Books on the ground.* Then they cleaned it up so promptly that it was almost impossible to notice, and these books they would open by turning their pages with an unimaginable speed. Other times *they would walk about with heavy footsteps in the House,* as if in a great urgency. At other times *they threw so many stones* in various places that the former Residents there were in mortal dread. How could the presence of guests so malign and so formidable not force them to abandon a dwelling so taxing and so dangerous to their lives?

What an affront that the Daughters, naturally so shy, would dare succeed them and take their place? They nonetheless did not cause the slightest difficulty after Father Billet, at their request, gave this House his Benediction. But he was not peacefully left to do so as these *invisible Troublemakers,* upset to find themselves compelled by his Conjurations to move out, caused as much aggravation as they could by the horrible Racket they made and by the *tumultuous Quantity of stones they threw* in one Room while he was blessing another. It was inevitable their rage would acquiesce to the power of the Exorcisms. They were driven from this House almost as they had been driven from Heaven; at least they never returned for as long as the nuns still lived there.

I say "for as long as they lived there" because as soon as they had left to dwell in the other House, about which I shall speak in good time, this infernal troop, seeing their former abode emptied of these Angels of the earth, whose Presence was as formidable and intolerable to them as that of the Angels of Paradise, they returned to make it their home and began at once causing the same disorders.[17]

Treated as malign spirits, the troublemaking brownies described above possess all the characteristics of the classic poltergeist: noise by day and night, dishes and books tossed to the ground, the sound of footsteps, the throwing of stones. It is easy to see why the original inhabitants had left! But the Bernardines were faced with the same problem. In their case the blessing of the orator, Father Billet, and his exorcisms were effective. A modern analysis explains that the good father broke the emotional resonance of the phenomena by refusing to surrender to the climate of anguish that had been prevailing in a house where the inhabitants were living in a state of "mortal dread."[18]

Charles Joisten, who has thoroughly studied these accounts,[19] indicates another one, a copy of which his wife, Alice Joisten, was kind enough to send to me. In 1615, in the house of a lord of the former Dauphiné region in southeastern France, a brownie was playing thousands of tricks on its occupants.

A no less remarkable thing was told, the Commander said, about a spirit that was said to have done several very strange things in the house of a Lord of the Dauphiné, not far from Valence.

One day a flask of rose water was broken by a stone, and, although it was at the feet of the Maiden of the house, the water that was in it nonetheless was all carried aloft and spilt upon her head. Those

who tell you this, says a jurisconsult who was also present, are telling
the truth, about which I am highly informed, having in fact been
brought to the scene and told by several eyewitnesses about what
had taken place.

This spirit was a brownie who manifested at the beginning of
the year 1615. He paid respect to the holy days of Sunday and the
Festivals, on which he never made noise or molested anyone. Several
times he was seen throwing things with such force that it seemed
they should knock the people they hit senseless; however, none of
the targets were ever injured, except very mildly when they vexed
it in some way. Ordinarily it was quite friendly; several bouquets
had been made in anticipation of a baptism the following day, and
it wished to make its own. It spent the night before loading the tapestry with cabbage leaves it had taken from the garden, and, for even
greater effect, it filled the vases on the buffet with them.

A certain person, whose identity I will not reveal, had come there
wearing a beautiful long beard. As he was conversing with the others
in the room, this spirit brought from another corner of the house
where a Potter was polishing the crockery a tin of polish, and so
covered the face to which this fine beard was attached with it, he
had the devil's own time getting it cleaned off again.

Here is something you will appreciate. Several clergymen had
come to the house to pray and perform other duties of their profession against this spirit. When the dinner hour came they were seated
at the head of the table with the others below. As if to flatter them,
this brownie begged their forgiveness for the meat being served and
replaced their plates with others of metal scraps and shot and so
many other such things it was only with the greatest of difficulty
that they could eat their meal. On similar occasions he could often
be heard laughing, and three days before he vanished he was heard
playing the fife, beating the drum, and singing some very melodi-
ous tunes, not that he uttered any recognizable words. A Huguenot,
after requesting and receiving from him anything that he wished for

in the household, asked again to be given a brace of pistols; instead of giving the pistols, he filled his soul with such dread that he left the house greatly bewildered. What seems more remarkable is that he often placed several things in sealed rooms, and none could say how they had been introduced there.

Some opening, the clergymen say, must have been there, for such penetration is reserved to God alone; but demons are subtle, and through a sudden localized movement they deceive (obfuscate) the eyes of spectators, just like those performing feats of sleight of hand, and undoubtedly this Brownie did likewise.

"I believe him," said the jurisconsult, and resuming his remarks eventually concluded that after Monsieur of Valence was requested to come there with some kind of remedy, he did so accompanied by six or seven priests to bless the house. They perfumed it with incense in all its rooms and spoke the exorcisms of the church, after which nothing was heard there ever again.[20]

Many of the elements here correspond to those in modern stories about poltergeists, for example, the water that moves contrary to the laws of gravity, the violently hurled objects that do not hurt anyone whom they strike, and the materialization of objects in a sealed room (R 4). On the other hand, the behaviors such as decorating the hall with cabbage leaves, coating someone's beard with a tin of polish, and making music and singing, all smack of brownies and kobolds. Here again we can observe their close kinship with knocking spirits. As an aside, we should keep in mind that Episcopal interventions were still officially sanctioned well into the eighteenth century, and there was a special exorcism for haunted houses: the *Exorcismus domus a daemonio vexatae*.[21] This exorcism was used until around 1869 in the diocese of Annecy, but there are others that also exist.[22]

In 1680 there was the problem of a spirit called "Master Brownie" haunting Ardivilliers Castle in the Picardy area of France:

[who] raised a dreadful racket there. Flames danced at night making it seem that the whole castle was on fire. There were dreadful howlings that occurred only at a certain time of year close to All Saints Day. No one dared stay there except the farmer who alone had tamed this Spirit. If some unfortunate traveler chanced to spend a night there, he would be beaten mercilessly.[23]

The interpretation vacillates between brownies and the undead, the date on which the incidents occurred—All Saints Day—strongly suggests the latter as do the flames and howling that evoke Purgatory or even hell. We should note finally that, in the 1890s, a poltergeist manifested on a number of occasions in the Capuchin Cloister of Saint Barnabas in Genoa, Italy. All religious measures—exorcisms, and so forth—failed, and people said it was the work of a *folletti* (spirit).

The close connection of knocking spirits and brownies can be quite easily discerned in one nineteenth-century account, although its author is unconscious of the comparison. Starting in October 1875, a poltergeist manifested in a castle in Calvados, Normandy, and did not vanish until January 28, 1876, when its owner had a novena of masses said in Lourdes and had exorcisms performed. One witness, Monsieur Morice, wrote to a Dr. Darieux in September 1891, "What I know is that sometimes in the castle stables the horses seemed scared, and they would sometimes be found in the morning drenched in sweat as if they had been ridden a long time." An abbé who was present on the premises stated in February 1893, "I believe the horses were also tormented; they would be found in the morning covered with sweat and their straw tossed behind them."[24]

We should not assume Monsieur Morice's description is an isolated one. The earlier account of the Tedworth poltergeist mentions the nighttime ride of a horse by a spirit ("one of my Horses was all in a sweat and look'd as if he had been rid all night"). In this same story Mr. Mompesson found one of his horses lying on the ground at the beginning of April 1663 with one of its hooves jammed in its mouth ("found

the Horse he was wont to Ride, on the Ground, having one of his hin-
der Leggs in his Mouth"). The narrator of the story about the "Devil of
Mâcon" notes that the spirit sometimes played the stable hand, currying
his horse and braiding its mane and tail, but it would place the saddle
backward with the pommel facing the tail. It so happens that since the
early Middle Ages household spirits had a bond with horses. They took
care of them, braiding their manes and tails, and riding them during
the night.[25] It therefore seems quite natural that what happened to the
horses was interpreted as the work of domestic spirits.

One final point is worth drawing attention to. Certain dwarves and
familiar spirits are connected with death and manifest when it is imminent, either making noise or showing themselves. In 1561 Pierre Viret
noted:

> In this catalog we must place those demons, which being familiars
> to several men reveal to them in plain day, or otherwise, the sign
> of their imminent death, which they do through some moaning,
> or by some noise and conflict, nailing a coffin to convey the body
> condemned to die, or else by showing in plain day the funeral pro-
> cession of an unknown conveyance, which afterward would always
> come to pass.[26]

But rationalists like Benito Jeronimo Feijoo (1676–1764) chal-
lenged these kinds of tales. For him "dwarves are neither good nor evil
angels, nor souls separated from their bodies. . . . They are certain species of aerial souls born from the putrefaction of corrupted vapors and
the air."[27]

From the elements we have just examined, it seems that the majority of
brownies, whatever they are called and in whichever land they reside,
act or can act like knocking and noise-making spirits. To a large extent,
then, their manifestations agree with the features of the poltergeist. Of
course the conflation is advanced much further in folk traditions, which

are often blendings of elements with various origins, with the emphasis falling differently depending on the occasion. Sometimes this attains the level of a burlesque or farce, which can also be a way of overcoming the fear inspired by hallucinations, be they acoustic or some other sort. The agents of the manifestations almost always remain invisible, which encourages diabolical or mythical interpretations.

7

Two Striking Tales

Be thou a spirit of health
Or goblin damn'd.

WILLIAM SHAKESPEARE,

HAMLET, ACT 1, SCENE 4

Among the accounts we have come across in the course of this study, two stand out in particular. The first, dating from 1678, is so ambiguous that without knowledge of the traditions and folk beliefs of the time, it would be indecipherable—and to a certain degree it remains so regardless! The second, dating from 1924, is much clearer and for the most part conforms to the idea of the poltergeist as a stone-throwing spirit. In their own way both texts reflect how the described phenomena were perceived, and both texts also have, among other things, the advantage of allowing a glimpse of the assumptions that underlie the mental attitude of their protagonists.

THE ACCOUNT BY JOSEPH GLANVIL

Joseph Glanvil has left us a story that defies classification because of the obscurity of its elements.[1] The text is divided into twenty

The beginning of Joseph Glanvil's account of the Medcalfe haunting from 1678

RELAT. IV.

A true Account how Alice *the Daughter of* William Medcalfe *Yeoman, in the Parish of* Leffingham *in* Lincolnfhire, *was difturbed by an* Apparition, *with other feats of* Witchcraft *practifed upon that Family, fent from Mr.* William Wyche *dwelling in the fame Parish, to Mr.* J. Richardfon *Fellow of* Emanuel *Colledge in* Cambridge.

1. IN the Year 1678. on the *Sunday* after Twelfth-Day, *William Medcalfe* and his Wife went to Church, leaving their only Daughter *Alice* at home, and whilft they were there the faid *Alice* heard a noife in the Yard, and looking out at the Window, fhe faw a Man of a middle Stature, with Light Flaxen-Hair, ftanding at the Stable-Door, upon which fhe called out at the Window, and demanded of him what he did there? He returned, that he came for a Horfe which he borrowed of her Father She made him anfwer again, that fhe knew nothing of it, and that he fhould have none till her Father came home. He received the anfwer, and went away for that day.

2. The next day her Father and Mother being gone to *Sleeford*-Market, fhe faw him again at the Stable-Door, and demanded of him as before. He told her, *She might go look.* Then he asked her where the Horfes were. She anfwered him again as fhort, told him, *He might go look,* Upon this he began to footh and flatter her, and gave her many foftening words going towards the Door as he fpake, as if he intended to go in to her : which fhe obferving, fhe haftened and bolted the Door faft. Upon which he threatned her, (what his Threats were fhe cannot recal) but fome body knocking at the Door on the other fide of the Houfe, and fhe underftanding it was a Neighbour, opened the Door, and told her Neighbour all that had paffed, and upon it they both

paragraphs and obviously consists of two parts. The first part is a relation of some alarming visitations with allusions to troubles (1–10), followed by a description of them (12–20), with both parts connected by an injection by the narrator: "Hitherto I have given you as exact an Account I could get from them as to the time."

1–10: The Sunday following Twelfth-day 1678, in the parish of Lessingham in Lincolnshire, a stranger showed up at William Medcalfe's home while he was absent and accosted his daughter Alice about a horse he supposedly had borrowed from her father.

Knowing nothing about such a loan, Alice sent him away. He returned the next day and threatened her, before suddenly disappearing. A short time later, two weeks before Shrove-tide, a cobbler named Follet came to the Medcalfe home and announced to them that their daughter would die within the year; he had seen it in certain books he possessed. A short while after, Alice fell sick but recovered. She then saw the unknown man again trying to break down the door with a large club. She asked him what he was doing and he slammed his club down on some clay milk pans without, however, breaking them, and fled. The next time he returned he threatened her with a knife. In July, while Alice was preparing gruel for her breakfast, Follet came by and asked if she had any shoes that needed repairing. She answered there were most likely some but that she did not know where to find them as her parents were away, and he left. She returned to finish her breakfast, but it had curdled although she had used fresh milk. She decided to set it aside to show her parents on their return, but once she turned her back the plate began dancing on the table, fell, and spilled all over the ground. The same day, while Alice was raking hay, she became lame, and this lasted three months.* One day the stranger reappeared and told her Follet was the cause of all these troubles, and then he left.

This is the first part of the story, which provides the context and circumstances of the manifestations that were occurring at this same time but which the narrator retrospectively—and for reasons that remain unclear—separated out and only revealed the details of what Alice had suffered.

12–20: Often after Alice went to bed the inside doors and those of a cupboard would open violently and noisily. One night all the chairs

---

*In the Middle Ages sudden lameness was interpreted as being wounded by the invisible arrow of an elf (elf-shot).

were found in the middle of the room instead of their customary corner by the chimney, and a sieve was set on one of them and a key of the inside door on another. The barn doors opened in the middle of the day without anyone being seen. Once while Alice was spinning the distaff leaped from the wheel into the middle of the room, and Alice said she thought "Follet was in it," but barely had she uttered these words when she saw him ride by toward William York's house. Another time Alice's petticoat was taken away, and several times her clothes, only to be later returned and left where she should be sure to see them. An apron was stolen, cut into pieces, and then returned, and the same happened to a spigot, which had been laid on five eggs, then, the next night, placed in a barrel whose contents were found where the spigot had been. Toward the end of the summer the daughter was stripped and her hair snarled and tangled so badly her mother was forced to cut it. Then something that looked like a cat sat on Alice, who had fallen, and as long as it remained there she was unable to get back up.* Another time she saw this same cat, which flew at her and slammed into her so violently several times it left her face black and swollen. Alice next found a note wrapped in a handkerchief on which was written: "I will make you leave!" She read it and stashed it in a trunk to show to her parents, but the note vanished. One Saturday night she left a clean shift on her bed, which disappeared. She borrowed another from her mother but returned it as it did not please her, and when her mother looked at it found it *cut and slashed in several places*.[2]

Two other incidents follow that affected Alice's father. He sold some of his animals for eight pounds and then discovered he was missing seventeen shillings but the next day found sixteen shillings six pence in his pocket, so that all he lost was six pence. Another time his knife was missing from his pocket. That night he dreamed

---

*The cat implicitly refers to witchcraft as it is the most common animal shape taken by witches.

where he would find it, but it still was not there the next morning. However, when he was looking to see how much money he had in his pocket after going to Sleeford, he found his knife there.

The reader will have to agree that this story is quite mystifying. There is first the unknown stranger who is described as a man of average size with blond hair who shows up at the stable and has the ability to vanish suddenly. After the visit of the cobbler, he returns with a club, but when he strikes the milk pans with it they do not break, which is astonishing given how violently he struck them ("with so great violence that she [Alice] could not conceive that he has broken many of them, but afterwards upon examination she found them all whole"). Alice sees him every day of the week, but when she tries to show him to her father, he never sees him.

Next there is the bizarre cobbler, whose name lends itself to the confusion.* The Medcalfes give him work because he threatened Alice in a way about which we know little ("what his threats were she cannot recall"). This Follet seems to be a bit of a sorcerer as he made a prediction after examining, he claims, certain books in his possession from which he learned much. And when he leaves the farm after finishing his work, his words are prophetic: "And when he had done his Work he bid them Farewell telling them He was sure they would think of Follet when they did not see him." Why does he say this? Is it because of his prediction about Alice's imminent demise—who, although she fell ill, did not die? Or does the narrator, whose perplexity can be sensed here, suggest it because they will be compelled to think of Follet in light of the household manifestations?

Finally there is the name and profession of the individual to whom the troubles are attributed: Follet, a cobbler. Used here as a proper name, Follet implicitly refers to the world of spirits, and more specifically to brownies (*folletti*), an impression reinforced by what we know about

---

*[*Follet* in French means "spirit," or "wisp." —Trans.]

these beings. In the early eleventh century Burchard of Worms mentions the offering of tiny shoes made to domestic spirits.[3] This mention of his trade draws attention to the fact that in the more remote past knocking spirits appeared to be connected with certain professions. For example, in the story about the devil of Glenluce, the narrator emphasizes the tools the weaver customarily uses and tells us that the "devil" forbade Thomas, the son of George Campbell, to enter the room where his father exercised his trade (see chapter 5). In the work of Notker the Stammerer and the Czech legend of Nebojsa, a forge is involved, while in Dom Calmet's story the incidents take place in a printing shop.

The tricks the invisible spirit plays on Alice essentially smack of the pranks of a brownie, with the added complication of a few malicious acts such as the tearing of the shift and the apron. One final element speaks in favor of some confusion between brownies and the man named Follet: Alice's hair is tangled and snarled exactly like the household spirit does to the horses at night.

We should take note of two other intriguing details. The first concerns the shift that Alice finds slashed and torn in several places, an element that opens a new lead for investigation. In her study of seamstresses among the living and the dead, Marie-Claire Latry notes that when the dead reveal their presence, they reputedly send pieces of cut cloth, "clothing cut as if with scissors."[4] Although this belief is confined to the Landes region in France, and we have only one account at our disposal, it is nevertheless suggestive enough to warrant deeper research into this point.

The second detail concerns Alice's sudden lameness. This motif is present only twice in our corpus, and it affects a woman and a horse (that of Mompesson of Tedworth). Limping can undoubtedly be interpreted as sign of a new status, the consequence of contact with a being from the Otherworld. In fact, if there is one motif that recurs from at least the Middle Ages on, it is definitely that of the mark borne by those who have either encountered a dead person or made a visit to the beyond.[5]

It is hard to resolve the question of the identity of the poltergeist of Lessingham and to explain its relationship with the stranger and the cobbler. The story seems to have been arranged, which is to say someone adulterated a coherent tale in which Follet was not the name of a cobbler but that of the troublemaking spirit. We get the impression that the stranger with the bizarre behavior could have been the incarnation of this spirit, but we do not have anything that would allow us to venture farther with deductions and hypotheses. In order to get close to the "truth," we would need more accounts, which unfortunately are lacking at present.

THE CHALET OF THE SPIRITS

The three major explanations put forth by the texts concerning poltergeists—to wit, the dead, devils, or brownies and other place spirits—reveal an astonishing solidity and durability. Even in the twentieth century they underlie more than one account of strange events, an excellent example being the story of the "chalet of the spirits," which, oddly enough, has escaped notice by the majority of researchers studying poltergeists. It is an account by the parish priest Grat Vesan (1870–1946) who, in 1924, described what had occurred from September 5 to 28, 1909, in the house of Édouard Stévenin, near Issime, Italy, located in the Gressoney Valley not far from Val d'Aosta. With startling precision this report tells how, at a chalet in Torrison valley, stones would suddenly strike herders and cows. A sensible man who simply recorded the facts of what he witnessed, it was Grat Vesan who summoned the archpriest Cyprien, an exorcist from the diocese of Aosta.

But let's allow him to speak for himself.

From 1909

Record of several important incidents that could be of interest to posterity?—They were recorded and written by the parish priest of Issime (Grat Vesan), pell-mell and without much order . . . but which do follow a chronological order to some extent for the succession of

Les Diables dans la Vallaise

Dans un châlet d'Issime-St-Jacques, se passèrent, il y a trois ans, des faits fort étranges, dont le récit intéressera peut-être les lecteurs de l'almanach val-dôtain.

Inutile d'affirmer que l'authenticité de ces faits est indiscutable, ayant en pour témoins oculaires une centaine de personnes encore vivantes, et bien dignes de foi.

Pour l'intelligence de mon récit, il faut que je rappelle à la mémoire des lecteurs comment sont construites les habitations de nos *alpages*. Au dessus du rez-de-chaussée, tout occupé par l'étable, il y a ordinairement une seule pièce, transformée en cuisine, chambre à manger et dortoir et recouverte immédiatement par le toit : c'est un de ces appartements qui fut le théâtre des faits qui suivent.

Les époux X. et leurs trois petits enfants, furent une nuit subitement réveillés par la chute d'une pierre, au milieu de l'habitation. Ce bruit n'était pas une illusion, car la pierre restait là pour le témoigner, mais l'on se rendormit assez facilement sans trop se préoccuper de la provenance. Le lendemain, le fait se répéta, à peu près à la même heure, et cette fois encore, l'insouciance ou mieux la fierté du montagnard, ne se démentit point, devant cet effet sans cause plausible.

Cependant les mystérieuses pierres continuaient à tomber à peu près toutes les nuits, avec des circonstances analogues, et, naturellement, un des effets de cette continuité, fut la crainte d'une intervention diabolique.

On fit appeler M. l'abbé V. vicaire au Gaby. En partant pour la mystérieuse montagne, celui-ci fit une visite à quelques-uns de ses confrères qui certainement ne prirent pas la chose au sérieux et se permirent même à son adresse quelques plaisanteries. Le lendemain, à son retour, M. l'abbé était vivement impressionné, et son langage traduisait les émotions d'une nuit passée dans le qui vive. « J'ai toujours été un peu sceptique là-dessus, disait-il, maintenant, je crois! J'ai vu tomber plusieurs pierres, je les ai prises dans mes mains, et je puis assurer qu'aucun moyen naturel n'aurait pû leur donner l'élan et la direction qu'elles avaient : c'est un mystère ! » De fait, ce mystère s'ébruita sans cependant créer dans l'opinion publique, autre effet que celui de la curiosité.

Un beau soir, quelques jeunes gens, avec l'intention sans doute de faire

The opening page of the article by Romain Vesan.

the facts—there has been no thought put to an elegant turn of phrase of selection of words—but one thing was kept in view: the truth of the historical fact. Nothing has been embroidered by the imagination; all there is here is the completely simple recording of proven facts.

In faith,

G. Vesan, curate,

Issime–Saint Jacques

Completely unexplainable phenomena in the Valley of Torrison noted at various instances in two chalets belonging to a certain Édouard Stévenin of Gaby.

In 1909 this Édouard Stévenin of Gaby was owner of three chalets (or more exactly, a mountain with three high mountain pastures, the highest of which was called Seinir; the middle pasture was called Fontana; and the lowest, Torrison, the name of the valley).

The phenomena that follow occurred only in two chalets: one at Seinir from September 5, 1909, to the twelfth of that same month, and finally from September 19 to the 28th of the same month in that of Torrison.

The undersigned priest was twice an eye witness—on the 24th and 27th—and he recounts quite faithfully what he saw those two days . . . and of the other days he can say no more than what he was told by serious and trustworthy persons such as His Worship the Abbé Hilarion Vection d'Arvier, then Vicar of Gaby, and several men of Issime and Gaby all of sound age and earnestness.

From September 5 to 12 in Seinir, various incidents were noted that were both impressive and frightening: *two cows attached to the same chain, two goats comically dressed in men's clothing,* cast stones striking people, the canvas of the umbrellas under which the owner's small children were sleeping was torn open, stones rolling in the house or making impressive zigzags before striking people or rolling to the ground.

Struck by these strange phenomena the owner of the chalet asked His Worship, the Vicar of Gaby, to be kind enough to climb up there, both to see for himself and to give the place his blessing. He gladly went there on several occasions and on his return would faithfully stop by the Issime parsonage to report what he had seen. The priest who wrote and the Vicar of Issime, Professor Albert Munier, appeared to find it hard to believe in these stories, and they seemed somewhat unbelievable; yet each day the phenomena were verified and a greater number of people hastened up the haunted mountain, and all were unanimous in their narration of the facts.

On the thirteenth the owners descended into the middle chalet, the one of Fontana, merely to stop for a few days, and nothing manifested. By the nineteenth they were in the first chalet, in Torrison, and there again the phenomena, which [text missing in the original] here each evening *stones raining down* in the room where they stayed . . . and in large quantity. They struck people and livestock; however, they did *not cause a very sharp pain* and that pain was temporary. . . .

These phenomena repeated every night, and the manifestation of these strange incidents almost always began in the evening and lasted several hours. These facts impressed everyone there and in the surrounding regions. From Gressoney to Donnaz, Carema, etc., no one spoke of anything else. Every night the number of the curious increased, and this small chalet, lost in the middle of a dark valley, became a popular meeting place.

I finally decided to go up there to examine these incidents personally. Men from Issime wished to go with me: Monsieur Christillin Hilaire, communal counselor and first assessor; Desiré Chouquer; Théophile Goyet, son of the local doctor; and Gustave Dandrès, recently released from military service. These last three were in their prime, and as they climbed they feigned an unfailing courage and determined desire to discover the key to this mystery at any price. I tried to temper their enthusiasm but with little success.

We arrived on the mountain (the haunted chalet) around seven o'clock, and people were milking the cows. But several steps before we got to the stable door we saw the owner of the house and several others already there who had arrived before us, emerge from the stable in terror yelling: "Now the stones are falling on the cows and it is impossible for us to milk them!"

We all entered the stable with a certain apprehension and truly saw the presence of a variety of stones of a certain size right next to the cows and the terror of these beasts that were pulling against their chains as if trying to escape. The poor owner was pale with fear and yet showed us compassion: we exchanged a few words outside, he then invited us into their living quarters to begin the story of all these inexplicable phenomena.

There were close to twenty of us in that room, almost all men in the prime of life; six were sitting around the hearth and feeding a good fire as it was already getting cold, and the others found a place as best they could in this sole room reserved for people. We were there for five minutes when the mysterious stones began coming again. The first came from below, it was filthy with dried dung, and it struck Desiré Chouquer in the forehead causing a sharp pain and a small bump about the size of an almond. Terror again gripped all present, but none moved and we stayed there to observe. We did not have to wait for the stones; we saw them traverse a short distance one after the other. . . . It was impossible to see their departure point, all that could be seen was their direction for about a yard . . . some came from above, others from the left . . . right side . . . from below, some fell into the middle of the [text missing] scattering sparks and ash, others fell hard directly onto the floor, and some, *after making the strangest zigzags,* struck people before falling to the ground. That evening three were struck directly, and despite their juvenile enthusiasm and pride one has between twenty and thirty years old, they were forced to abandon this dwelling room and find refuge in a neighboring chalet.

Desiré Chouquer, a courageous young man of twenty-four, was the first to leave, after receiving three stones—gladly retreating after him was Théophile Goyet, age twenty-two, son of the famous doctor Jean Goyet, consortial doctor for the Vallaise . . . he had received two stones, but how violently? Still remaining was Gustave Dandrès, a strapping lad who had just completed his military service. He was determined not to become distressed . . . he wished to resist at all cost, he had said in the beginning and quite loudly that he was scared of nothing . . . yet despite his promises and apparent bravado, his courage failed, and he was also forced to leave the room after being struck for the eighth time. This one struck him on the nape of the neck after reaching him in a stranger fashion than any of the previous ones. As for me, I was sitting a little away from the hearth in a corner of the room near a small pile of wild hay. In front of me was a small table holding two oil lamps; both were lit to illuminate the room. This room, by the way, was greatly lit by the roaring fire that people were still feeding in the hearth. Gustave was sitting near the fire with several other people, and it was there that stones struck him repeatedly. He had just been hit for the seventh time and had quit his post in fright, and he came to sit near me, resting his back against the small pile of wild hay. The stones appeared to pursue him—one came across with extraordinary violence and directly hit one of the two oil lamps, the one farthest from me, and shattered it into tiny pieces in the middle of the room—while another, quite soon after, came out of the middle of the pile of hay and rolled on the ground after striking the courageous Gustave in the nape.

Finally he could not take it any longer, and so at my urging he also left this room, white as a piece of paper, to rejoin his two other companions in the neighboring chalet. It was then 10:30 in the evening, and during the period of three hours that we were in this room no less than 25 to 30 stones [were hurled]. I handled and examined almost all of them . . . nothing peculiar or abnormal—they were ordinary stones of different sizes, but none any bigger than a person could easily throw by hand. *People saw these stones coming from a distance of one yard and no more*—it could be said that an invisible hand was throwing them with uncommon violence from this starting point. After the departure of the third young man, Gustave Dandrés, the phenomenon stopped for a good while and we thought it was over. It was eleven at night and then, addressing the various people present there, I told them: "Let's recite the rosary and the litanies." I was up then and walking around the room—well, it was at the precise moment when I said, "Let's recite the rosary"—a relatively large stone fell at my side, without touching me though, and this was the last one for that night.

I did not try to huddle into a corner but continued to walk about, calmly reciting the rosary and the litanies—resigned to taking the stones if they came. Thank God, none came to strike me . . . nor any of the other people who spent the final part of that night there. However, I remained there with a good deal of apprehension—I had a lot of trouble believing in the often repeated story of these phenomena, repeated by trustworthy individuals—and now that I was a witness with both eyes and ears, I had no choice but to succumb to the facts. I stayed most of the time seated at the corner of a little table, reciting my sermon and prayers by the light of an oil lamp. At a certain moment—when I saw the stones coming one after the other and one had just broken one of the two lamps on the table— I decided to offer myself to God as victim by praying to Him—*if he had bequests or some other matter left pending*—to strike me and spare the others. I was at that moment convinced I would be fatally struck . . . but no: God in his lovable designs had other arrangements, and I was spared all.

There is a related fact here that does not enter directly into the story of these inexplicable phenomena, but a fact that I cannot pass over, however, in silence.

The wife of the owner of the chalet, Louise Stévenin, née Fresc de J. Jacques, born in Gaby, was pregnant with her third child, and the day of its birth was approaching. That same evening, around ten o'clock, at the moment the stones were falling most furiously in the room, I saw *this poor woman in a state of great agitation;* she was going back and forth across the entire space. Finally her husband, Édouard, called me outside to talk and, nearly in tears, presented the situation. He told me, "As you can see, Father, my wife is in this interesting condition and she feels quite poorly at this moment— I am fearful she might give birth this evening—what are we to do? The neighbors are making a fuss about taking her in because they fear her presence will cause the stones to start falling on their houses, too—an absurd prejudice—and how could anyone want her to stay here in the middle of everyone and under the falling stones? Please give me some advice."

This brave man was quite emotional and rattled, and so was I at hearing this painful story. They had with them a good servant, a woman about thirty years old, and with total resolve I told Édouard, "Be courageous and the Good Lord will help you. Give a lantern to that girl and she can accompany your wife immediately to your house in Issime."

They followed my advice and these two good women left the high grounds around 10:30 in the evening to make the long and painful descent. I leave it to those people with heart and feeling to imagine the difficulty of such a situation! But God is a father and his Providence is the best of mothers. Édouard's poor wife arrived without incident to her house in the county center of Issime at around one in the morning, and at two o'clock, an hour after her arrival, the child was born peacefully, safe and sound, and in robust health. He was baptized on October 3 by the undersigned priest and given the names of Augustin Louis (Stévenin). If he reaches old age, he can tell his grandchildren then about the adventures surrounding his birth!

To continue our story . . . I am happy to say that since 11:00, at the beginning of the recitation of the rosary, no more stones fell. Toward midnight, all those remaining in the room went to bed— dressed (of course) on a pile of hay. A lantern was left lit for several hours . . . then someone chanced to extinguish it, ready to relight it at the first signal. Thank God, no more noise, but not a person among those there slept a wink; the impression was too vivid to allow sleep to come. That morning around 5:00, the aforementioned three young men left the chalet where they had spent the night to come see us. They had agreed when leaving that they would get an early start to go back down to their homes.

At the moment the three young men neared the house, the stones began falling again, one, two . . . ; the three arrivals knocked at the door, and they opened it but retreated immediately without trying to enter, because as soon as they were on the threshold, three stones came at them, one after the other, with the speed of lightning. They retreated in terror and waited for us outside. And these five stones that fell that morning were hot. I made sure to examine all of them; it was hard to hold these five in my hands, and judging by touch, *they could have been 45 to 50 degrees Celsius.* The young men wrapped them in their handkerchiefs to bring them back home, but after making a short leg of their journey, they threw them in the valley because *they feared they would be carrying the curse and terror into their houses.* By eight o'clock we had all returned home, and during the day everyone was keen to listen to us and hear the story of all these incidents.

That same evening, the 25th, the number of curious spectators was even larger, and a fine caravan left Issime in the afternoon, although I was not one of them. There were many young folk including three carabinieri [policemen] garrisoned at Issime. They made the ascent on the order of their [text missing] and to punish the guilty parties, if ever a hoax could be found. On the next day, the 26th, the land seemed even more animated by the story of the phenomena that seemed to be intensifying more and more. There were more than forty there that evening; some were part of the Issime party including the three carabinieri, and the others had come from Fontainemore, Lillianes, Perloz, Pont St. Martin, Donnai, and Carêma.

The number of the inquisitive onlookers just kept growing. Oh well, according to the story of those involved, this is what happened that night. One carabiniere stood guard outside the house, and the other two were in the inhabited room; the stones fell as on the previous nights, and no visible cause could be seen. At someone's advice everyone formed a circle, holding hands, and *they tried to dispel the spirits by pronouncing kabbalistic spells together.*

Misfortune beset them—at this moment a hail of stones fell on them, striking everyone from the first to the last—one carabiniere had his hat knocked off, one was struck in the arm, and another in the head. He received a bloody nose from it—in short, the moment was tragic, and at precisely midnight, after this hail of stones, everyone deemed it best to leave this house and return home. The next day, Sunday, this was all people talked about in Issime and the neighboring parishes. People were gripped with terror.

September 27. The owners of the chalet and the family members (Stévenin) had become more and more alarmed by the strange phenomena that were manifesting with increasing intensity in their dwelling and begged the undersigned priest of Issime to invite an exorcist to come without delay to say liturgical prayers there. At this time the authorized and accredited exorcist for the diocese of Aosta was the abbé Cyprien Gorret, a curate from La Thuile, a good and venerable elderly man and a holy priest. Adolphe Stévenin, the brother of the haunted chalet's owner, went to La Thuile together with a letter written by the priest from Issime. The venerable archpriest Gorret left at once and on Monday the 27th, he was in Issime to perform his holy ministry. They left from the Issime parsonage around two in the afternoon; at this time I alone was making my way to the chalet with the Father from La Thuile. We spent almost that entire long and painful journey in prayer—and we arrived at the designated spot about 4:30.

At five o'clock the reverend curé from La Thuile began the liturgical prayers of the exorcism . . . and on they continued, with a few short breaks, until eight in the evening. The number of curious onlookers continued to swell, and by eight o'clock there were about fifty people who had come from various parishes in the Valleise and the surrounding area. As there was a bit of racket and confusion, the exorcist, Father Gorret, and the undersigned priest, had deemed it wise to go into the neighboring chalet, the property of a certain Amédée Stévenin. When leaving the haunted house we asked the witnesses who had hastily gathered there to call us at the first sign of manifestations. Ordinarily these began as nightfall came on, between seven and eight o'clock. This time there was not a sign—everything was perfectly tranquil . . . 7, 8, 9, and 10:00, and nothing. We all were delighted about the effectiveness of the prayer.

At around 10:30 we were summoned: "Come quick, the stones are beginning to fall!" Among the curious onlookers who hastened there this time was a certain Joseph Clérin, a native of Perloz but a resident of Pont St. Martin, where he ran a general store. He was a tall young man around twenty-five who was strong and robust . . . a real strapping fellow and a freethinker to boot—someone who believed in nothing and scoffed at everything. He had spent some time in Paris and, wanting to be superior to the others, thought he had greatly elevated himself by feigning a great skepticism. Sitting back on the pile of wild hay that had been placed in a corner of the room, he ridiculed the belief of the others as well as their fear. Misfortune took him—one moment while in the midst of his verbal outbursts a large stone, coming from no one knew where, struck him smack in the chest. He stood back up furiously, shouting, "Who threw that at me?" No one answered; you can easily see that not one of us has moved. However . . . at that moment *another mysterious stone that made various zigzags through the room* appeared and then hit the same person, striking him hard. No more room for doubt, the mysterious stone was there again. At the first call the reverend curé Gorret, the exorcist, and I immediately made our way to the spot and found all the men there agitated and worried. Someone began retelling the story—but we did not have time to listen to the whole thing to be convinced, because a third stone passed through our midst with dizzying speed to strike the wall and ricochet back to again strike the same individual, Clérin. He was hit painfully on his funny bone and let out a cry. The exorcist immediately began saying the liturgical prayers again, and everyone present became composed and contemplative; all with hats off and in an attitude of the greatest respect. Among this large crowd of men there was an Italo Angeloni of Turin, a professor of literature, vacationing in Issime; as well as the brigadier of the carabinieri, also vacationing there; a Russian professor; and the pharmacist of Issime, a certain Cagliero de Carmagnola.

All at once, while they were praying, a fourth stone arrived—followed almost immediately by *the formidable sound of a slap,* whose loud noise froze everyone in terror. The individual targeted was still the same—the famous Clérin who had transformed from a petulant rabble-rouser into a timid rabbit. At the noise of this formidable smack, the whole place was gripped by fear, but poor Clérin had not only heard it but had also felt a very sharp pain on the nape of his large, fat neck. In fact, there was a very visible bright red mark there the size of a large hand. Clérin, when being hit, said it felt like this brutal strike had come from a *glacial hand.*

It was then midnight and the sound of this solemn slap prompted everyone to leave this post. The unfortunate Clérin could take no more and wished to leave at any price. Several people therefore left with Clérin, including the exorcist and me. On the road home the good Clérin sang an entirely different tune than he had before, and he said, "I truly could not believe at all in what people were telling me; well, I had to convince myself at my own expense . . . there was something there—I believe—it is mysterious but there is something. If I have to, I will sign what I just saw, heard, and felt with my own blood." When we got to Issime, as there was plenty of moonlight, Clérin took his bicycle and went home to Pont St. Martin. Here with precision, step by step, is what I personally observed with my own eyes and ears and for which I testify with complete certainty. Perhaps others later will explain the key to the mysteries?

September 28. With the reiterated plea of the chalet's owner, Édouard Stévenin, the reverend curé from La Thuile, the delegated exorcist, stayed on for another day and the next day went back up to the chalet to begin saying the liturgical prayers for exorcism again. I had to leave Issime for family reasons, and consequently I was not able to accompany my dear colleague again. So I can only relate the narrative based on the testimony of some of those in attendance.

The number of the inquisitive had grown even larger than that of the previous days and may even have reached as many as seventy. As they were making quite a racket and some of them were seeking to provoke the spirits, the exorcist asked the owner to strictly forbid them from entering his house. The order was given and the owner held firm despite the threats from some of the onlookers. The night was cool, and the large crowd built a large fire a little distance from the haunted chalet. They quickly grew agitated, and, as the door of the chalet was closed to them, they eventually left in small groups one after the other—after launching a tirade of abusive words against the exorcist who had this order carried out. Therefore in the room where these strange phenomena were verified as occurring, that evening there was only the owner of the house with the servants and the exorcist, accompanied by a seminarian, a certain Nasso, a nephew of Monsieur Nicco, canon of the Cathedral of Aosta.

This seminarian came from Donnaz; they repeated the exorcism prayers for two hours in a row . . . and during this night saw only the arrival of two mysterious stones, but they struck no one. The exorcist consoled the owner; he told him not to concern himself about it anymore—that he hoped it had all stopped. He moreover recommended that he place his faith in God and to perform several particular devotions for the good souls of his household.

That very day they came down from the chalet with their livestock, and they would not be returning until the next year. Then, that is to say, the next year, it was over, and since then nothing more has been seen or heard.

However, these strange phenomena had keenly stirred and troubled the chalet's owner, the good Édouard Stévenin, as well as his elderly father. They both died the following year, and everyone presumed that these painful incidents had certainly had affect on their health. Édouard was about forty, but his health was in a delicate state, while his father had recently turned seventy but was still robust. Édouard had three brothers who lived several years after him; he left his young, robust wife and three handsome boys, one of whom had been born in the sad circumstances I just described.

Several years later my brother Romain, like myself a priest and then vicar of Issime, sought to interest the Valdostan almanac, *Le Messager*, by sending a long, somewhat embellished account of this incident. The caricaturist worked up a little scene of his own device to illustrate the almanac even more. Here in the preceding narrative there is nothing but the pure truth recounted without images, without embellishments, and without poetry for the reader.

The story should be based solely on the facts. Below are the signatures of several witnesses who vouch with me for the truth of the facts recounted.

In faith,
Abbé Grat Vesan curé
Hilaire Christillin, the assessor
Teofilo Goyet
Désiré Chouquer
Gustave Dandrès
Brigadiere dei R. R. Carabinieri Bonetto
Carabiniere dei R. R. Osch
Carabiniere Pillistrelli
Issime, September 1924[6]

The number of witnesses, among whom we find clergymen and administrators, and therefore educated people, is all quite impressive. All vouch for the veracity of the phenomena. This intermittent rain of stones is an exemplary case of a poltergeist, even if nothing or practically nothing in the story enables us to detect its source. Was it Édouard Stévenin's pregnant wife? This would then be one of the rare known cases where an adult takes the place of an adolescent in crisis in the role of "medium" or "sensitive." Details that we have come across in other cases reemerge here and there: the heat of certain stones, their aberrant trajectories, their sudden materialization inside the chalet within a few yards of the people present, and the fact that they did not hurt anyone. There was also the punishment of the freethinker Joseph Clérin who, in addition to the stones, was the recipient of a magisterial slap. It is also noticeable that the most courageous and intrepid individuals end up gripped by fright, and, typical of poltergeists, there is the short duration of the phenomenon: twenty-four days.

Grat Vesan alludes to the article that his brother Romain (1882–1966) published in 1912 in *Le Messager valdôtain*.[7] Its conclusion is extremely revealing.

Each person, on returning home, recounted his impression and way of interpreting the mysterious phenomena, but I believe that everyone in his heart believes and thinks like me, which is to say that

The illustration of the phenomenon that appeared in
Le Messager valdôtain *in 1912*

upon our wretched earth there are evil spirits who have the sad mission of teasing, harming, and frightening poor mortals.

Here we get a glimpse of the oral traditions that were able to develop out of similar events: the intensifications, embellishments, slippages, and alterations of all kinds, which ensure such manifestations, will enter into the realm of legend with the passage of time.

Those who preferred to see this as a case of deviltry found easy points of reference in the two cows attached to the same chain, the goats comically dressed in people's clothing, and the heat of the stones; while those who saw it as a case of a soul in torment, like our good priest, looked for a legacy or unfinished business—in other words, a situation in which a dead person's wishes were not respected. Others seemed to believe in witchcraft and began reciting kabbalistic spells. As for the cold invisible hand, we shall see what to make of that later.

8

Singular Manifestations

We know that spirits are rarely satisfied with knocking and making some noise. They throw stones, speak, deal out slaps to people, and sometimes partially or completely reveal themselves. I will now draw attention to several rarer manifestations—fire, voices, the apparition of a hand, and the persecution of a specific individual—as well as to several details that remain inexplicable to this day.

FIRE

In the chapter dedicated to the Middle Ages, we saw that the evil spirit active near Bingen (see page 86) brought fire with him into the houses he entered. To my knowledge this is the oldest account of a fire-starting spirit. Then, after a silence of several centuries, knocking and fire-starting spirits reappear in the seventeenth century, in the work of Glanvil cited earlier. In 1654 a knocking spirit was at work in the house of the weaver Gilbert Campbell of Glenluce, Scotland (see pages 88–89).

> The racket began anew, and on the next day, which was a Sunday, *the house was set on fire*. It was put out, however, by neighbors return-

ing home from church and thus caused little damage. Fasting and prayers were prescribed for the following day, but despite this, the house was again set on fire at nine o'clock in the morning Tuesday; yet again it was speedily extinguished with little harm done.

The protagonists of this drama assume that it is the devil at work.

In the nineteenth century Alexander Aksakoff (1832–1903), imperial counselor to the Czar, had the accounts of phenomena that took place in 1853 drawn from the Russian archives in the Kharkov Government, and Walter Leaf published them.[1]

In January 1853, a small cavalry post (*etape*) at the hamlet of Liptsy, in the Government of Kharkoff, was commanded by a Captain Jandachenko, who, with his wife, lived in a small four-roomed house, which had been taken by the village community for his official residence. It had previously belonged to peasants, in whose time nothing abnormal had occurred in it. It seems, indeed, that in the beginning of January 1852, something mysterious had happened there, but, as this is only casually alluded to by one of the witnesses, we must fast forward a year, to January 9th, 1853, when the present story opens.

On that day it appears that the house was occupied by Captain Jandachenko and his wife, who had a bedroom and sitting room on one side of the passage; on the other side were a storeroom and the kitchen, in which the servants also slept. On this evening there were five of them, two maids named Efimia and Matrona, the latter hired, the former a serf of the captain's, and three soldiers: one of them, Vasili (Basil), being the captain's orderly, and the other two attached to him temporarily.

After the servants had put out the light, but before they had gone to sleep—such is the account, which they give without variations—*sundry small objects, such as cups and wooden platters standing on the stove, were thrown about the room.* A light was struck, but the throwing continued when no one was looking, and no cause could be found for it. Next day, the fifth, Captain Jandachenko mentioned this to his parish priest, Victor Selyezneff, who came with his church officers on the sixth, the Epiphany, after the ceremony of blessing the water in the river. "On entering the house," he says, "I saw a small stone fall in the passage; a cup full of dumplings fell at my feet in the midst of the attendants who were carrying the icons, and I heard repeated knocks." Captain Jandachenko adds that after the house had been sprinkled with holy water—the object of the priest's visit—*"an ax was thrown from the loft in the passage against the doors with remarkable velocity and noise."* Another priest, Father Lobkovsky, whose curiosity had been aroused by what he had been told during the blessing of the river, was also present, with several other official visitors to the captain. They went into the kitchen, when, "in the sight of all of us, there was smashed against the door in the passage, where no human being was, a bottle of varnish, which, according to the captain, had been standing in the sitting room cupboard under lock and key." Moreover, a soldier reported—though this, as we know, is "not evidence"—that a tub full of vegetables in the cellar had left its place and upset its contents.

Undaunted by the small success of the aspersion, the good priests brought the heavy artillery of the church into play next day. With the assistance of a third father of the church officials and the icons, a solemn service was read. Hardly had they begun when *a stone was thrown in the kitchen,* which was empty, *and smashed a window in the sight of all.* Then *a piece of wood, followed by a pail of water, flew out* of the kitchen into the midst of the assembly, the latter upsetting in their midst. The culminating horror was *the fall of a stone into the basin of holy water itself.* The house was again thoroughly sprinkled, and the holy objects carried back to the church; but as the phenomena still continued, the captain begged two of the priests to return and read the formal prayers for the exorcism of evil spirits.

This seems to have had little more effect than the previous service. The phenomena continued in the presence of several fresh witnesses, and on the eighth took a new turn. *The bed in the room of the captain and his wife caught fire* in the presence of both; they put it out, but it immediately blazed out in a fresh place and had to be again extinguished. At the same time *two blows were struck on the window by a brick, and four panes of glass were broken.* Captain Jandachenko was at last driven to change his quarters but moved back after a few days. At the same time he again had recourse to the services of a priest, which for the time were successful, as *the phenomena were now reduced to nothing worse than some "human groaning"* of a most doleful description, heard by the servants in the kitchen.

But after a few days it all began again; and on January 22, Captain Jandachenko brought some friends in to witness what was going on. On this occasion the orderly, Vasily, *was slightly wounded in the head by a knife thrown* by the evil agency. Things grew worse and worse, and a number of peasants were brought in to the house to watch: but, in spite of all care, next afternoon (the twenty-third) *the roof of the house caught fire* and was burned off, the efforts of the firemen being much hindered by a peculiarly thick and malodorous smoke blown in their faces. This led to an inquiry by the local "ispravnik" (head of the district police), which took place on February 4th and 5th.

The evil spirits yielded for a time to government interference; and though, as appears from the very full report of the evidence, nothing was found to direct suspicion against any one, all was quiet for some months. Captain Jandachenko had in the meantime permanently moved to another house, and here, on July 23, *the old games began once more. In one room the pillows were thrown off the beds, in another jars of water were upset.* The captain at once applied officially for help, and again a guard of peasants was set all about the house. In vain, things were more lively than ever through the 24th, and in the morning of the 25th the most serious troubles of all began. At eight o'clock *the thatched roof was suddenly found to be on fire.* It was extinguished before the fire engine came, but for precaution, engine and firemen were kept on the spot. At three o'clock in the afternoon thick smoke was seen coming from a shed in a wing of the house. A soldier crawled in on hands and knees and dragged out *a hay mattress full of smoldering fire, which was put out*. Finally, at five o'clock a sudden gust of wind arose, and with it the whole roof of the wing burst into flames. The fire spread so rapidly that the men not only could not start the engine, but had great difficulty in dragging it into a place of safety; *and with the captain's house four neighboring cottages were completely burned to the ground*.

. . . This lasted for five days, from July 27th to 31st, after which, no result having been arrived at, the matter was transferred to the civil court at Kharkoff, where it was duly pigeon-holed.

Two elements should be noted here. First is that the visits by the clergy and the Christian methods—relics, icons, holy water, services— remained ineffective. Next, there was a gradual progression of the manifestations that gained in intensity and eventually culminated in inexplicable fires. We pass from the throwing of objects to blows, and from broken windows to arson. Then there is a kind of pause that ensues after the intervention of the exorcist: the phenomena are reduced to dismal moaning, but when everything resumes, the Jandachenkos move out, and the manifestations repeat themselves in their new abode until it is burned down.

Another account also comes by way of Russia. It describes what happened on the outskirts of the city of Lletzky in the Government of Orenburg,[2] in the house of a Mr. Shchapoff.

On November 14, 1870, a shade was seen and drumming was heard on the shutters all night. Investigations turned up nothing. On the fifteenth, the phenomena repeated, but there were knockings on the window and then on the wall of the room, and then other noises and dancing was heard. On the sixteenth the knocks occurred again, as well as noises in the chimney, and the objects in the room began sailing around and made a noise far out of proportion to their size when they fell to the ground.

On January 8, 1871, a small ball of light the size of a plate appeared. On the ninth the raps began knocking in the afternoon and followed the mistress of the house everywhere. The Shchapoff couple went to consult Dr. Shustoff in the neighboring town. While they were there nothing happened at their home, but when they returned on the twenty-first things resumed with even more intensity than before. Everything began flying about the house, even dangerous utensils like knives, with no one ever able to stop the objects when they started moving but only when they were sailing by or falling.

The Shchapoff family left their house again only to return in March, and the phenomena resumed anew, *then a cotton shirt on a table caught fire.* It was easily put out, but the next day *some furniture caught fire* spontaneously and the neighbor, a man named Portnoff, burned his hands extinguishing the flames. These flare-ups were preceded by an apparition: Mr. Portnoff recounted to me how "on the evening of my departure the phenomena had begun with *the apparition of bright meteors,* which appeared dancing in the veranda in front of the sitting-room window. There were several of them varying in size from a large apple to a walnut. Their shape was round, their color deep red or bluish pink; they were not quite transparent but rather dull. This curious dance continued for some time, and it seemed as though the globes were trying to get in at the window."

The following day when Portnoff returned home he found his own bed in flames, which were then successfully extinguished. But the most terrifying thing was yet to come, for which all that preceded had only been a prologue: "I was sitting playing the guitar," Portnoff said. "The miller, who had been with us, got up to leave and was followed by Helena Efimovna (Mrs. Shchapoff). Hardly had she shut the door behind her when I heard, as though from far off, a long, deep, drawn wail. The voice seemed familiar to me; overcome with an unaccountable horror I rushed to the door, and there in the passage I saw a literal pillar of fire in the middle of which, draped in flame, stood Helena Efimovna, the lower portion of her dress was on fire and *the flames came from below and almost concealed her.* I supposed that the fire was not violent as her dress was quite a thin one, and rushed to put it out with my hands, but I found it burned them badly as though they were sticking to burning pitch. *A sort of cracking noise came from beneath the floor,* which also shook and vibrated violently. The miller came back from outside to help, and between us we carried off the unconscious victim in her burned dress.

My wife recounted in turn that when she went back into the hallway the floor shook beneath her *with a hellish roaring,* and a bluish spark lit up from below to strike her. She hardly had time to even cry out as she lost consciousness when the flames enveloped her. Notable was the fact *she suffered not the slightest burn; and although her dress was burned to above her knees,* even her lower limbs were left unscathed.

The miller told how when he was crossing through the garden he had heard a dreadful noise followed by a pitiful cry; at the same time he caught glimpse of a fire in the corridor. He felt such a rush of fear that his legs barely allowed him to race to their assistance.

After this terrible adventure there was nothing left to do but run away. This we did, asking refuge at a nearby Cossack's hut, where we stayed until the floods subsided. As soon as possible I sold the house and bought another one. When we moved into the new home, the phenomena did not reoccur, and calm was restored to our family.

Numerous clues allow us to assume that the cause of all this was Shchapoff's wife. The knocks sounded while she slept and followed her when she moved. Once she went to bed, objects flew at her and so forth. Moreover, there is the following extraordinary detail: the flames that consumed her robe did not burn, and the lady was left unscathed.

One other detail, that of the fiery globes, is not a novelty as we have encountered them before, in 1533, in the story of the evil spirit of Schildach in the Wurttemberg (see page 85): this entity spread fires thanks to globes of fire. "What was so unusual about this is that balls of fire (*globi ignei volitantes*) were raining here and there onto the houses." The same thing reappeared in another form in 1654, in the story of the spirit of Glenluce. There a voice could be heard saying, "If you want to see me, extinguish the light and I shall appear in your midst like a ball of fire."

Here is one final account. In Quebec, from September 15 to November 17, 1889, a knocking spirit was at work in the home of farmer George Dagg. Fires erupted spontaneously in his house, with eight in one day, six indoors and two outside; the curtains burned in the middle of the day while family and neighbors were there.[3]

VOICES

The sounds produced by knocking spirits (B 6) cover the lower frequencies of the scale with a clear predominance of the bass notes. The noises sound like things rustling or sliding, dull blows, a loud racket, or an all-out din. The reverse is true when voices are involved: they are most often soft, high, childish, sometimes interrupted by laughter, but sometimes husky or similar to grunts.

In the accounts thus far cited we have seen that it is not uncommon to hear a voice—as, for example, in *The Life of Saint Caesarius* where a voice challenges passersby before pelting them with stones. Sometimes a dialogue even ensues as was the case with the late Garnier, as recounted by Hugues du Mans in the twelfth century, or in the account of the spirit that was disturbing the home of Gilbert Campbell in 1654. The voices are not always intelligible, whereas those of demons and spirits, on the other hand, are. In the story of the "Devil of Mâcon" in September 1612, the diabolical spirit sang a little jingle, repeated the word "shepherd" several times, let out a hunting call, recited prayers that he truncated, and provided exact revelations, notably on the death of the father of the narrator, Perrault. The spirit of the Glenluce account (see chapter 5) threatens, prevaricates, and tells lies when attacked by the minister. The demons of Vauvert have horrible voices, but that of Shildach is capable of imitating the birds and charming the ear with sweet melodies. On June 2, 1713, just before the manifestations of the knocking spirit haunting Dr. Gerstmann's house stopped once and for all, a voice was heard saying, "Ended. Ended today. Evil end. Sacred end." In 1889 the noisy spirit haunting the house of George Dagg, resident of Clarendon in Pontiac County, Quebec, spoke in a gruff voice.[4] From the Middle Ages to the present, cries and voices could be heard, and it is worth noting that coercion was often required to make the spirit speak, and this task often fell to a clergyman, which is logical since the poltergeist is regarded as a devil.

THE HAND

Among the most surprising things in poltergeist stories, the apparition of ghostly hands is quite noteworthy. Their appearance generally occurs in tandem with the hearing of voices.

In 1654 the knocking spirit in the house of Gilbert Campbell showed his hand and his arm up to the elbow and struck the floor so hard with it that the house shook ("a naked Hand and an Arm, from the Elbow down, beating upon the Floor till the House did shake again").[5] Four years later, near Daventry in Northamptonshire, a ten-year-old girl vomited water and stones, then chests and boxes moved of their own accord, the covers were torn from the beds, a Bible changed location several times, a knife flew up into the air, and knocking was heard that seemed to be made by a hand holding a hammer. One night, the young girl started crying that she felt a hand in her bed that no one could catch hold of. This hand was cold, and the little girl died four days later.[6] In the month of June 1682, the hand of a poltergeist was seen haunting the house of George Walton in New England.[7] In 1695 the reverend Alexander Telfair witnessed a poltergeist whose manifestations naturally included stone throwing as well as a small white hand and arm striking the walls.[8]

Around the same time Dr. Gibbs, the prebendary of Westminister, at the request of his friends, visited a house haunted by spirits; a young girl had felt herself touched by a cold hand and died soon after ("a young Girl, who was plucked by the Thigh by a cold Hand in her Bed, who died within a few days after"). Several weeks later the mistress of the house confided to Gibbs when he chanced to pass by that the house was haunted, especially on the second floor, and that stones, bricks, and objects were flying about of their own accord ("there was such a flinging of things up and down, of Stones and Bricks through the Windows, and putting all in disorder"). Then he witnessed some bizarre phenomena: a window opened by itself, a piece of a wheel flew in, then the window shut itself and reopened to cast out a piece of tile. The doctor climbed to the room upstairs and saw seats, benches, torches, beds, and so on, hurled about in the greatest disarray. In short order the inhabitants were forced to abandon the premises.[9] Contrary to the examples cited earlier, the hand triggered the poltergeist phenomenon, which, in this account, is closely connected to the death of the young girl. In 1761 the brothers and sisters of Molly Durbin avowed they had seen the hand that attacked and scratched her (we will return to this later).

Among the misfortunes of the Shchapoff family, which we examined above, the reporter specifies at the end of his account that he forgot one manifestation: "It was a small and delicate pink hand like that of a child, who my wife surprised drumming on the window panes."[10] The narrator then added:

> I saw a tiny pink hand, like a child's, spring up from the floor, disappear behind my wife's coverlet, and pull at the folds so that I could see the unnatural quickness with which the folds moved, beginning from the lower end to the point by her side where the hand had disappeared. I was horrified, because from my wife's position, it was absolutely impossible that the hand could be her own.

Between August and September 1862, the house of the national counselor Joller in Niederdorf, Switzerland, fell prey to a knocking spirit, and the counselor stated, "The most insupportable thing was the contact with a frozen hand and its fingertips, as well as a current of glacial air . . . which all the inhabitants of the house could feel, mostly at night but also during the day."[11]

When they are freezing to the touch, these phantom hands appear to be those of the dead. When they are not freezing and are comparable to the hands of children, it is possible we are faced with different aspect of the same phenomenon. To my knowledge the oldest story of such a hand can in fact be found in the *Memorable Histories* of Henry of Hereford (died 1370), a Dominican from Minden.[12] In 1349, in Cyrenbergh, a town in the Landgrave of Hesse, "a small and gracious human hand let itself be seen and touched . . . No other part of this being was seen or felt, but something like the hoarse voice of a man could be heard distinctly." On interrogation, this creature revealed that it was a man named Reyneke, but the bulk of the story gives the impression he is a kind of household spirit, a familiar spirit that serves the family with whom it lives. One day when guests arrived, "there arose an incredible din in the house and above them," coming from Reyneke, who warned them: "It is your shamelessness that is the cause of this racket." It seems that Henry of Hereford preserved fragments from a poltergeist story that is blended with beliefs concerning domestic spirits and dwarves.*

The apparition of hands raises the problem of the corporeal nature of knocking spirits, for, in order to make sound, it is necessary, according to sound physical logic, that these hands have substance. There is another detail, however, that reveals they are indeed three-dimensional: when persecuting an individual, the slaps bestowed by the spirit can be heard and leave a mark on the victim's face. This inevitably brings up another question: Why does only a hand appear? At the current stage of

---

*In fact, like dwarves, Reyneke and his fellows lived in a hollow mountain.

my research, I can only offer the following conjecture: the hand would in some way be a *pars pro toto* intended to demonstrate the reality of the knocking spirit, who, for some unknown reason, does not have the ability to let itself be seen entirely. These corporeal apparitions are distinct from the apparitions of ghostly spirits, of which we will provide a glimpse in the following examples.

In his *Chronicle,* Ralph of Coggeshall (died 1127) speaks of a spirit (*fantasticus*) who makes revelations and which a young maidservant saw a single time in the form of a small infant dressed in white.[13] In 1686 only Alice Medcalfe was able to see a stranger who was either closely connected to the poltergeist knocking at her parents' house, or was the knocking spirit itself. In September 1889, one of George Dagg's children (see page 163), at whose house a poltergeist was active, cried out: "O mama, the handsome man! . . . he rose into the sky and was all red." No adult could see anything at all, but two other children when questioned spoke of a very handsome man dressed in white, with long black hair and wearing a crown of stars on his head. A magistrate in Indes (France) told of the manifestations of a poltergeist that victimized him in March 1920, and his story informs us that on the night of the thirteenth and morning of the fourteenth of this month he saw the silhouette of a woman who he asked several times, "Who are you?" only to hear the response, "O father." On December 25, 1910, the late Leah, aunt of the pastor of Tweedal was seen by her husband, children, and two servants, but although the pastor could hear her voice, he did not see her.[14]

PERSECUTIONS

While the cast stones and objects generally do not harm or only cause mild bruises, it can also happen that people will be literally persecuted, harassed, and injured by the poltergeist. We can truly describe these as attacks against an individual, and those that concern women specifically come in the form of bites, stones, and pinching. There is therefore a notable difference between the projectiles that cause no harm (except, by chance, to freethinkers), and these accounts of malignant actions.

In 1654 Gilbert Campbell's son was persecuted by a spirit and sent away from his father's house. When he wanted to return he said that "he heard a voice forbidding him to step foot into the house. He went inside nonetheless, *but was mistreated so badly he was obliged to return to the minister's.*" During the months from June to August 1682, a spirit attacked the house of George Walton, a New England farmer, and then the man himself. It all began with a shower of hot stones, then a door was torn from its hinges, the windows were broken, a hammer was slammed down next to a person, a candlestick was swept from the table, and the spit was spirited up the chimney and then cast back down, point-end first, where it embedded itself in a log. The stones struck most often those locations where George Walton was to be found, even when in the middle of the fields or barn, and on August 2 the farmer was seriously injured by the stones. After an interruption during the winter, the phenomena resumed in the spring of 1683.[15] On December 18, 1761, in the Durbin home in Bristol, one of the young daughters, Molly, was pinched and this occurred repeatedly until January 1762. She was then bitten on the back, shoulder, and on the nape, and the mark of eighteen teeth and saliva could be seen, and then she was stuck with needles, which generally occurred at night. Priests coming to the rescue interrogated the spirit in Latin and received responses in the form of scratching.

Around 1820, Schuppart, a professor of theology at Giessen, was pelted with stones for a period of six years, while his wife was the recipient of blows and slaps; she was also stuck with pins and bitten. Around 1863 thirteen-year-old Maddalena Rimassa was the constant target of thrown objects that struck her head but never left an injury no matter their size. In 1916 Ireland a farmer lost his last-born child, and a poltergeist manifested that went after his wife and ten-year-old daughter in particular. In the story about the knocking spirit in Clarendon (Quebec), the spirit pulled four-year-old Dinah's braid so hard it almost tore it off.[16] In the autumn of 1926 a Romanian servant girl, aged thirteen, working in England, was bitten ceaselessly, and it was said that the tooth marks were visible on her.

We can see evidence for an entire range of malignant actions—always remaining, however, within the sphere of contusions—exactly as if someone had it in for the victim.

Outside the persecutions, we have what could be called the self-defense reactions of knocking spirits. In fact, although accounts describing the throwing of stones or similar objects (bricks, tiles, and so on) predominate, we should not overlook the showers of filth, ashes, or excrements that essentially target the churchmen who have come to exorcise the houses. Everything suggests that the poltergeist attempts, by these means, to drive off the priest who threatens it by means of the power invested in him and the sacraments he brings with him. The choice of disgusting objects is also a way of deriding the adversary and scoffing at his authority, and it further smacks of a kind of mischievousness that can be found in medieval charivaris. These showers of objects imply that the poltergeist sees and hears everything that is going on; even though it remains invisible, it is always able to make its presence felt. Swearing and curses, or the sweeping declarations of a freethinker who refuses to accept the phenomenon is real, are immediately paid back.

THE HOT STONES

In 1612–1613, in the story of the "Devil of Mâcon" (see page 87), one of the protagonists, Monsieur Tornus, marks a stone thrown by the demon and tosses it outside. It returns scorching hot (W 1), and he concludes it must have been briefly in hell. In 1682 some of the stones cast at George Walton were also hot. In the account of the haunted chalet in Issime, the narrator states:

And these five stones that fell that morning were hot. I made sure to examine all of them; it was hard to hold these five in my hands, and judging by touch, they could have been 45 to 50 degrees Celsius.

Investigators of poltergeist phenomena have advanced a hypothesis that is worth mentioning as it admirably documents the attempts to formulate scientific explanations. Observing that the rocks traveled through walls without leaving any trace, E. Bozzano imagines a dematerialization followed by a remateralization (R 4) once they are inside the house, and he suggests this:

> Now, by virtue of the law of the transformation of physical forces, this is precisely what should happen if the "conveyed" stone or object underwent a process of extremely swift disintegration and reintegration, which is to say, in this case a more or less noteworthy verified thermic reaction should occur in accordance with the different molecular constitutions of these stones or objects.[17]

Readers will have to determine for themselves just what is scientific in that!

OBJECTS TRAVELING ERRATICALLY

Anything that is not solidly attached inside a house is capable of sailing off into the air or moving (R 3), it all depends on how much it weighs. Dishes, lights (candleholders), and other domestic accessories, as well as shoes, travel through the air. Furniture, primarily chairs and beds, moves of its own accord. Other elements, like shutters, doors, and windows, start moving back and forth or opening and closing with no apparent cause.

All the witnesses of poltergeist phenomena have noted surprising things, mainly the course taken by the stones was unnatural. Their trajectory can be curved or parabolic, but does not follow a straight line and can take a sharp turn as if the projectiles were being remote controlled in some way. Stones sometimes fall from the ceilings and emerge from the walls with extreme violence, but their impact often has no relation to the height they have fallen or the violence with which they were thrown. Enormous stones arrive with extreme rapidity and slow their course before hitting someone who, thanks to this, is not injured. Others that are quite tiny fall gently but make a huge racket. In 1723 Jeremias Heinisch, the pastor of Gröben, a town outside Berlin, noted such phenomena in his description of a knocking spirit's manifestations that disturbed his presbytery. After it broke the windows rocks began falling straight down as if their force had been suddenly exhausted: "One would say that an invisible hand had been holding them up." He also noted that they turned sharply around the corner of the house, which was "something impossible for anything thrown naturally." These ninety-degree turns are also present with the poltergeist of Resau,[18] and, here, too, the projectiles came to a sudden stop as if held back on their course by an invisible hand.

Herr Grottendieck, who witnessed a poltergeist in Sumatra during September 1903, noted:

> The stones fell with remarkable slowness, in such a way that even suspecting a hoax, there was something mysterious about it all the same. One would say they were lingering in the air, describing a parabola and forcefully hitting the ground. But the noise they produced was abnormal, as if it was too loud relative to the slowness of their fall.[19]

On the night of February 1, 1843, in a Philadelphia home, among other manifestations a mirror zigzagged through a room. In Milwaukee, at the Giddings home in 1874, an egg struck a person there after following a course parallel to the ground. In 1849, in the workshop of Mr. Bristow, a carpenter from Swanland near Hull, England, a poltergeist sowed disorder and one witness said:

> Except in some special cases, the projectiles fell and hit without any noise, although they came at such a speed that in normal circumstances they would have produced a fairly large clatter. *Nobody ever saw a missile at the time it started.* One would have said that they

could not be perceived until they had traveled at least six inches from their starting point. Which brings one to consideration of another aspect of the mystery—namely that the missiles only moved when nobody was looking, and when they were least expected. Now and again one of us would watch a piece of wood closely for a good number of minutes, and the piece would not budge; but if the observer stopped looking at it, this same piece would jump on us . . . *Sometimes the direction taken by the projectiles was a straight line, but more often it was undulating, rotatory, spiral, serpentine, or jerky.*[20]

The projectiles visibly defy the natural laws of physics. This implies that they are obeying other laws, and the specialists in the psychic sciences speak of telekinesis or psychokinesis. In 1836 Joseph von Görres noted this concerning a poltergeist visitation in the home of a certain man named Obergemeiner in October 1818.

The masses set in movement were often large, and their speed was great. However, their result was inevitably so mediocre that these objects sometimes remained stopped at the windows or fell perpendicular to the feet of the persons they struck. The force that set them in motion could therefore increase or shrink at will, and it was easy to see that these masses did not follow the whims of chance but were directed by a reasonable purpose, to wit, to cause no harm to anyone.

If we suppose this force is by its nature good (*Gutartigkeit*), we have to accept that it is self-regulating and self-moderating, and if it is malevolent by nature (*Bösartigkeit*), a higher law must govern it, thus in either case it is a will guided by reason. It this is so, if the facts are incontestable, and if these conclusions are rigorous, then we have to acknowledge that there are invisible, incorporeal spirits (*unsichtbare, unleibliche Geister*) at work here or at least physical individuals capable of becoming invisible and taking action. Regardless of which hypothesis is maintained, this is why we see that these incidents smack of magic.

All this is only the rigorous conclusion from incontestable premises. To deny these facts because they cannot be explained is folly. To shunt them aside without taking the trouble to study them is pathetic mental cowardice and is good for nothing (*elende Geistesfeigheit und Nullität*).[21]

Görres therefore retains only two possibilities: spirits or magicians. Furthermore, he emphasizes that the driving force (*bewegende Kraft*) operates according to its own whim, that it is free, intelligent, and spiritual and even capable of moral motivations as it avoided injuring those present and respected the crucifix sitting on the table. All the characteristics extracted by Görres apply much more to human beings than to spirits. We will now look at a particular case in more detail.

THE SCANDINAVIAN DIFFERENCE

The diachronic examination of knocking spirit stories has cast light on the way in which they were perceived and interpreted through the ages. The connections between the various interpretations, whose internal logic has been revealed, shows that we are confronting a large complex that has occupied and still occupies an important place in the history of mental attitudes. Knocking spirits have allowed men to believe in the supernatural, whether it is represented by creatures of popular mythology, demons, or the dead. It is worth noting, however, that certain European countries do not appear in our inquiry—notably the Scandinavian countries. This is quite surprising, and the specialists I consulted were unable to answer the question: "Do you know of any poltergeists in your homeland?" Furthermore, when a knocking spirit is involved, it is always in connection with spiritualism, and the Swedish terms *klapp-ande* and *knack-ande,* the names for poltergeists in that country, do not seem to have come into use until the nineteenth century. The Norwegian term *bankeånd,* meanwhile, is a calque, or loan translation of the German word *poltergeist.*

This "absence" of poltergeists can be explained by a different mental attitude of the people of the north with respect to what we call the "paranormal." Even today ghosts and revenants are almost an everyday occurrence in Iceland, as the excellent study directed by Christophe Pons in the 1990s has shown.[22] In Norway hauntings are common and heavily exploited in both literature—see *Trommereisen* (In Search of the Drum) by Ailo Gaup[23]—and the press. Reading a contemporary investigation, conducted by the *Glåmdalen* newspaper of Kongsvinger, a small village in southwest Norway, can provide us with some elements of an answer, because it shows, from the example below, that poltergeists are combined with ghosts and revenants.

The house of the couple Inger Marit and Roar Lunde in the old quarter of Kongsvinger, in southwest Norway, was so haunted they were obliged to request the assistance of a priest and a healer to obtain peace in their rooms. Peace was only restored once the priest Vibeke Bergsjø Aas and the healer Lise Lyseggen had performed several ceremonies in the house.

When Inger Marit and Roar Lunde moved into the house at 27 Vollgata on April 22, 1994, they noted they were not alone! They saw that their six-year-old child was very nervous in his room on the second floor. When he was sitting on his bed, he asked: "Is this house a haunted house?"

All the time they heard *the noise of footsteps and people talking on the second floor,* but when they got there, they would hear them on the first floor.

They would hear the door open although they had locked it, but when they replaced the door, they no longer heard anything.

One day a black cat appeared on the floor; it then left through the door and suddenly vanished without leaving a trace. They then noted that it was walking across the comforter on the bed. When they bought their own cat, the sinister black cat disappeared.

Roar was the first to see mysterious shapes appear on the floorboards.

One day when Inger Marit was in the kitchen, she and her husband saw *a little woman* wearing a shawl and an apron who walked close by them, then left the house without leaving a trace.

They installed a new kitchen, and one day while Marit was making dinner a shade then manifested, which hastened to a corner of the kitchen where it turned the roasting spit under Marit's nose, while she was gripped by panic.

When Roar and Marit bought some old objects at an auction, the inexplicable events started again. They had placed an *ancient wardrobe* in their bedroom; *that night it gave off creaking sounds. Both of them felt that someone wanted to strangle and beat them. An old stemmed glass rose off the table* in the room; then lay back down on its side before rolling off and breaking when it hit the floor.

Three witnesses confirmed that all of this happened. The cat had attacked them numerous times. A dog that paid them a short visit began barking frantically and then hid trembling beneath the sofa. Their friends and acquaintances who visited them were reluctant to return because they were too frightened.

Roar's father definitely saw something strange. Certain chairs screeched, and a woman had approached him, spun around, and said something to him point blank in a croaking voice before vanishing through the roof.

After the exorcism performed by the healer and the priest, everything became calm and peaceful again. Vibeke Bergsjø Aas (the priest) told a newpaper reporter that he was quite happy to have had an opportunity to restore peace and order into this house that had been so haunted and troubled.[24]

We can see, then, that the elements of poltergeists—the creaking noises of the wardrobe, the screeching of the chairs, the glass that flew up, the noises of feet and voices, the door that opened by itself—are buried in the midst of apparitions—a malefic cat, a little woman, a shade. To put an end to the phenomena, the priest sprinkled holy water in the house during the exorcism ceremony and used the sign of the cross. When he learned of this, Per Oskar Kjølass, Bishop of Nord-Hålogaland, stated that the Norwegian church should reintroduce the practice of blessing new houses into which one is moving for the first time.

Aware of this pattern and reexamining ancient narratives, we can find in the *Saga of Snorri the Godi*,*[25] which dates from around 1230, the following narrative sequence in which the dead, noises, and apparitions form an inseparable whole.

> Before dying at Froda [the name of an Icelandic farm], Thorgunna asked that all her bedding be burned after she was no more. Because it was beautiful, this was not done, with disastrous consequences. A fatal moon cast its light in the common room at Froda: a shepherd died, revenants were seen, and six people passed away before Advent. At that time *noises were heard* in a cupboard where dried fish was stored, as if something was rending it to pieces; six men died at sea on a fishing expedition. Then a seal's head appeared, which emerged through the floorboards, and stared at Thorgunna's bedding, and *noises were constantly heard in the cupboard* day and night. The day arrived when they needed these stores. A man opened the cupboard and saw a large tail that looked singed and was as large as an ox tail and thick and covered with short seal hair. People pulled on it but it disappeared, never to be seen again; of the fish there was nothing left but the skin.[26]

In these northerly latitudes, poltergeists seem to lack diabolical and goblinlike dimensions that have been evident in many of their southern counterparts. But in order to get a more complete picture of

---

*[Also known as the *Eyrbyggja saga.* —*Trans.*]

what is going on, we would have to take a new look at all the northern folktales about kobolds and deviltry, which is a future research project of mine. Based on what we currently know, there is only one hypothesis that would have the merit of explaining the "Scandinavian difference": poltergeists are implicitly component elements of manifestations of the dead.

Conclusion

There is nothing new about stone throwing, pranks, collisions, and the spontaneous movement of objects; there have always been stories concerning them. We have seen how over the course of the centuries there were several interpretations of poltergesits. During the Middle Ages, folk beliefs offered three explanations: devils, unspecified spirits, and the dead. The perspective has changed in modern times, and some psychologists and psychiatrists connect these manifestations to unconscious conflicts in order to advance psychoanalytical interpretations. All that varies is the interpretation of the facts, which reflect the mental attitudes and bases of knowledge that prevailed in successive eras. Each era has believed in poltergeists and finds what it expects to find in the phenomena—completely subjectively! The chart on page 179 provides a glimpse of these developments.

During the Middle Ages the devil and his auxiliaries were omnipresent, whether as succubi and incubi, or as some other form. All paranormal manifestations were attributed to the devil or to demons and theologians and preachers alike sang the same tune: protect yourself from Satan and his glamours. Hagiographic literature abounds in attacks of saints by demons, and stone throwing is not absent from such books as, for example, *Lives of the Fathers*. Knocking spirits are devils,

POLTERGEISTS DUE TO THE PRESENCE
OF LIVING BEINGS

Reading A	Reading B	Reading C	Reading D
Pagan Middle Ages	*Christian Middle Ages*	*Post-Medieval Era, 16th–17th Centuries*	*Modern Era*
Spirits	The devil	Witchcraft	The Dead
Genies	Demons	Hoax	People with sixth sense, or with psychokinetic abilities
The dead	The dead		

even for a nineteenth-century priest. In the Christian world this is the one explanation that is left when all others have been exhausted; it is more "rational," but varies in accordance with the religion of the person passing judgment. Therefore it is logical that Christians turn to a priest or pastor who will come to perform exorcisms, reciting and having others recite prayers, sprinkling the site with holy water, or carrying relics to every corner. Purification by fasting of the individuals involved is also recommended. It is what we will call the "religious response."*

However, in accordance with a process that demonized the creatures of popular belief, a process I have demonstrated in several earlier studies† so there is no need to reiterate it here, the phenomena that clerics maintain to be the work of devils are perceived differently by the common people—the *paganus, rusticus,* or *illiteratus.* They see in such situations the confirmation of the existence of the (visible or invisible) fantastic and supernatural beings who inhabit our universe, figures that answer to a thousand different names depending upon the country, province, and century, beings who in the West were finally encompassed by the generic terms of "brownie" ("kobold"), "sprite," and "household spirit."

---

*In other parts of the world it would be Buddhist monks who come to say mantras.
†See my various studies on ghosts and revenants, dwarves and elves, and spirits of place.

What criteria were used to achieve the attribution of poltergeists to these beings? Besides the general behavior of knocking spirits described in chapter 4, one of the criteria with the greatest influence is certainly their fantastical nature and the mischievousness that can be glimpsed behind many manifestations. In the texts where brownies are expressly mentioned, their actions smack of tricks and pranks, mockery, and bad jokes. These beings seem to make sport of the living, vexing and pestering them. The reader will have seen that humans are rarely hurt by these unusual manifestations. The considerable disorder these creatures cause seems to indicate they are unhappy and view the inhabitants as intruders, or else their behavior displeases the invisible dwellers there.

In medieval accounts we are generally dealing with place spirits, which is to say those that live in the house and/or outbuildings of the farm, as well as local spirits that dwell in woods or fields. Beliefs have existed from the dawn of time maintaining that the ground belongs to supernatural beings with whom the man who builds or settles there must make arrangements; in light of such beliefs, poltergeist phenomena have been interpreted as the sign of a disagreement. By throwing stones, ashes, or filth, by turning houses upside down, our invisible neighbors, our "co-owners," let us know a taboo has been violated, that an unspoken agreement has been broken. One such violation might be, for example, that they did not receive their regular offering. They avenge themselves in their own distinct style, and their deeds and gestures smack of the symbolism of disorder. According to Saint Augustine, order is the guarantee of happiness. Because they transgress all laws of physics, paranormal phenomena therefore are given an interpretation in this sense: that of messages. To restore order we must know how to decipher them and discover what prompted the wrath of our invisible neighbors.

The presence of the dead in this belief complex remains to be explained. Several factors figure into this connection between knocking spirits and the deceased. According to an opinion that has been widespread over the centuries, there is both a world of spirits and a world of the dead that exist parallel to our own. The first is called the Otherworld and is peopled by elemental spirits—fairies, dwarves, elves, and so forth—and the second is called the Beyond. Both worlds communicate and interfere with the world of the living. In ancient times the Beyond opened up on a regular basis, and the dead had license to roam over the earth. In Greece this took place during the time of the Anthesteria festival, in Rome during the Lemuralia, with the Celts during Samhain (November 1), and with the Germanic peoples during Jól (Yule), the period spanning from Christmas to Epiphany, the time called the "twelve days" that is rich with supernatural manifestations.

According to some mythologists[1] the Beyond preceded the birth of the Otherworld, for which it would be the root. The former remained the land of the dead, whereas the other developed to offer a euphemistic and mythical vision of it. This is why there is no need to underscore the kinship of white ladies* and fairies, as well as that of dwarves and the wicked dead, and that of the elves with the good dead.[2] Over the course of the centuries the reintegration of the dead into our close environment took place in the form of what one commonly and improperly called "spirits"—a more vague term than one might wish for, but convenient as it functions more abstractly, encompassing all sorts of manifestations.

The difference between the world of the dead and that of the so-called spirits gradually blurred to produce a single universe, the world of the others, to borrow the title of a recent film (*The Others,* 2001). Furthermore, in the accounts cited in the present study the name of the entities often varies: we go from the devil to evil spirits, from brownie to sprite, from boggart to familiar. Some names for the spirits ("knocker," and so forth) emphasize the confusion, or rather the collusion, of rapping spirits and the dead. From the medieval sources we

---

*[A "white lady" is a type of female ghost who often appears in rural areas and who probably suffered trauma in life. —*Ed.*]

might remind ourselves of the *pilosus,* also called a *larva,* who installed itself in a forge, and of that "faun," the late Garnier, who haunted the house of the prefect Nicolas.

Through multiple sources we thus know that the dead share in common with these demonized spirits the habit of making noise to alert the living to their presence. The merging of the one with the other is logical if we accept the points of convergence and the above-noted phenomena of shifts and substitutions—phenomena that are interdependent with the culture of the witnesses and the recorders of the incidents.

It is here that the tradition of folk beliefs plays a large role: when these beliefs have not been acculturated or led astray by the dominant religion, other explanations emerge that reflect the mind-sets of an era. A poltergeist is grasped in this way, as we have seen, as a deviltry, a manifestation of the dead—and let's clearly note Christianity's influence here, as most of the time these dead are souls in torment—and, more rarely, these manifestations are seen as caused by magic or witchcraft.

The dead are at the center of the interpretations, and, from antiquity to modern times, a recurrent theme grabs our attention: the influence of human remains. Whether in the story of Athenodorus or that of Saint Germain of Auxerre, or in those collected by C. Flammarion, E. Bozzano, M. E. Vaugeois, or E. Auricoste de Lazarque,[3] a corpse or a skeleton is responsible for the phenomena of noise and stone throwing. This is a primal explanation. The belief attached to human remains is corroborated by the stories of howling skulls, for which Great Britain offers a particularly savory version with that of Wardley Hall (Lancashire).[4]

Subsequently, the racket, din, noise, and the movement of objects were attributed to the dead seeking something, which allowed the church to accept them in its bosom after making them, as noted earlier, into tormented souls seeking suffrages, masses for the most part, or the reparation of a misdeed committed while they were still among the living.

Outside of these two major sections of the history of poltergeists, some accounts receive no explanation, perhaps because the testimonies were unintentionally incomplete. Why point out the presence of this or that person if we do not know who the medium or intermediary for these manifestations is? All the phenomena of spontaneous combustion, for which the story of Alexander Aksakoff provides a fine example, represent an extreme of poltergeists. Again, in a Christian society it is completely natural to see this as the devil's hand at work.

The ineffectiveness of priests and exorcisms in at least 50 percent of the cases seems to contradict the theory that diabolism is the culprit. This ineffectiveness is nothing new, and many examples can be found in the Middle Ages. The intervention of a cleric in the other cases, however, is enough to restore things to order. Philip Wallon proposes the following explanation for this: as an individual who does not know the protagonists in the poltergeist drama, the cleric is not influenced by the "affective contagion" that tends to intensify the phenomena. "The synergies of minds can bring about major effects. . . . It is the very principle of emotional resonance or affective contagions,"[5] a contagion that tends to amplify the phenomena. The telekinesis that "underscores the close relationship between the unconscious and the appearance of the objective facts"[6] is based on what Carl Jung once called, in a conversation with Freud, the "catalytic exteriorization phenomenon."[7]

For many people, if a minister or priest can put an end to poltergeists, it is clearly because they are diabolical manifestations, and the process of mythicization is relaunched as the witnesses see their deductions confirmed. We then enter into the realm of oral transmission, the peddling of facts, which when passed from person to person become distorted—but always in the direction of an intensification or accentuation of the initial interpretation. Certain details end up being added to the objective facts, as is attested by the so-called memorates. Spreading like a rumor, the phenomenon becomes intensified, inspiring other accounts. Eventually, after a varying span of time, it acquires an air of undeniable authenticity. Fed on presuppositions that fall within the area of pre-logical thought, the accounts give credit and additional nourishment to the beliefs. Some see it as confirmation of what they know, others are inclined to believe it, and each appearance of an analogous phenomenon rejuvenates the tradition, which has centuries-old roots. The influence is reciprocal: the manifestation finds its veracity in the tradition, and the tradition's veracity is confirmed by the manifestation.

An unrecognized facet of human history, poltergeists are marked by a thorough syncretism of mythic thought and rationalist desires. All unexplained facts prompt a need for explanation, and this one is based on a vision of the world that accepts the presence of the supernatural and does not sever it from daily life, seeing proof of its existence in these strange manifestations. Swaying between faith and reason, man believes in the experience (*Erfahrung*) of the phenomena. Once upon a time it was the church seeking to impose its notions of diabolical illusion and deviltry; more recently, rationalists have lent credence to those of fantasy and hallucination. But ancient beliefs prove impossible to uproot, surviving all attempts at acculturation once they are linked to man's fundamental questions about another world—a realm that is clearly the home of the dead as well as the spirits.

*Consummatio igitur opera utcumque potuimus, a discreto lectore veniam postulamus.**

---

*[To the extent we have been able to achieve the aim and consequently the work, we ask the indulgence of the distinguished reader. —*Trans.*]

Appendices

I

Rite for the Exorcism of a House
Tormented by a Demon[1]
(Exorcismus domus a daemonio vexatae)

The priest should wear a surplice and stole and begin with these words:
"In the name of the Father and of the Son and of the Holy Ghost,
Amen" while simultaneously making the sign of the cross three times.
He will then recite the *Adjutorium nostrom*[2] and *Dominus vobiscum,*
followed by this prayer:

> Almighty and powerful God who has bestowed such grace upon
> Thy priests that whatever is worthily and conscientiously performed
> by them in Thy name is accounted to be done by Thee, we beseech
> Thy immeasureable clemency that where we are about to visit,
> Thou also wouldst visit, that what we are about to bless, Thou also
> wouldst bless, that Thou wouldst lend Thy mighty right hand of
> power to all which we are about to do, and that at the coming of
> our humble person (by the merits of Thy saints) the demons may fly
> away and the angels of peace many enter in. Through Jesus Christ
> our Lord. Amen.

O God of angels, God of archangels, God of prophets, God of apostles, God of martyrs, God of confessors, God of virgins and of all right-living men, O God and Father of our Lord Jesus Christ, I call upon thee and I suppliantly invoke Thy holy name and the compassion of Thy radiant Majesty, that Thou wouldst lend me aid against the spirit of all iniquity, that wherever he may be, when Thy name is spoken, he may at once give place and take to flight. Through Jesus Christ . . .

Conjuration

I abjure thee, O serpent of old, by the Judge of the living and the dead; by the Creator of the world who hath power to cast into hell, that thou depart forthwith from this house. He that commands thee, accursed demon, is He that commanded the winds, and the sea and the storm. He that commands thee is He that ordered thee to be hurled down from the heights of heaven into the lower parts of the earth, He that commands thee is He that bade thee depart from Him. Hearken, then, Satan and fear. Get thee gone, vanquished and cowed, when thou art bidden in the name of our Lord Jesus Christ who will come to judge the living and the dead and all the world by fire. Amen.

The priest will then recite the first five Gradual Psalms (119–123) while he visits every part of the house, sprinkling it with holy water; he will then bring this stage of his labor to an end with a few biblical passages as an introduction to the following prayer.

Do Thou O Lord, enter graciously into the house that belongs to Thee; construct for thyself an abiding resting place in the hearts of Thy faithful servants, and grant that in this house no wickedness of malicious spirits may ever hold sway. Amen.

The second set of five Gradual Psalms will then be recited while the priest again sprinkles holy water throughout the entire house, before reciting this prayer:

> O God, omnipotent and never-ending, who is in every place subject to Thee, pervadest all and workest all Thy Will, comply with out entreaty that Thou be the protector of this dwelling, and that here no antagonism of evil have power to resist Thee, but that, by the cooperation and virtue of the Holy Spirit, Thy service may come first of all, and holy freedom remain inviolate. Through Jesus Christ . . .

The house will then be sprinkled with holy water a third time while the final five Gradual Psalms are recited, ending with another prayer.

> O God, who in every place subject to Thee are present as guardian and protector, grant us, we beseech Thee, that the blessing on this house may never slacken, and that all we who join in this petition may deserve the shelter which Thou affordest. Through Jesus Christ . . .

The priest will then read the passage from Luke 19:1–10,* then incense will be placed in the thurible, and the entire house incensed. Next, after the prayer *Visita, quaesumus, Domine habitationem istam*,[3] the priest will give his blessing, sprinkle yet more holy water, and leave.

II
A Hoax (1649)

Belief in poltergeists was so deeply rooted in mental attitudes that it gave rise to hoaxes and fueled novels and fictional literature. The best example of this is the story of the spirit haunting the royal castle of

---

*The story of Zacchaeus the publican.

Woodstock, upon which Sir Walter Scott (1771–1832) based a novel in 1826. After his study of the matter, he presented the results of his research in *Letters on Demonology and Witchcraft*.[4] Located about eight miles northwest of Oxford, Woodstock was built in the twelfth century by Henry II to hide the beautiful Rosamund. First, here are the facts as they were originally told about the events that ensued when Cromwell sent commissioners to take possession of the royal palace of Woodstock in 1649.[5]

The Commissioners, October 13, 1649, with their Servants being come to the Mannor house they took up their lodging in the King's own Rooms the Bed Chamber and Withdrawing Room, the former whereof they also make their Kitchen, the Council Hall, their Brewhouse, the Chamber of Presence, their place of sitting to dispatch business, and a Wood house of the Dining Room where they laid the wood of that ancient Standard in the High Park known of all by the name of the Kings Oak, which that nothing might remain that had the name of King affixed to it, they digged up by the Roots. October 14 and 15 they had little disturbance but on the 16 there came as they thought somewhat into the Bed Chamber, where two of the Commissioners and their Servants lay, in the shape of a Dog, which going under their beds did as it were gnawing their Bed cords. But on the morrow finding them whole and a quarter of Beef, which lay on the ground untouched, they began to entertain other thoughts.

October 17. Something to their thinking removed all the Wood of the Kings Oak out of the Dining Room into the Presence Chamber, and hurled the Chairs and Stools up and down that Room. From whence it came into the two Chambers where the Commissioners and their Servants lay, and hoisted up their Bed's feet so much higher than their heads that they thought they should have been turned over and over, and then let them fall down with such a force that their bodies rebounded from the bed a good distance, and then shook the Bedsteads so violently that themselves confessed their Bodies were sore with it.

October 18. Something came into the Bedchamber and walked up and down and fetching the Warming pan out of the Withdrawing Room made so much noise that they thought five Bells could not have made more. And October 19, Trenchers were thrown up and down the Dining Room and at them who lodged there whereof one of them being awakened put forth his head to see what was the matter, but had Trenchers thrown at it.

October 20, *The Curtains of the Bed in the Withdrawing Room were drawn to and fro, and the Bedstead much shaken, and eight great Pewter Dishes and three dozen of Trenchers thrown about the Bedchamber again. This night they also thought whole armsfull of the Wood of the Kings Oak were thrown down in their Chambers but of that in the morning they found nothing had been moved.*

October 21. The Keeper of their Ordinary and his Bitch lay in one of the Rooms with them which night they were not disturbed at all. But October 22 though the Bitch kenneled there again to whom they ascribed their former nights rest both they and the Bitch were in a pitiful taking, *the Bitch opening but once, and that with a whining fearful yelp.*

October 23. They had all their clothes plucked off them in the Withdrawing Room and the Bricks fell out of the Chimney into the Room. And on the 24 they thought in the Dining Room that all the Wood of the Kings Oak had been brought thither and thrown down close by their Bed side, which being heard by those of the Withdrawing Room, one of them rose to see what was done fearing indeed that his Fellow Commissioners had been killed, but found no such matter whereupon returning to his Bed again *he found two or three dozen of Trenchers thrown into it and handsomely covered with the Bed clothes.*

October 25. The Curtains of the Bed in the Withdrawing Room were drawn to and fro and the Bedstead shaken as before and in the

Bed Chamber, Glass *flew about so thick and yet not one dozen of the Chamber windows broken* that they thought it had rained money. Whereupon they lighted Candles but to their grief they found nothing but glass.

October 29. Something going to the window opened and shut it, then going into the Bed Chamber *it threw great stones for half an hour's time, some whereof lighted on the High bed, others on the Truckle bed, to the number in all of above fourscore.* This night there was also a very great noise as if forty Pieces of Ordinance had been shot off together. At two several knocks it astonished all the Neighboring Dwellers, which is thought might have been heard a great way off. During these Noises, which were heard in both Rooms together, both Commissioners and their Servants were struck with so great horror that they cried out to one another for help, whereof one of them recovering himself out of a strange Agony he had been in, snatched a Sword and had like to have killed one of his Brethren coming out of his Bed in his Shirt, whom he took for the Spirit that did the mischief. However at length, they got all together yet the Noise continued so great and terrible, and shook the Walls so much, that they thought the whole Manor would have fallen on their Heads. At its departure it took all the Glass of the Windows away with it.

November first. Something as they thought walked up and down the Withdrawing Room and then made a noise in the Dining Room. *The stones, which were left before and laid up in the Withdrawing Room, were all fetched away this night and a great deal of Glass not like the former thrown about again.*

November 2. There came something into the Withdrawing Room treading as they conceived much like a Bear, which first only walked about a quarter of an hour; at length it made a noise about the Table and threw the Warming pan so violently that it quite spoiled it. It threw also a Glass and great Stones at them again, and the bones of Horses, and all so violently that *the Bedstead and the Walls were bruised by them.* This night they planted Candles all about the Rooms and made fires up to the Rantle trees of the Chimneys but *all were put out, no Body knew how, the Fire and Burn wood which made it being thrown up and down the Rooms, the Curtains torn with the Rods from their Beds* and the Bed posts pulled away that the Tester foil down upon them and the feet of the Bedstead cloven into two. And upon the Servants in the Truckle Bed who lay all the time sweating for fear there was first a little which made them begin to stir but before they could get out *there came a whole Tubfull as it were of stinking Ditch water* down upon them so green that it made their Shirts and Sheets of that color, too. The same night, *the Windows were all broke by throwing of Stones,* and there was most terrible noises in three several places together to the extraordinary wonder of all that lodged near them. Nay, the very Rabbet Stealers who were abroad that night were so afrighted with the dismal Thundering that for haste they left their Ferrets in the holes behind them beyond Rosamond's Well. Notwithstanding all this one of them had the boldness to ask in the Name of GOD what it was, what it would have, and what they had done that they should be disturbed after this manner. To which no answer was given but it ceased for a while. At length it came again, and as all of them said brought seven Devils worse than itself. Whereupon one of them lighted a Candle again and set it between the two Chambers in the Doorway, on which another fixing his eyes saw the similitude of a Hoof striking the Candle and Candlestick into the middle of the Bedchamber, and afterward making three scraps on the snuff to put it out. Upon this, the same person was so bold as to draw his Sword, but he had scarce got it out but there was another Invisible hand had hold it, too, and tugged with him for it, and prevailing struck him so violently that he was stunned with the blow. Then began violent Noises again, insomuch that they calling to one another got together and went into the Presence Chamber, where they said Prayers and sang Psalms, notwithstanding all, which the Thundering noise still continued in other Rooms. After this November 3, they removed

their Lodgings over the gate and next day being Sunday went to
Ewelin where how they escaped the Authors of the Relation knew
not. But returning on Monday *the Devil,* for that was the name they
gave their nightly Guest, left them not unvisited nor on the Tuesday
following, which was the last day they stayed.[6]

Everyone will agree that all the ingredients are in place here for pro-
ducing an excellent poltergeist story. Specifically, the combinations of
the facts and the way they are staged makes easily apparent that poltergeists (however they may be interpreted) were common knowledge
in the seventeenth century—at least sufficiently so to spark reactions
of fear and terror. At the same time, this reveals the distribution such
phenomena could enjoy as it is almost a law of sorts: every peculiar
and mysterious fact, quickly described and interpreted as supernatural,
spreads by word of mouth like a spark follows a trail of gunpowder.[7]
And beginning in the sixteenth century, such stories spread farther by
broadsheets, the ancestor of gazettes and other newspapers. The appe-
tite for the sensational is nothing new! Seeing how the media handled
the poltergeist of the Arcachon Clinic in 1963,[8] and that of the Delain
Church in 1998,[9] one can only imagine how they would have handled
them in earlier eras.

Sir Walter Scott's Perspective

The whole matter was, after the Restoration, discovered to
be the trick of one of their own party, who had attended the
Commissioners as a clerk, under the name of Giles Sharp. This
man, whose real name was Joseph Collins of Oxford, called "Funny
Joe," was a concealed loyalist and well acquainted with the old man-
sion of Woodstock, where he had been brought up before the Civil
War. Being a bold, active-spirited man, Joe availed himself of his
local knowledge of trap doors and private passages so as to favor the
tricks that he played off upon his masters by aid of his fellow domestics. The Commissioners' personal reliance on him made his task

the more easy, and it was all along remarked that trusty Giles Sharp saw the most extraordinary sights and visions among the whole party. The unearthly terrors experienced by the Commissioners are detailed with due gravity by Sinclair, and also, I think, by Dr. Plott. But although the detection or explanation of the real history of the Woodstock demons has also been published, and I have myself seen it, I have at this time forgotten whether it exists in a separate collection, or where it is to be looked for.

Görres' Opinion

J. J. von Görres, however, has provided us with a more nuanced opinion, which is worth citing.

We should recognize that there could well be some kind of hoax involved in this incident, and the purpose of this noise was to frighten the commissioners out of the castle. But, on the other hand, these phenomena offer a perfect analogy with all the others of this nature; and it is hard to believe that in a house with so many people that the imposture, if it existed, was not discovered. It is regrettable, though, that a very exacting inquiry has not placed this incident above all suspicion. As the commissioners demonstrated intrepid boldness and only gave in to force, we should presume they did all they could during the day to discover the true cause for this disorder, and only retreated from the scene when they were convinced it was no longer possible to stay any longer.

The source for both Scott and Görres is *The Natural History of Oxfordshire* by Robert Plott[10] (1640–1696), a royal professor and historian. Plott recorded this story using documents from eyewitnesses, including one written by a highly educated and trustworthy individual who lived during the time and in the place where these events took place. He was consulted on the personal circumstances of other eyewitnesses and gave all the pieces of testimony to one of the commissioners, who said what this person wrote was the pure and honest truth, thus it appeared incontestable to Robert Plott. However, he does not permit himself to swear to its basis a priori, but to the contrary discusses the various phenomena that occurred, concluding that it was impossible to attribute it to deceit. Scott sums up his own position thusly:

> Similar disturbances have been often experienced while it was the custom to believe in and dread such frolics of the invisible world, and under circumstances that induce us to wonder, both at the extreme trouble taken by the agents in these impostures, and the slight motives from which they have been induced to do much wanton mischief. Still greater is our modern surprise at the apparently simple means by which terror has been excited to so general an extent, that even the wisest and most prudent have not escaped its contagious influence.

Finally this Joseph Collins played on the superstitious credulity of his contemporaries like so many others who came after him, especially in the nineteenth century when frauds and rigged phenomena[11] were prevalent in the spiritualist circles, which appropriated knocking spirits into the context of table-tipping: "Spirit, are you there?" The French singing group Les Frères Jacques made a spoof of such activity by a medium in one of their songs.

III
A Poltergeist in Turin (1900)

On the 16th of November, 1900, in Turin, Via Bava No. 6, in a little inn run by a man named Fumero, *there began to be heard in the daytime, but to a greater extent at night, a series of strange noises.* In seeking out the cause, it was found that full or empty wine bottles had been broken in the wine cellar. More frequently they would descend from their places and roll along the floor, heaping themselves against the closed door in such a way as to obstruct the entrance when it was opened. In the sleeping chamber on the upper floor (which communicated by a staircase with the servants' room near the small public room of the inn) *garments were twisted up and some of them transferred themselves downstairs into the room beneath. Two chairs in coming down were broken. Copper utensils, which had been hung upon the walls of the servants' dining room, fell to the floor and slid over long reaches of the room, sometimes getting broken.* A spectator put his hat on the bed of the upper chamber; it disappeared and was later found in the filth heap of the courtyard below.

Careful examination failed to disclose any normal cause for these performances. *No help could be got either from the police or the priest.* Nay, when the latter was performing his office, a huge bottle full of wine was broken at his very feet. A vase of flowers that had been brought into the inn descended safely onto a table from the molding above the door where it had been placed. . . . Five or six times, even in the presence of the police, a little staircase ladder, which leaned against the wall at one side of the main room of the inn, *was slowly lowered to the floor yet without hurting anyone.* A gun went across the room and was found on the floor in the opposite corner. Two bottles came down from a high shelf with some force. They were not broken, but they bruised the elbow of a porter, giving him a slight black-and-blue spot.

The people kept crowding in to see, and the police during their investigations made the Fumero family understand that they suspected them of simulating, so that the poor creatures decided to suffer the annoyance in silence. They even gave out that it had ceased (after an imaginary visit from me) so as to escape at least the ridicule, if not the damage. I began attentively to study the case.

I made a minute examination of the premises. The rooms were small. Two of them served the purpose of a wine shop, one was used for a servants' eating room and was connected by a small stairway with a bedchamber above. Lastly, there was a deep wine cellar, access to which was obtained by means of a long stairway and a passageway.

The people informed me that they noticed that whenever anyone entered the cellar, the bottles began to be broken. I entered at first in the dark, and, sure enough, I heard the breaking of glasses and the rolling of bottles under my feet. I thereupon lit up the place. The bottles were massed together upon five shelves, one over the other. In the middle of the room was a rude table. I had six lighted candles placed upon this, on the supposition that the spiritistic phenomena would cease in bright light. On the contrary, I saw three empty bottles, which stood upright on the floor, spin along as if twirled by a finger and break to pieces near my table. To avoid a possible trick, I carefully examined, by the light of a large candle, and touched with my hand all the full bottles standing on the shelves and ascertained that there were no wires or strings that might explain the movements. After a few *minutes two bottles, then four, and later others on the second and third shelves separated themselves from the rest and fell to the floor without any violent motion, but rather as if they had been lifted down by someone;* and after this descent rather than fall, six burst upon the wet floor (already drenched with wine), and two remained intact. A quarter of an hour afterward three others from the last compartment fell and were broken upon the floor. Then I turned to leave the cellar. As I was on the point of going out, I heard the breaking of another bottle on the floor. When the door was shut, all again became quiet.

I came back on another day. They told me that the same phenomena occurred with decreasing frequency, *adding that a little brass color grinder had sprung from one place to another in the servants' room* and striking against the opposite wall, jammed itself out of shape—as indeed I observed. *Two or three chairs had bounced around* with such violence that they were broken, without however hurting anyone standing by. A table was also broken.

I asked to see and examine all the people of the house. There was a tall waiter lad of thirteen, apparently normal; another, a head-waiter, also normal. The master of the house was a brave old soldier who from time to time threatened the spirits with his gun. Judging

from his flushed face and humorous state, I judged him to be somewhat under the influence of alcohol. *The mistress of the inn was a
little woman of some fifty years, lean and very slender. From infancy
up she had been subject to tremors, neuralgia, and nocturnal hallucinations, and had had an operation for hysteron-ovariotomy.* For all
these reasons I counseled the husband to have her leave the premises
for three days. She went to Nole, her native town, on the 25th of
November and there *suffered from hallucinations—voices heard at
night, movements, persons that no one else saw or heard. But she did
not cause any annoying movements of objects.* During these three days
nothing happened at the inn. But as soon as she got back, the performances began again at first furiously, but afterward more mildly.
The occurrences were always the same—utensils, chairs, bottles, broken or displaced. Seeing this, I again counseled that the wife absent
herself anew, and she did so on November 26.

On the day the woman left (she was in a state of great excitement
and had cursed the alleged spirits), all the dishes and bottles that had
been placed on the table were broken and fell to the floor. If the family
was going to dine, the table had to be prepared in another place and
by another woman, because no dish touched by the mistress remained
intact. *Hence one naturally suspected that she had mediumistic powers,* or would have done so had it not been that during her absence
the phenomena were repeated in just the same way. That is to say (to be
specific), a pair of shoes of hers that were in the bed chamber, on the
dressing cloth, came downstairs in broad daylight (half past eight in
the morning), traversed the servants' room through the air, passed into
the common room of the inn, and there fell down at the feet of two
customers who were seated at a table. This was on November 27. The
shoes were replaced on the dressing cloth and continually watched but
did not move until noon of the next day; and at that hour, when all
were at dinner, they disappeared entirely. A week afterward they were
found, with heels to the floor, under the bed of the same chamber. . . .

When it was seen that the phenomena continued just the same, the woman was recalled from Nole, and they were repeated with the same continuity as before. A bottle of effervescent liquor, for example, in the inn, in full daylight, in the sight of everybody, *slowly, as if accompanied by a human hand,* passed over a distance of twelve or fifteen feet, as far as the servants' room, the door of which was open, and then fell to the floor and was broken.

After all this it occurred to the host to dismiss the younger of his two waiters. When he left (December 7), all the phenomena ceased. This of course makes one surmise that the motive force emanated from him. Yet he was not an hysteric and was the cause of no spiritistic occurrences in his new home, or that we can accept that the hysterical woman, even when she was in Nole, could influence the objects in her Turin home, as we shall see has happened elsewhere.[12]

IV
The Haunted House of Iasi (1995)[13]

In this more recent account of a Romanian poltergeist, which represents an extraordinary synthesis of what I presented above, we can find no less than seven different explanations depending on the profession of the witnesses and their level of education. But magic and tormented souls recur here as leitmotifs, and deviltry can be read between the lines; the influence of human remains is also suggested. The other interpretations are divided between parapsychology, psychiatry, and physics (energies, electromagnetic waves).

November 15, 1995
5 Trei Ierarhi Street, Iasi, the Home of the Rener Family

It all began around 12:00, when Lidia Rener, the mother of Constantine Rener was alone in the house. *The pots filled with water sitting on the stove burners overturned, and the wardrobe doors noisily opened and closed by themselves,* and the dogs began barking in terror, although no intruder was bothering them at all.

Scared, Lidia Rener talked to her daughter-in-law Doina about it. She and the doctor Gabriela Untu, the most important witness of the events, went to fetch the elderly priest Theodor Irimia, who had witnessed several uncommon incidents during his life, but never anything like this.

"I went there immediately. I could not open the door to the main room. I pushed it a little and, repelled by an invisible force, it came back toward my head, but I was able to get in. I saw water everywhere, and the pots that were overturned and open cupboard doors . . . I immediately read the Prayers of Saint Basil, cast holy water throughout the house, and the phenomena calmed down a little. From the beginning, *I suspected a negative power was involved* that was hanging over the family members and the house, which had been possessed at that moment by a *diabolical spirit*," the priest Irimia recounted of the first day he went there.

Explanations were suggested all at once. While the priest and Lidia Rener suspected that everything was occurring as answer to a prayer (by Lidia Rener, who had revealed it to the priest), a prayer intended to heal Dr. Rener of his carnal desires, others imagined other explanations. But all their friends knew that the doctor had relations with other women, even gypsies. Only the priest and Lidia thought *it might be the white magic practiced by the gypsies (Doar preotul si doamna Lidia au indraznit sa se gindeasca la faptul ca ar fi putea fi vorba despre magie alba practicata de catre tiganci)*, because the man had touched women of their ethnic group. It was also thought that the house was haunted by restless spirits, *in fact by the negative energies of those who had once lived in Madame Lidia's house (De asemenea, s-au gindit si ca locuinta ar fi putut fi bintuita de spirite nelinistite, de fapt energiile negative provenite de la cei care au locuit inainte in casa doamnei Lidia)*. While Lidia Rener's and the priest's opinions leaned toward these explanations, the daughter-in-law and doctor Gabriela Untu presumed the origin [of the phenomena] was the child Cezar Rener, but the hypothesis did not seem valid as he was only seven years old. He was skinny and incapable of work around the house that required strength. "At first, I thought it was a paranormal phenomenon, then I thought it was the work of a human being. I do not put my trust in such events, but I finally came to believe it was something out of the ordinary, because several incidents took place there in the house where my friend Doina Rener still lives," Dr. Gabriela Untu admitted.

November 16, 1995, 8:00. The priest remembers it again because this was when the incidents went "crazy." "They came to bring me back in the morning. Things had calmed down after the first mass, but everything started up again the next day. I do not know exactly what happened or how; there were now carpets that had been taken from the house and thrown into the courtyard and a bathrobe on the hedge. Corn that had been put on to boil was spread all over the house. These were things that I had never seen in my fifty years as a priest. I got scared and alarmed. I had brought the church singer with me, who was also a witness, and together *we again recited the Prayers of Saint Basil.*" This is why the priest kept being summoned back, day after day, because the incidents continued to occur in identical fashion. The incidents would calm down for a while, then resume with the same intensity. Each time the doctor Gabriela Untu, close to Doina Rener, was a witness. "*I saw the television fall but nothing went with it, I saw the table move and banknotes torn to pieces.* I thought it was the child [who did that] but it was too much. *The table in the middle of the house was turned over and actually broken,* and the child did not have the strength to do that. The money was torn up and the eyeglasses twisted out of shape. We thought it might be the dead, or curses (*Ne-am gindit cu totii ca era vorba de morti, blesteme*); it was truly a house turned upside down. One day I saw all the bottles of mineral water broken. They flew around, and then fell, after heading toward Madame Lidia and toward Doru also. The carpets were piled up behind the house. At first glance I thought it was dogs, but they could not pull and carry them behind the house where they were found, so dogs could not have been responsible for doing this. My husband was also a witness—more or less because he worked and did not have a lot of time—of shocking things, at least for the moment, because things have since calmed down. I remember thinking it was electromagnetic rays, all sorts of physical things (*putea fi vorba de unde electromagnetice, de fel de fel de chestii fizice*). It was really something quite strange," Dr. Gabriela Untu insisted.

Cezar, Lidia Rener's nephew, was the chief suspect for causing the incidents. But he remembered these days with fear: "I don't recall it very well, I know that all the objects fell, money I received for shopping was torn to pieces, but it was when we were all sitting at the table and all the dishes, the knives and forks especially, flew at my parents, that I was most scared. Then my grandmother came in to say that the television had fallen; it was right at the center of the house, and everything you have already learned. I don't want to and I could not make up what happened," recalled the boy.

When learning of this case, the physicists of A. I. Cuza University expressed the desire for the possibility to reproduce the incidents. "No well-founded explanation has yet been found for their appearance. The phenomenon exists, and it is possible that it has taken place there also. Experts have verified in the laboratories the possibility of making objects move through concentration, even a good distance, by energetic powers. We have even taken readings," we were told by Dorina Creanga, instructor for the biophysics and medical physics departments of A. I. Cuza University.

"Every day I recited the Prayers of Saint Basil, sometimes even several times a day. Everything calmed down after a memorial mass (*Totul s-a calmat abia dupa efectuarea unui praznic*), on Friday the second week," said the priest Irimia. One year following the incidents the stomatology specialist Dr. Constantine Rener died, and all those who had witnessed these events chose to guard their silence— a silence that emerged from their feelings of powerlessness.

The president of the Iasi Regional Council remembers: "There was a curse in this house, like curses made by the Gypsies *(In casa aceea a fost vorba de un blestem, vraji facute de tiganci)*, who resorted to this kind of magic to punish the sinful impulses of Madame Rener's late son." The phenomenon manifested for two weeks, then silence reigned—a silence that heralded misfortunes. "Just after losing her only descendant, Lidia Rener decided to break this silence," the priest Irimia said. He believes it is possible that negative energies induced by black magic *(energiile negative induse de magia neagra)* had overturned the energetic balance of the house. "In any event, it was the first case of such scope that I have seen since the beginning of my priesthood."

In addition to Lidia Rener (eighty-one years old), her son Constantine Rener, now deceased, and her daughter-in-law, the other witnesses besides some Iasi officials to these incidents were: Gabriela Flaiser, sister of the current president of the regional council, the doctor Gabriela Untu, and the head of the Department of Culture, Bogdan Birleanu. Although skeptical with regard to the credibility of their testimonies, they held their tongues about what they saw, for the sake of protecting their reputations. "My sister told me what she saw. Paranormal phenomena really do take place. *The objects of the house moved, because of an invisible hand (Fenomenele paranormale s-au petrecut cu adevarat. Lucrurile din casa se miscau, minate de o forta nevazuta).* I did not put my trust in her, but she can talk to you about these events. I learned that everything became calm again after repeated interventions by the priest. I don't think any explanation can be found for a phenomenon like this," said Flaiser.

I was a witness, every day, of all the events that took place both inside and outside the house, because I was in retirement and spent a lot of time at home. The unknown forces would be at work, as much when I was there alone as when I was there with relatives, friends, the priest, and so forth. All of it can be confirmed.

The clairvoyant Valentina also visited at one time, and she saw a foreign presence. That is all I can say; I believe in everything I saw; if I had not seen anything, perhaps I would not have believed it. Then my son died. It is good because everything became calm again, and my nephew Cezar Rener is safe and sound.

V
The Ghost of Titina (2005)[14]

Here is how a Romanian newspaper explained a poltergeist phenomenon taking place in Oltenia, one of the country's provinces. The value of this sensational news item is what it shows us about the reactions of the living. Interpreting the facts as proof that a soul in torment was unhappy with her fate, they exhumed the body.

Phenomena without any scientific explanation have been taking place for the past five months in the home of the Grecu family in the Cernele quarter of the city of Craiova. Lightbulbs would break when installed, and the electrical wires in the walls would short-circuit.[15] Things had become intolerable. "The house is haunted," Constantine Grecu, the owner of the dwelling, told us. "Agents from the Oltenia Electrical Company have done tests on site and tell us they cannot explain what is happening and that from the technical perspective, there is nothing wrong with our electrical system. No one knows the causes for the phenomena in the house."

The family made the decision to disinter the person they thought was haunting the house. This is why, at the request of her parents, the tomb of Titina Ciorobea, located in the Cernele cemetery, was opened on Saturday around one o'clock in the afternoon. *The girl's remains were transferred to a new coffin and another burial mass was performed.* Those present for it included the members of the Grecu family, the relatives of the deceased, and

Father Ilie, who had come from Athos,* *to drive the evil spirits* from the haunted house. A week before, the monk Ilie said he had seen a young girl when he was visiting the Grecu family home. The whole family therefore assumed it was the spirit of Titina, who had died there twenty years earlier. Aurelia Firicel, one of the exhumed girl's sisters, believed she had to be disinterred, *so that her soul could find rest,* and the events taking place in the house of their other sister be brought to an end.

Father Bita of the Cernele parish hopes that now all will return to normal and the Grecu family will experience no more problems. "Exhumation is the final resort, so that the spirit of the deceased finds rest, and likewise the family."

The monk from Greece remained impressed by what he had seen in the house. "I am going to go back to Mount Athos and present the case to the other monks there. We all hope the spirit is now at peace," he said at the end of the procession.

---

*According to E. Timotin, this detail lacks much credibility as the monks of Mount Athos have the habit of never leaving their monastery.

Notes

INTRODUCTION.
THINGS THAT GO BUMP IN THE NIGHT

1. Flammarion, *Les Maisons hantées.*
2. Wallon, *Expliquer le paranormal.*
3. Lecouteux, *Les Nains et les Elfes au Moyen Âge; Démons et Génies du terroir au Moyen Âge; La Maison et ses Génies: Croyances d'hier et d'aujourd'hui.*

CHAPTER ONE.
WHAT IS A POLTERGEIST?

1. Mozzani, *Bouqins Collection,* 1454–1455. The book points to several relatively recent cases involving poltergeists: the case of the Cidreville rectory (Normandy); that of the park of an Arcachon clinic in 1963; that of a Munich lawyer's office in 1968; and that of a house in northern France in 1985.
2. *Dictionnaire alphabétique et analogique de la langue française,* vol. 2, 634 b.
3. Trousset, *Nouveau Dictionnaire encyclopédie illustré,* vol. 5, 341.
4. *Nouveau Larousse illustré. Dictionnaire universal encyclopédique,* vol. 4, 298b.
5. Because of the film's success, Brian Gibson made a sequel, *Poltergeist* II (1986).

6. *Collins English Dictionary.*

7. *Harrap's Standard French and English Dictionary,* pt. 2, 931.

8. *Gentleman's Magazine,* issue 3, 1764.

9. Lavater, *Von Gespänsten / unghüren / fälen u. anderen wunderbaren dingen / so merteils wenn die menschen sterben söllend /oder wan gross sachen und enderungen vorhanden sind / beschähend / kurtzer unnd einfaltiger bericht.*

10. Lavater, *Trois livres des apparitions des esprits, fantosmes, prodigies et accidents merveilleux qui precedent souventes fois la more de quelque personage renommé ou un grand changement ès choses de ce monde.*

11. Scot, *The Discoverie of Witchcraft.*

12. Bodin, *De la Demonomanie des Sorciers,* pt. 1.

13. Thyraeus, *Daemoniaci, hoc est, de obsessis a spiritibus daemoniorum hominibus.*

14. James I, *Daemonologie, in Forme of a Dialogue, Diuided into three Bookes.*

15. Maioli, *Canicular Days.*

16. Le Loyer, *A Treatise of Specters or Straunge Sights, Visions and Apparitions appearing sensibly vnto men.*

17. Guazzo, *Compendium maleficarum ex quo nefandissima in genus humanum opera venesica, ac ad illa vitanda remedia conspiciuntur.*

18. Del Rio, *Les Controverses et Recherches Magiques.*

19. Baxter, *The Certainty of the World of the Spirits.*

20. Sinclair, *Satan's Invisible World Discovered.*

21. Glanvil, *Saducismus Triumphatus: or full and plain Evidence concerning Witches and Apparitions.*

22. Bovet, *Pandaemonium, or The Devil's Cloyster.*

23. Alberus, *Novum dictionarium genus.*

24. Luther, *D. Martin Luthers Werke. Kritische Gesamtausgabe.*

25. Ibid., vol. 3, 3814.

26. Ibid., vol. 5, 5358b. The Latin phrases were intended to reinforce his argument.

27. Ibid., 5358b, cited as a footnote.

28. In 1517, in his *Vocabulorum rerum promptuarium,* Baldassar Trochus used *polternacht* as an equivalent to *hymenalia.*

29. Pfeifer, *Etymologisches Wörterbuch des Deutschen,* vol. 2, 1297–98; and see the entry for "*poltern*" in Kluge, *Etymologisches Wörterbuch der deutschen Sprache.*

30. Prätorius, *Anthropodermus Plutonicus. Das ist, eine neue Welt-Beschreibung von allerlei wunderbarlichen Menschen,* pt. 1, 314–15.

31. *Report of the mysterious Noises at Hydesville,* Canandaigua, April 1848.

32. Wallon, "Poltergeist," in Sbalchiero, *Dictionnaire des miracles et de l'extraordinaire chrétien,* 629; similarly, *Explorer le paranormal,* 188–212; similarly, *Le Paranormal* (Que sais-je? 3424), 81–97.

33. The IMI maintains an internet site: www.metapsychique.org. See also the special edition of *Sciences & Vie* (Sept. 2006) dedicated to *Miracles: concevoir l'inconcevable,* 110–14.

34. Thompson, *Motif-Index of Folk-Literature.* Poltergeists are classified under the references F 470–F 473:

F470. Night-spirits. Poltergeister; goblins; hobgoblins.

F473. Poltergeist. Invisible spirit (sometimes identified as ghost or witch) responsible for all sorts of mischief in or around a household.

F473.1. Poltergeist throws objects.

F473.2. Poltergeist causes objects to behave contrary to their nature.

F473.2.1. Chair is rocked by invisible spirit (Cf. D1601.28).

F473.2.4. House burns for no apparent reason.

F473.3. Poltergeist mistreats people.

F473.4. Poltergeist mistreats animals.

F473.5. Poltergeist makes noises.

F473.6. Miscellaneous actions of poltergeist.

35. Cf. Lecouteux, *Dictionnaire de mythologie germanique,* 111–12.

36. Zobel, *Historische und Theologische Vorstellung des Ebentheüerlichen Gespenstes / Welches In einem Hause zu S. Annaberg / 2. Monat lang im neüligst 1691sten Jahr / viel Schrecken / Furcht und wunderseltsame Schauspiell angerichtet,* 60.

37. Brückner, *Volkserzählung und Reformation. Ein Handbuch zur Tradierung und Funktion von Erzählstoffen und Erzähllitteratur im Protestantismus;* and especially Peuckert, *Die große Wende,* which describes the troubled period of transition from the fifteenth to the sixteenth century, and the accompanying host of superstitious ideas.

In chap. XXXIX of his *Discoverie of Witchcraft,* Reginald Scot writes: "In all ages moonks and preests have abused and bewitched the world with counterfet visions; which proceeded through idlenes, and restraint of marriage, wherby they grew hot and lecherous, and therefore devised such meanes to compasse and obteine their loves. And the simple people being then so superstitious, would never seeme to mistrust, that such holie men would make them cuckholds, but forsooke their beds in that case, and gave roome to the cleargie." In chap. XL he also provides Cardan's opinion on the bizarre noises that can be heard in houses: "Cardanus speaking of noises, among other things, saith thus; A noise is heard in your house; it may be a mouse, a cat, or a dog among dishes; it may be a counterfet or a theefe indeed, or the fault may be in your eares. I could recite a great number of tales, how men have even forsaken their houses, bicause of such apparitions and noises: and all hath beene by meere and ranke knaverie. And wheresoever you shall heare, that there is in the night season such rumbling and fearefull noises, be you well assured that it is flat knaverie, performed by some that seemeth most to complaine, and is least mistrusted."

38. Heinisch, *Das Zeugniß der reinen Wahrheit von der Sonder-und wunderbahren Würckungen eines insgemein sogenannten Kobolds, Oder Unsichtbaren Wesens in der Pfarr-Wohnung zu Gröben,* 40.

39. Bräuner, *Physicalisch und Historisch Erörterte Curiositaeten. Oder: Entlarvter Teufflischer Aberglaube,* 278.

40. Wegner, *Philosophische Abhandlung von Gespenstern worinn zugleich eine kurze Nachricht von dem Wustermarckischen Kobold gegeben wird,* 69ff.

41. Zedler, *Grosses vollständiges Universal-Lexikon,* vol. 15, col. 1181.

42. *Der vielförmige Hintzelmann,* 77–78.

43. *Meyers Konversationslexikon,* vol. 14, 22.

CHAPTER TWO.
A SMIDGEON OF OBJECTIVITY

1. Roll, "The Changing Perspective on Life after Death," 212–17.

2. Wallon, *Expliquer le paranormal,* 198.

3. Bozzano, *Les Phénomènes de hantise,* chap. 7.

4. Wolman, *Encyclopedia of Psychiatry, Psychology, and Psychoanalysis.*

5. Clarke, *Memoirs of the Wesley Family,* 161–200.

6. De Montalembert, *Histoire merveilleuse de seur Allis de Thésieux, laquelle est apparue,* which recounts an anonymous narrative published in 1528.

7. Ibid., 109, based on Taillepied (died 1589); *Traicté de l'Apparition des Esprits. A sçavoir, des Ames séparées, Fantosmes, Prodiges et autres accidens*

merveilleux, qui précèdent quelquefois la mort des grands personnages ou signifient changement de la chose publique, in-12; Lenglet-Dufresnoy (1674–1755), *Recueil de Dissertations sur les Apparitions, les Visions et les Songes,* 4 vol. in-12.

8. Chassande, "Monographie du Mandement d'Avallon and Bayard et de la commune de Saint-Maximin, canton de Goncelin (Isère)," 189–90.

9. Görres, *Die christliche Mystik,* vol. 3, 360–68.

10. *Gazette des Tribunaux,* December 20, 1849.

11. Flammarion, *Haunted Houses.*

12. Bozzano, *Les Phénomènes de hantise,* chap. 7, case XXIV.

13. Hertlé, *Sorciers, magiciens et enchanteurs de nos terroirs,* 80.

14. Bozzano, *Les Phénomènes de hantise,* chap. 7, case XX.

15. Poulain, *Sorcellerie, revenants et croyances en Haute-Bretagne,* 234.

16. Ibid., 235.

17. Ibid., 233.

CHAPTER THREE.
MISCHIEF-MAKING SPIRITS OF THE MIDDLE AGES

1. Augustine, *The City of God,* 490.

2. *Acta sanctorum,* August 27.

3. De Lyon, *Vita Germani,* chap. 10.

4. Martine, *Vie des Pères du Jura,* chap. 53, 296–98.

5. Gregory of Tours, *Liber vitae Patrum* I, in *Monumenta Germaniae Historica, Scriptores rerum Merovingium* I, 2, 663–68.

6. Coulton, *Social Life in Britain from the Conquest to the Reformation,* 415–20.

7. Dawes, *Three Byzantine Saints: Contemporary Biographies of St. Daniel the Stylite, St. Theodore of Sykeon and St. John the Almsgiver,* chap. 129.

8. Alcuin, *Vita s. Willibrordi,* chap. 22, in *Acta sanctorum,* November 7. English translation: Alcuin, *Life of Willibrord,* 17.

9. Sigebert de Gembloux, *Chronica,* in Migne, *Patrologia latina* 160, col. 165; *Chronographia,* universal chronicle of 381–1111, published in *Monumenta Germaniae Historica, Scriptores,* vol. VI. It was continued by different authors until 1163. Other authors have recorded this story with variations: Jacques Sprenger and Henry Kramer (or Institoris), *Malleus maleficarum* I,

15; Vincent de Beauvais, *Speculum historiale* IV, 24, 37; Nider, *Preceptorium* I, 11, 15, published in Paris in 1507 by Udalric Gering and Jehan Petit.

10. Jacobus de Voragine, *Legenda aurea,* vol. 2, chap. 177, 438.

11. *Aventinus refert historiam, quae in pago Camontino ad Rhenum accidit sane memorabilem, de mirificis illussonibus diaboli, quae ut rectius cognoscatur, eius verba inserere volui. Ibidem, inquit, hisce diebus desertor ac perfuga spiritus, multa miracula edidit, circulatorias praestigias lusit, incolas infestavit. Primo umbra feralis, a nemine quidem conspecta, lapides in homines iactare, pultare fores coepit. Mox sub humana effigie pestilens ac nequissimus ille genius delitescens, responsa reddidit, furta prodidit, criminatus quoscumque nota infamiae aspersit: discordias, simultares excitavit. Paulatim horrea, casas omnes succendit atque exussit. Sed uni molestior exstitit, perpetuo eius lateri, quocumque diverteret, haerens atque domum comburens. Et ubi viciniam universam in necena innocentis concitaret; ob scelera illius hunc locum infamem ac devotum esse, pravus mendaciorum faber iactabat. Coactus est homo sub dio manere. Ab omnibus enim, quasi lemuribus nocturnis sacer, tecto arcebatur. Atque ut ille confinibus satisfaceret, candens ferrum manibus portavit, ac quum non vilaretur, insontem se comprobavit. Nihilominus tamen in agris frumenta eius in aceruos composita, idem Lar contaminatus ac perditus combussit. Et quum odiosus indies magis atque magis esse pergeret, coacti pagani rem ad Pontificem Moguntinum deferunt. Sacerdotes missi agros, villas, sacris ac comprecationibus, lustraliaqua, salequelustrico expiant, atque conlustrant. Prava ac conturbata mens primo quidem renitebatur, ac lapidibus quosdam vulneravit. Verum divinis carminibus incantatus, efficacibusque supplicamentis adiuratus, tandem conticuit, nec usquam gentium apparuit. Ubi discesserunt Mystae spiritus ater atque pestilens rursus adest. Interim dum illi, inquit, calvastri sacrificuli, nescio quid immurmurarent, sub lineo amiculo sacerdotis (nominatim huncce notabat) qui meo suasu filiam hospitis sui superiore nocte compressit, delitui; cf. Ph.* Camerarius, *Operae horarum subcisivarum,* chap. 74.

12. *Notkeri Balbuli Gesta Karoli Magni imperatoris* I, 23. French translation: Lecouteux and Marcq, *Les esprits et les morts,* 41–42.

13. Holtzmann, "Die Chronik des Bischofs Thietmar von Merseburg und ihre

Korveier Überarbeitung," in *Monumenta Germaniae Historica, SS rerum Germanicarum,* Nova Series, vol. 9. English translation from Warner, *Ottonian Germany: The Chronico of Thietmar of Merseberg,* 355.

14. Holtzmann, "Die Chronik des Bischofs Thietmar," I, 13 [p. 77 in English edition].

15. De Nogent, *De vita sua sive monodiae,* II, 11.

16. Ibid., I, 24.

17. Dimock, ed., *Giraldi Cambrensis Opera,* VI, 93–94. English translation from Gerald of Wales, *The Journey to Wales and the Description of Wales,* 151.

18. *Itinerarium Kambriae,* I, 12, in Dimock, *Giraldi Cambrensis Opera,* VI.

19. *Des Gervasius von Tilbury Otia imperialia,* 6–7. *Otia imperialia,* I, 18.

20. *De Universo,* 2 vols., Paris, 1674.

21. Mamoris, *Flagellum maleficorum.*

22. Kirk, *La République mystérieuse des elfes, faunes, fées et autres semblables,* 46. This book was published for the first time in Edinburgh in 1691 under the title: The secret commonwealth; or an essay on the nature and actions of the subterranean (and for the most part) invisible people heretofoir going under the name of faunes and fairies, or the lyke, among the low country Scots, as they are described by those who have the second sight, then republished in 1815. [It has been reprinted on occasion since then, most recently in 2006. —*Trans.*]

23. *De Universo,* vol. 2, 849 D; 924a G; 856b H; 958b G; 1062a G.

24. *De Universo,* 841b B.

24. Ibid., 856b H.

26. "Das Schrätel und der Wasserbär" in von der Hagen, *Gesamtabenteuer, hundert altdeutsche Erzählungen,* vol. 1, 257–70.

27. Ibid.

28. Ibid., ll. 92–97: "des tiuvels vâlant / und sîn gespenste *ist zuo mir komen / in mînen hof.* . . . / *mit niht ich daz ervaren kann,* / waz krêatiuren ez sî." I have emphasized the important terms in italic.

29. Ibid., 107–15.

30. Du Breul, *Théâtre des Antiquitez,* 345–46.

31. Nider, *Formicarius.*

CHAPTER FOUR.
THE KNOCKING AND NOISE-MAKING DEAD

1. Cf., e.g., Probe, *Hispanic Legends from New Mexico. Narratives from the Rev. D. Jameson Collection,* 59–60, 64, 99, 123, 125, 210, 431.

2. Stöber, *Die Sagen des Elsasses,* 99. The Alsatians used two terms: *d's Gespenst* and *d'e Geischt.*

3. De Marliave, *Trésor de la mythologie pyrénéenne,* 213.

4. Sauvé, *Le folk-lore des Hautes-Vosges,* 301–2; Markale, *Contes de la mort des pays de France,* 49. Cf. also Michel, *Légendes et fauves du pays des lacs,* 193.

5. Markale, *Contes de la mort,* 53.

6. Lascaux, *Contes et légendes de Bretagne, recueillis dans le pays de Rennes,* 57–59.

7. Jaffé, *Geistererscheinungen und Vorzeichen. Eine psychologische Deutung,* with many examples of a dead person taking leave of those close to him or her.

8. Piniès, *Croyances populaires des pays d'Oc,* 55–56.

9. Ibid., 65–66.

10. Seignolles, *Les Évangiles du diables. Le Grand et le Petit Albert,* 477.

11. Ibid., 530.

12. Thurston, *Ghosts and Poltergeists,* 86–87.

13. Pliny the Younger, *Letters,* Letter LXXXIII. Italics mine; Latin from the original text.

14. Görres, *Die christliche Mystik,* 402.

15. Guillaume, *L'âme du Morvan,* 120.

16. Jalby, *Le folklore du Languedoc. Ariège, Aude, Lauraguais, Tarn,* 116.

17. De Marliave, *Trésor de la mythologie pyrénéenne,* 213.

18. Béraud-Williams, *Contes populaires de l'Ardèche,* 173; Jalby, *Le folklore du Languedoc,* 119.

19. *Revue des Traditions populaires* 13 (1898), 145.

20. Ibid., 129–30.

21. Fabre and Lacroix, *Légendaire du Languedoc-Roussillon,* 45.

22. Pfleger, *Das Talbuch, Melkersagen und Bauerngeschichten,* vol. 2, 33–34.

23. Sébillot, *Littérature orale de l'Auvergne,* 160.

24. Leser, *La vallée de Munster,* 119–20.

25. Flammarion, *Les maisons hantées,* 208–9.

26. Fabre and Lacroix, *Légendaire du Languedoc-Roussillon,* 46–47.

27. Hertlé, *Sorciers, magiciens et enchanteurs de nos terroirs*, 70.

28. Pfleger, *Das Talbuch, Melkersagen und Bauerngeschichten*, vol. 2, 36–37.

29. Lecouteux, *La maison et ses génies*, 52–53.

30. Doerflinger and Leser, *Toute l'Alsace. A la quête de l'Alsace profonde. Rites, traditions, contes et légendes*, 122.

31. *Revue des Traditions populaires* 13 (1898), 137–39.

32. Thurston, *Ghosts and Poltergeists*, 80ff.

33. Bozzano, *Les Phénomènes de hantise*, 39, 213.

34. Lang, *Cock Lane and Common-Sense*.

35. Görres, *Die christliche Mystik*, vol. 3, 402ff. Görres calls the printer Labhart.

36. Calmet, *Traité sur les Apparitions des Esprits et sur les vampires ou les Revenans de Hongrie, de Moravie, etc.*, vol. 2, chap. XLVIII. English Translation: Calmet, *This Phantom World*, 271–72.

37. Flammarion, *Les Maisons hantées*, 178–80 [171–73 in English translation —*Trans.*].

38. Sands, *Légendes rustiques*, 107–9.

39. Sands, *Correspondence*, vol. 4, 203–4.

40. Bozzano, *Les Phénomènes de hantise*, chap. 6.

41. De la Salle, *Croyances et Légendes du cœur de la France*, vol. 1, chap. VI.

42. Liebrecht, *Zur Volkskunde. Alte und neue Aufsätze*, 8.

43. Thurston, *Ghosts and Poltergeists*, 107–8.

44. Ibid., 244.

CHAPTER FIVE.
DEVILTRY, MAGIC, SORCERY, AND POLTERGEISTS

1. Jean of Winterthud, *Chronica Iohanni Vitodurani*, in *Monumenta Germaniae Historica, Scriptores*, Nova Series, vol. 3, 51.

2. Camerarius, *Operae horarum subcisivarum*, chap. 74.

3. Grosse, *Magica seu mirabilium historiarum*, folio 29.

4. *Annales ducum Baioariae*, bk. IV.

5. Camerarius, *Operae horarum subcisivarum*, chap. 74.

6. Görres, *Die christliche Mystik*, V, 23.

7. *L'Anti-démon de Mâcon, etc. en la maison du Sieur F. Perreaud* (Geneva: 1653). As this pamphlet was never at my disposal, I used the detailed summary provided by Thurston in *Ghosts and Poltergeists*, 40ff.

8. Lecouteux, *Les nains et les elfes au Moyen Âge,* 179–81.

9. Brognoli, *Alexicacon hoc est de maleficiis,* vol. 2, no. 429.

10. Burnet, *The History of the Reformation of the Church of England.* It can also be read in *The Hydrostaticks* (Edinburgh: 1672) by George Sinclair, who reused it in *Satan's Invisible World Discovered.*

11. Seignolles, *Le diable dans la tradition populaire,* 157–58.

12. Verpoorten, *De daemonum existentia,* 24.

13. Thurston, *Ghosts and Poltergeists,* 14–27.

14. Chapisseau, *Le folklore de la Beauce et du Perche.*

15. Chervet, *Contes du Tastevin,* 125–26.

16. Martin and Vurpas, *Le Beaujolais: contes, légendes, récits, chansons,* 111.

17. Pfleger, *Das Talbuch, Melkersagen und Bauerngeschichten,* vol. 2, 30–31.

18. Unedited document cited in Jalby, *Le Folklore du Languedoc,* 271.

19. Joisten, *Êtres fantastiques du Dauphiné,* 336, 409, 420.

20. Bardin, *Le pays de Septème,* 104ff. Cited from Joisten, *Êtres fantastiques du Dauphiné,* 506–7.

21. Dvoráková and Meidinger, *Contes de Bohême,* vol. 1: *De justes et des épouvantables,* 85ff.

22. *Animadversioni critiche sopra il notturno congresso delle Lammie,* 168.

23. Bozzano, *les Phénomènes de hantise,* 37.

24. Boncœur, *Le diable aux champs,* 68–69.

25. Bozzano, *Les Phénomènes de hantise.*

26. Valk, *The Black Gentleman: Manifestations of the Devil in Estonian Folk Religion,* 71–72.

27. Boncœur, *Le diable aux champs,* 74.

28. Lascaux, *Contes et légendes de Bretagne,* 40–41.

29. Glanvil, *Saducismus Triumphatus.*

30. Zernecke, *Thornische Chronica,* 335.

31. Taillepied, *Psichologie,* 182–83.

32. Chervet, *Contes du Tastevin,* 136.

33. Joisten, *Récits et contes populaires de Savoie,* 99.

34. Pourrat, *Légendes du Pays vert,* 127.

35. Mirville, *Pneumatologie. Des esprits et de leurs manifestations diverses. Mémoires adressés aux Académies,* 336ff.

36. Wallon, *Expliquer le paranormal,* 188–213.

37. For more on this see Lecouteux, *Witches, Werewolves, and Fairies.*

38. Thurston, *Ghosts and Poltergeists,* 130.

39. For more on the strigoï, see Claude Lecouteux, *The Secret History of Vampires,* 82–83.

CHAPTER SIX.
BROWNIES AND POLTERGEISTS

1. Claude Le Petit, *La Chronique scandaleuse* (1668), cited in Sébillot, *le Folklore de France,* vol. 4, 195.

2. When discussing demons Ricardo Argentini Anglo mentions these beings: "*daemones mites Germani ita vt Graeci Cobalos vocent, aly virunculos montanos, aly Gutulos & trullos.*" Cf. Anglo, *De praestigiis et incantationibvs daemonvm et necromanticorvm,* chap. 20.

3. Lindig, *Hausgeister. Die Vorstellungen übernatürlicher Schützer und Helfer in der deutschen Sagenüberlieferung,* 50, 83, 94, 119–23, 143–44.

4. The brownies:

Pulling off the covers: Meier, *Deutsche Sagen, Sitten und Gebräuche aus Schwaben,* no. 96; 339.

Sitting on sleepers like a heavy weight: Meier, *Deutsche Sagen,* no. 96; 339.

Tossing sleepers to the bottom of the bed: Bodens, *Sage, Märchen und Schwank am Niederrhein,* no. 407.

Preventing people from working by bombarding them with all kinds of objects: Eisel, *Sagenbuch des Voigtlandes,* no. 124; Grässe, *Sagenbuch des Preußischen Staates,* vol. 1, no. 191.

Making people fall: Birlinger, *Volksthümliches aus Schwaben,* vol. 1, no. 64; Waibl and Flamm, *Badisches Sagenbuch,* vol. 1, 215–16.

Spoiling and stealing food: Assion, *Weiße, Schwarze, Feurige. Neugesammelte Sagen aus dem Frankenland,* no. 208.

Overturning benches, tables, lamps: Reiser, *Sagen, Gebräuche und Sprichwörter des Allgäus,* vol. 1, no. 170; Schambach and Müller, *Niedersächsische Sagen und Märchen,* no. 153, II.

Attacking children, hitting them, overturning their cradles: Wossidlo, *Mecklenburgische Sagen,* vol. 2, no. 898 ; Reiser, *Sagen,* vol. 1, no. 170.

Ceaselessly opening and slamming doors: Beitl, *Im Sagenwald, neue Sagen aus Vorarlberg,* no. 350.

Causing an enormous din: Peuckert, *Niedersächsische Sagen*, 6 vols., no. 3026.

5. Joisten, *Êtres fantastiques.*

6. Ibid., 182 (Oisans), 190 (Oisans), 214 (Saint-Barthélemy), 235 (Matheysine), 242 (Matheysine), 339 (Villard-de-Lans).

7. *Dictionnaire languedocien–français*, 247.

8. Brueyre, *Contes populaires de la Grande-Bretagne*, 247.

9. Fleury, *Littérature orale de la Basse-Normandie*, 49.

10. Pluquet, *Contes populaires, préjugés, patois, proverbes, noms de lieux, de l'arrondissement de Bayeux*, 12.

11. Cérésole, *Légendes des Alpes vaudoises*, 37–38.

12. Bett, *English Legends*, 90. Stories about poltergeists in the German-speaking countries can be found in Kuoni, *Sagen des Kantons St. Gallen*, no. 28, 17; Gräße, *Der Sagenschatz des Königreichs Sachsen*, vol. 1, no. 359, p. 318; Alpenburg, *Deutsche Alpensagen*, no. 55; Heyl, *Volkssagen, Bräuche und Meinungen aus Tirol*, 229–30; Hupfauf, *Hifalan & Hafalan, Sagen aus dem Zillertal*, 46.

13. Torquemada, *Jardin de Flores curiosas*, 147.

14. Menghi, *Compendio dell Arte essorcistica seu possibilità delle mirabili.*

15. A Christian amulet; for more on this see Claude Lecouteux, *Le Livre des amulettes et talismans*, 93–94.

16. Del Rio, *Disquisitionum Magicarum Libri Sex*, bk. II, question 26. This book was reprinted twenty-four times between its first publication in 1633 and 1755!

17. Grossi, *La Vie de la Vénérable Mère Louise-Blanche Terese de Ballon*, 223–25. I would like to thank Alice Joisten for bringing this marvelous text to my attention.

18. Wallon, *Expliquer le paranormal*, 199–200.

19. Joisten, "Quelques attestations de récits légendaires antérieurs au XVIIIe siècle en Savoie et Dauphiné," *Le Monde alpin et rhodanien* 1974/2 (1974): 119–30; here at 125.

20. Jacquinot, *Adresse chrétienne pour vivre selon Dieu dans le monde, avec Méditations pour chaque jour du mois, divisées en quatre semaines*, 182–93.

21. *Manuale dioecesi Genevensis*, 99–105. Here is an older one: *Remedia pro domo à spectris uexata: Si aliqua domus igitur spectris, aut alia diaboli infestatione sit inquieta, statim habitatores conscientiam expurgent, conterantur,*

*& de peccatis consessionem Sacramentalem instituant: omnia de domo aufer-
ant, quæ Deo displicere possunt. Deuotè se insuper Deo, B. Virgini Mariæ,
& Sanctis commendent, & interea dum durat vexatio, quotidie, mane, &
vesperi Sacerdos habitu Sacerdotali indutus, cum stola, cruce, & aqua bene-
dicta accedat, & lustret omnia domus habitacula, deuotè recitans psal. Qui
habitat in adiutorio altissimi &c. Euangelium S. Ioannis. In principio erat
verbum &c. & alias preces pias, ac exorcismos. Ponantur per angulos domus
rami benedicti, palmarum, & candelæ benedictæ: curent missas celebrari à
deuotis Religiosis pro pace, & quiete domus illius, vt cesset ira Dei, & mit-
tat Angelum suum custodem, qui de domo illa diabolum excutiat. Interim,
caueant domestici, ne cum diabolo sermonem vllum habeaut, nec loqueti illo,
quidquam respondeant, multoque magis caueant, ne alique Magum vocent,
nec vllis superstitiosis remedijs, pro vexatione redimenda vtantur.* This is taken
from chap. X of the *Compendium maleficarum ex quo nefandissima in genus
humanum opera venefica, ac ad illa vitanda remedia conspiciuntur per fratrum Franciscum Mariam Guazzium, Ord. S. Ambrosij ad Nemus Mediolani
compilatum. In hac autem secunda æditione ab eodem authore pulcherrimis
doctrinis ditatum, exemplis auctum, & remedijs lo eupletatum. His additus
est Exorcismus potentissimus ad soluendum omne opus diabolicum; nec non
modus curandi febricitantes, ad Dei gloriam, & hominum solatium* (Milan:
Ambrosiani typographia, 1626).

22. We can find two other exorcisms for haunted houses in: *Manuale exorcismorum* (Antwerp: Plantin, 1619), pt. 3: *Exorcismus domus a malis spiritibus vexatae* and *Alia formula benedicendi domum intestatam a malignis
spiritibus.*

23. *La Fausse Clélie* (Nimegen: 1680), 253–54; quoted in Sébillot, *le Folklore,*
vol. 4, 188.

24. Bozzano, *Les Phénomènes de hantise,* chap. 32, case II.

25. Lecouteux, *La maison et ses génies,* 144–45, 168–69, *et passim;* similarly,
Lecouteux, *Les nains et les elfes,* 179ff.

26. Viret, *Le Monde a l'Empire et le Monde Demoniacle fait par Dialogues,* chap.
16.

27. Feijoo, *Teatro crítico universal,* vol. 3, 4th discourse, 72: *"Duendes y Espíritus
familiares; los Duendes ni son Ángeles buenos, ni Ángeles malos, ni Almas
separadas de los cuerpos . . . son cierta especie de animales aéreos, engendrados
por putrefacción del aire, y vapores corrompidos."*

CHAPTER SEVEN.
TWO STRIKING TALES

1. Glanvil, *Saducismus Triumphatus*, 490–96.

2. Once *she found a Note wrapped up in a Handkerchief,* with these words written in it, "I would have you go from." After she had read it, she locked it up in her Trunk, designing to shew it to her Father and Mother when they came home (for they were gone to church) but when she went to look for it again, it was gone out of her Trunk, and she never saw it any more.

    The last thing that happened was this, one Saturday night Alice going to Bed, *laid a clean Shift in her Bed, intending to put it on the next morning; but in the morning looking for it, she could not find it.* The next night she borrowed one from her Mother, and laid that also on her Bed, as before. In the morning, when she went to put it on, it did not please her, whereupon she gave it to her Mother, desiring her to change it; the Mother took it to change, and opening it, *found it cut and slashed in many places,* and they are both very certain that it was whole before. And the same morning when they came into the Hall, they found the other, which was first taken away, laid upon the Table.

3. Lecouteux, *La Maison et ses génies,* 100.

4. Latry, *Le fil du rêve. Des couturières entre les vivants et les morts,* 98.

5. Cf. Lecouteux, *The Return of the Dead.*

6. I follow here the transcription of the handwritten manuscript provided by Luisa Sasso in his splendid article "Le phénomène des pierres frappantes d'Issime (Val d'Aoste) en 1909. Le témoignage du curé Grat Vesan," *Le Monde alpin et rhodanien* 1999/4 (1999), 39–54.

7. Romain Vesan's article was published in *Le Messager valdôtain* of 1912, pages 84–87, under the title: "Les Diables dans la Vallaise" [The Devils in the Vallaise]. This is how it opens: "Three years ago in a chalet of Issime-St-Jacques, some very strange incidents took place, whose story may perhaps interest the readers of the Valdoastan almanac. There is no need to state that the authenticity of these incidents is beyond dispute as there were more than a hundred eyewitnesses who are still living and quite trustworthy."

CHAPTER EIGHT.
SINGULAR MANIFESTATIONS

1. In the *Proceedings of the Society for Psychical Research* XII (1897): 319–22.

2. Bozzano, *Les Phénomènes de hantise,* chap. 7, case XXVI.

3. Thurston, *Ghosts and Poltergeists,* 162.

4. Ibid., 164.

5. Glanvil, *Saducismus Triumphatus,* 489ff.

6. Finucane, *Appearances of the Dead: A Cultural History of Ghosts,* 139.

7. Thurston, *Ghosts and Poltergeists,* 125ff.

8. *Eclectic magazine of foreign literature, science, and art,* 557.

9. Glanvil, *Saducismus Triumphatus,* 421ff.

10. Bozzano, *Les Phénomènes de hantise,* chap. 7, case XXVI.

11. Ibid., 216.

12. Hervordia, *Liber de rebus memoriabilioribus sive chronicon Heinrici de Hervordia,* 279ff.

13. Thurston, *Ghosts and Poltergeists,* 190–91.

14. Ibid., 51.

15. Ibid., 126ff.

16. Ibid., 17, 29, 164.

17. Bozzano, *Les Phénomènes de hantise,* chap. 7.

18. Puls, *Spukgeschichten. Der Spuk von Resau;* Müller, *Der Spuk von Resau.*

19. Bozzano, *Les Phénomènes de hantise,* chap. 7, case XVIII.

20. Ibid., chap. 7, case XXIII.

21. Görres, *Die christliche Mystik,* 369–70.

22. Pons, *Le spectre et le voyant. Les échanges entre morts et vivants en Islande.*

23. Gaup, *Trommereisen.* This book was translated into French by Olivier Gouchet in 2001. [An English translation titled *In Search of the Drum* was published in 1993. —*Trans.*]

24. *Glåmdalen,* March 27, 2006, 4–5. I would like to thank Ronald Grambo, who provided me with this information and did an analysis of it, from which I quote: "My information: The property is located close to Galgebakken (gallows mound) where criminals were customarily hung, especially thieves and the slaves of the city fortress (the convicts working in the fortress were called "slaves"), who could easily find their death there if they committed a crime during their forced labor. The haunted house is located in close proximity to the fortress. Here they once had barbers with the difficult task of

amputating feet and hands . . . Here there was much pain and sorrow, and many brutal, painful deaths."

25. *Saga of Snorri the Godi; Erybyggja Saga,* chapters 50–54.

26. Lecouteux, "Les bruits de l'au-delà": 113–24.

CONCLUSION

1. Krappe, *La genèse des mythes.*

2. Lecouteux, *Les nains et les elfes au Moyen Âge.*

3. See the bibliography.

4. Cohen, *Encyclopédie des fantômes,* 259–64.

5. Wallon, *Expliquer le paranormal,* 199, 211.

6. Ibid., 190.

7. "Ein sogenanntes katalytisches Exteriorisations Phänomen" in Jung, *Erinnerungen, Träume und Gedanken,* 160. Jung indicates that Freud was interested in opinions about precognition and parapsychology. Jung spoke these words in one of their discussions.

APPENDICES

1. *Manuale dioecesi Genevensis,* 99–105; Thurston, *Ghosts and Poltergeists,* 206–8. Two other exorcisms for haunted houses can be found in *Manuale exorcismorum,* third part; *Exorcismus domus a malis spiritibus vexatae,* and *Alia formula benedicendi domum intestatam a malignis spiritibus.*

2. Prayer that forms part of the hours. There is an example of its use in the *Life of Saint Friard,* who lived during the sixth century: And when he reached the place where was that cloud of wasps, he made the sign of the Cross and said, "*Adjutorium nostrum in nomine Domini, qui fecit cœlum et terram,*" and losing all use of their will they flew down a hole in the ground, never to reemerge.

3. *Visita, quaesumus, Domine, habitationem istam, et omnes insidias inimici ab ea longe repelle: Angeli tui sancti habitent in ea, qui nos in pace custodiant; et benedictio tua sit super nos semper. Per Christum Dominum nostrum. Amen.*

4. Harper's Family Library, *XI (1830).*

5. Glanvil, *Saducismus Triumphatus,* 403–9; Sinclair, *Satan's Invisible World,* 32–39; Görres, *Die christliche Mystik,* vol. 3, 404–7.

6. This is how Walter Scott summarized the entire incident: "The most celebrated instance in which human agency was used to copy the disturbances
imputed to supernatural beings refers to the ancient palace of Woodstock,
when the Commissioners of the Long Parliament came down to dispark
what had been lately a royal residence. The Commissioners arrived at
Woodstock, October 13, 1649, determined to wipe away the memory of
all that connected itself with the recollection of monarchy in England.
But in the course of their progress they were encountered by obstacles,
which apparently came from the next world. Their bedchambers were
infested with visits of a thing resembling a dog, but which came and
passed as mere earthly dogs cannot do. Logs of wood, the remains of a
very large tree called the King's Oak, which they had splintered into bil-
lets for burning, were tossed through the house, and the chairs displaced
and shuffled about. While they were in bed the feet of their couches were
lifted higher than their heads, and then dropped with violence. Trenchers
'without a wish' flew at their heads of free will. Thunder and lightning
came next, which were set down to the same cause. Specters made their
appearance, as they thought, in different shapes, and one of the party saw
the apparition of a hoof, which kicked a candlestick and lighted candle
into the middle of the room, and then politely scratched on the red snuff
to extinguish it. Other and worse tricks were practised on the astonished
Commissioners who, considering that all the fiends of hell were let loose
upon them, retreated from Woodstock without completing an errand
which was, in their opinion, impeded by infernal powers, though the
opposition offered was rather of a playful and malicious than of a dangerous cast."
7. See Schenda, *Von Mund zu Ohr. Bausteine zu einer Kulturgeschichte volkstümlichen Erzählens in Europa.*
8. The June 1966 issue of the *Revue métapsychique* reports: From mid-May
until the beginning of September 1963, the Orthopedic Clinic in Arcachon
was harassed by projectiles consisting of stones, pieces of cinder blocks, and
brick fragments, whose origin remains unknown. . . . During this time the
patients, the majority stretched out on carts, were the recipients of approxi-
mately two to three hundred pebbles of all sizes. . . . The trajectories of
the stones and the direction they took, the speed, the number, and nature
of the projectiles varied highly. The time they also occurred also appeared

to be quite capricious . . . , but most particularly at nightfall. Never were any of the patients injured and if two among them were touched, it was only quite lightly. The sole condition, apparently necessary and sufficient, was the presence in the immediate area of Jacqueline R., who was seventeen years old, which provided justification for all the suspicions concerning her [as agent of the phenomenon]. But, despite the close surveillance on the part of the other patients, no evidence was ever unearthed. To the contrary . . . she was the target of a large number of stones. . . .

Dr. Cuénot points out that the stones began falling at the moment the personnel and the patients of the clinic learned it was scheduled to be closed or sold. During this period, one patient, Angélina M., was a favorite target of the stones. It was only after the departure of Angélina (July 7) that the focus was transferred to Jacqueline in some way. . . . The showers of stones became increasingly prevalent with a marked preference for Jacqueline's surroundings. . . . She only needed to spend several minutes in any part of the outside terraces for the pebbles to start raining down around her. If she was absent from the clinic, the thrown stones ceased. Once she returned, they would resume with a lapse of about five to ten minutes each time. At the same time, the weight, the force, and the number of stones thrown at the patients increased to an alarming degree in July and August. Some days there were as many as thirty.

9. See Becker, *L'église "hantée" de Delain.*

10. Plot, *The Natural History of Oxford-Shire.* A facsimile edition was published in 1972.

11. Wallon, *Le paranormal,* 102.

12. Bozzano, *Les Phénomènes de hantise,* chap. 7, case XXII, quoted from Lombroso, *Ricerche sui fenomeni ipnotici e spiritici,* 246.

13. Article by Christ Popa, "Casa bintuita din Iasi," *Evenimentul Zilei,* March 6, 2004. I have included key passages in the original language.

14. Olaru, "Strigoiul a fost dezopat. Necazurile familiei Grecu au fost provocate de fantoma Titinei."

15. This is reminiscent of the "Rosenheim poltergeist," studied by Hans Bender, a professor in Freiburg, Germany: "On a cold November morning in 1967, most of the lawyer Sigmund Adam's employees were already at work in in his offices in the Bavarian town of Rosenheim. One of the last people to arrive was Anne-Marie Schneider, a recently hired eighteen-year-old secre-

tary. She entered the lobby and took off her coat. While walking beneath a hanging lamp, it started to sway but the young girl took no notice of it. She headed to the coatroom, and the movement of the lamp intensified. Suddenly the lightbulb in the coatroom began swinging back and forth. An employee who had spotted it while entering shouted: 'Watch out! The lamp!' Anne-Marie bent down and covered herself with her coat for protection. A moment later, the lightbulb in the lobby exploded, projecting a shower of glass shards in Anne-Marie's direction. The cord stopped swinging and with a few words of thanks to the employee who warned her, Anne-Marie grabbed a broom to sweep up the glass. . . ." The fluorescent tubes attached to the ceiling kept breaking down. Once a string detonation occurred and the entire lighting system went out all at once. Even when they were not on, the incandescent lightbulbs would explode without damaging the filament. The fuses popped for no apparent reason, and sometimes would eject themselves from the fuse box. The dysfunctions of the telephone system were particularly serious." For more details, see Broughton, *Parapsychologie, une science controversée.*

Bibliography

OLDER WORKS

Alberus, Erasmus. *Novum dictionarium genus.* Leipzig: Chr. Egenolphum, 1540.

Alcuin, *Life of Willibrord.* In C. H. Talbot, trans. and ed. *The Anglo-Saxon Missionaries in Germany.* New York: Sheed and Ward, 1954.

Anglo, Ricardo Argentini. *De praestigiis et incantationibvs daemonvm et necromanticorvm.* Basel: R. Silver, 1568.

Animadversioni critiche sopra il notturno congresso delle Lammie. Venice: 1751.

Annales ducum Baioariae. 1521.

Ausgustine, Aurelius. *The City of God.* In Rev. Marcus Dods, trans. *The Works of Aurelius Augustine, Bishop of Hippo,* vol. II. Edinburgh: Clark, 1871.

Baxter, Richard. *The Certainty of the World of the Spirits. Fully evinced by the unquestionable Histories of Apparitions and Witchcrafts, Operations, Voices, &c. Proving the Immortality of Souls, the Malice and Misery of the Devils, and the Damned, and the Blessedness of the Justified. Written for the Conviction of Sadduces & Infidels.* London: Printed for T. Parkhurst at the Bible and Three Crowns in Cheapside, and J. Salusbury at the Rising Sun over against the Royal Exchange, 1691.

Bodin, Jean. *De la Demonomanie des Sorciers. À Monseignevr M. Chrestofle de Thou, Cheualier, Seigneur de Cœli, premier President en la Cour de Parlement, & Conseiller du Roy en son priué Conseil. Reueu, corrigé, & augmenté d'vne grande partie. Par I. Bodin, Angevin.* Paris: Jacques du Puys, 1587.

Bovet, *Richard. Pandaemonium, or The devil's cloyster: being a further blow to modern sadduceism, proving the existence of witches and spirits, in a discourse deduced from the fall of the angels, the propagation of Satans kingdom before the flood, the idolatry of the ages after greatly advancing diabolical confederacies, with an account of the lives and transactions of several notorious witches: also, a collection of several authentick relations of strange apparitions of dæmons and spectres, and fascinations of witches, never before printed*. Printed at the Black Lion in Chancery over against Lincolns Inn, 1684.

Braüner, Johan Jacob. *Physicalisch und Historisch Erörterte Curiositaeten. Oder: Entlarvter Teufflischer Aberglaube*. Frankfurt: Johann David Jung, 1737.

Brognoli, Candido. *Alexicacon hoc est de maleficiis*, vol. 2. Venice: Nicolaus Pezzana, 1714.

Burnet, Gilbert. *The History of the Reformation of the Church of England*, 3 vols. London: Chiswell, 1679–1714.

Calmet, Dom Augustin. *Traité sur les Apparitions des Esprits et sur les vampires ou les Revenans de Hongrie, de Moravie*, 2 vols. Einsiedeln: Jean Everhard Kälin, 1749.

Camerarius, Philipp. *Operae horarum subcisivarum*. Frankfurt: n.p., 1602.

Clarke, Adam. *Memoirs of the Wesley Family*. London: Lane and Scott, 1823.

Compedium maleficarum ex quo nefandissima in genus humanum opera venefica, ac ad illa vitanda remedia conspiciuntur per fratrum Franciscum Mariam Guazzium, Ord. S. Ambrosij ad Nemus Mediolani compilaatum. In hac autem secunda aeditione ab eodem authore pulcherrimis doctrinis ditatum, exemplis auctum, & remedijs lo eupletatum. His additus est Exorcismus potentissimus ad soluendum, omne opus diabolicum; nec non modus curandi febricitantes, ad Dei gloriam, & hominum solatium. Milan: Ambrosiani typographia, 1626.

De Gembloux, Sigebert. *Chronica*. In Jacques-Paul Migne, ed. *Patrologia latina*, vol. CLX. Paris: Migne, 1854.

Del Rio, Martin. *Les Controverses et recherches Magiques*. Translated by Andre du Chesne. Paris: College de Cambray, 1611.

———. *Disquisitionum Magicarum Libri Sex*. Cologne: Peter Henning, 1633.

Dictionnaire languedocien–français. Saint-Hippolyte-du-Fort: n.p., 1798.

Dimock, James F., ed. *Giraldi Cambrensis Opera*, vol. VI. London: Longmans, Green, Reader and Dyer, 1868.

Du Breul, Jacques. *Théâtre des Antiquitez*. Paris: Chevalier, 1639.

Eyrbyggja Saga. In Ó. Sveinsson, ed. *Islenzk Fornrit IV,* Reykjavík: 1935 (BPhG 24).

Feijoo, Benito Jerónimo. *Teatro crítico universal,* vol. 3. Madrid: Pantaleón Aznar, 1777.

Gentleman's Magazine. Issue 3 (1764).

Glanvil, Joseph. *Saducismus Triumphatus: or full and plain Evidence concerning Witches and Apparitions, in two parts. The First treating of their Possibility; The Second of their Real Existence. The Third Edition. The Advantages whereof above the former, the Reader may understand out of Dr H. More's Account prefixed thereunto. With two Authentick, but wonderful Stories of certain Swedish Witches; done into English by Anth. Norneck, D.D.* London: Printed for S. Lownds at his Shoppe by the Savoy-Gate, 1688.

Grosse, Henning. *Magica seu mirabilium historiarum.* Eisleben: n.p., 1597.

Grossi, R. P. Jean. *La Vie de la Vénérable Mère Louise-Blanche Terese de Ballon.* Annecy: Humbert Fontaine, 1695.

Guazzo, Francesco Maria. *Compendium maleficarum ex quo nefandissima in genus humanum opera venesica, ac ad illa vitanda remedia conspiciuntur.* Milan: Ambrosiani typographia, 1626.

Heinisch, Jeremias. *Das Zeugniß der reinen Wahrheit von den Sonder- und wunderbahren Würckungen eines insgemein sogenannten Kobolds, Oder unsichtbahren Wesens in der Pfarr-Wohnung zu Gröben.* Jena: Meyer, 1723.

Jacobus de Voragine. *Legenda aurea.* Compiled ca. 1260. Translated by J. B. M. Roze. Paris: Garnier-Flammarion, 1967.

Jacquinot, Barthélemy, S.J. *Adresse chrétienne pour vivre selon Dieu dans le monde, avec Méditations pour chaque jour du mois, divisées en quatre semaines.* Lyon: Regnauld Chaudière, 1621.

James I, King of England. *Daemonologie, in Forme of a Dialogue, Diuided into three Bookes.* Edinburgh: Printed by Robert Walde-graue, printer to the Kings Majestie, 1597.

Jean of Winterthud. *Chronica Iohanni Vitodurani.* Edited by F. Baethgen and C. Brun in *Monumenta Germaniae Historica. Scriptores.* Nova Series III.

Kirk, Robert. *The secret commonwealth; or an essay on the nature and actions of the subterranean (and for the most part) invisible people heretofoir going under the name of faunes and fairies, or the lyke, among the low country Scots, as they are described by those who have the second sight.* Edinburgh: n.p., 1691.

Lavater, Ludwig. *Trois livres des apparitions des esprits, fantosmes, prodigies et accidents merveilleux qui precedent souventes fois la more de quelque personage renommé ou un grand changement ès choses de ce monde.* Zurich: G. Des Marescz, 1581.

———. *Von Gespänsten / unghüren / fälen u. anderen wunderbaren dingen / so merteils wenn die menschen sterben söllend /oder wan gross sachen und enderungen vorhanden sind / beschähend / kurtzer unnd einfaltiger bericht.* Zurich: G. Des Marescz, 1569.

Le Loyer, Pierre. *A Treatise of Specters or Straunge Sights, Visions and Apparitions appearing sensibly vnto men. Wherein is delivered, the Nature of Spirites, Angels, and Divels: their power and properties: as also of Witches, Sorcerers, Enchanters, and such like.* London: Printed by Val. S. for Mathew Lownes, 1605.

Lenglet-Dufresnoy, Nicolas. *Recueil de Dissertations sur les Apparitions, les Visions et les Songes,* 4 vols. in duodecimo. Paris: Jean Musier, 1715.

Leo, Johannes. *Historia Prussiae.* Brunsberg: n.p., 1725.

Maioli, Simeone. *Canicular Days.* 1597.

Mamoris, Petrus. *Flagellum maleficorum.* Lyon: Nikolaus Philippi, 1621.

Manuale dioecesi Genevensis. Annecy: n.p., 1747.

Manuale exorcismorum. Antwerp: Plantin, 1619.

Megiser, Hieronymus. *Annales Carinthiae.* Leipzig: Abraham Lamberg, 1612.

Meier, Ernst Heinrich. *Deutsche Sagen, Sitten und Gebräuche aus Schwaben.* Stuttgart: J. B. Metzler, 1852.

Menghi, Girolamo. *Compendio dell Arte essorcistica seu possibilità delle mirabili.* Bologna: Giouanni Rossi, 1580.

Meyers Konversationslexikon. Leipzig and Vienna: Bibliographisches Institut, 1897.

Montalembert, Adrien de. *Histoire merveilleuse de seur Allis de Thésieux, laquelle est apparue.* 1580.

Nider, Johannes. *Formicarius.* Augsburg: Anton Sorg, 1484.

———. *Preceptorium.* Paris: Udalric Gering and Jehan Petit, 1507.

Prätorius, Johannes. *Anthropodermus Plutonicus. Das ist, eine neue Welt-Beschreibung von allerley wunderbahrlichen Menschen,* part 1. Magdeburg: Lüderwald, 1666.

Pliny the Younger. *Letters.* New York: P. F. Collier and Son Company, 1909–14.

Plot, Robert. *The Natural History of Oxford-Shire.* Oxford: n.p., 1677.

Saga of Snorri the Godi. ca. 1230. *Eyrbyggja Saga,* ed. Ó. Sveinsson, in *Islenzk Fornrit IV,* Reykjavík: 1935 (BPhG 24).

Schott, Gaspar. *Magia universalis naturae et artis.* Wurzburg: H. Froidevaux, 1675.

Scot, Reginald. *The Discoverie of Witchcraft.* London: William Brome, 1584.

Sinclair, George. *Satan's Invisible World Discovered.* Edinburgh: John Reid, 1685.

Summers, Montague. *A Treatise of Ghosts.* London: Fortune Press, 1933.

Taillepied, François-Noël. *Psichologie. Traicté de l'Apparition des Esprits. A sçavoir, des Ames séparées, Fantosmes, Prodiges et autres accidens merveilleux, qui précèdent quelquefois la mort des grands personnages ou signifient changement de la chose publique.* Paris: Jean Corrozet, 1616 [1588].

Thyraeus, Petrus. *Daemoniaci, hoc est, de obsessis a spiritibus daemoniorum hominibus.* Cologne: Goswin Cholinus, 1598.

Torquemada, Antoine de. *Jardin de Flores curiosas.* Salamanca: Alonso de Terranova y Neyla, 1577.

Trochus, Baldassar. *Vocabulorum rerum promptuarium.* Leipzig: Melchior Lot, 1517.

Valvasor, Johann Weichard von. *Ehre deß Herzogthums Crain,* 3 vols. Laibach: n.p., 1689.

Verpoorten, G. P. *De daemonum existentia.* Gdansk: n.p., 1779.

Der vielförmige Hintzelmann. Leipzig: n.p., 1704.

Viret, Pierre. *Le Monde a l'Empire et le Monde Demoniacle fait par Dialogues.* Geneva: Guillaume de Laimarie, 1561.

Wegner, Georg Wilhelm. *Philosophische Abhandlung von Gespenstern worinn zugleich eine kurtze Nachricht von dem Wustermarkischen Kobold gegeben wird.* Berlin: Haude & Spener, 1747.

Zedler, Johann Heinrich. *Grosses vollständiges Universal-Lexikon.* Leipzig and Halle: Zedler, 1732–1754.

Zernecke, Jacob Heinrich. *Thornische Chronica.* Berlin: Haude, 1727.

Zobel, M. Enoch. *Historische und Theologische Vorstellung des Ebentheüerlichen Gespenstes / Welches In einem Hause zu S. Annaberg / 2. Monat lang im neüligst 1691sten Jahr / viel Schrecken / Furcht und wunderseltsame Schauspiell angerichtet.* Leipzig: Lanckisch, 1692.

STUDIES, ANTHOLOGIES, AND TEXTS

Acevedo, Manuel Otero. *Über die Gespenster. Wahrheit für die moderne Psychologie.* Translated by F. Feilgenhauer. Leipzig: Spohr, 1896.

Alpenburg, Johann Nepomuk Ritter von. *Deutsche Alpensagen.* Vienna: Braumüller, 1861.

Annales des Sciences Psychiques (1892–1893): 1905.

Appel, Johann A., and Friedrich Laun. *Gespensterbuch,* 4 vols. Stuttgart: Deutsche Verlags Anstalt, 1814–1815.

Assion, Peter von. *Weiße, Schwarze, Feurige. Neugesammelte Sagen aus dem Frankenland.* Karlsruhe: Badenia-Verlag, 1972.

Auricoste de Lazarque, E. "Histoires surnaturelles de Boulay." *Revue des Traditions populaires* 19 (1904): 257–68, 408–16.

Becker, Elisabeth. *L'église "hantée" de Delain.* Paris: Agnières, 2000.

Beitl, Richard. *Im Sagenwald, neue Sagen aus Vorarlberg.* Feldkirch: Montfort-Verlag, 1953.

Béraud-Williams, Sylvette. *Contes populaires de l'Ardèche.* Paris: Editions Curendera, 1984.

Bett, Henry. *English Legends.* London: Batsford, 1952.

Bilz, Friedrich Eduard. *Tote leben und umgehen uns, nebst einem Anhang: neue Theorie über Entstehung der Welt und der Menschheit sowie Wunder der Astronomie und anderes mehr.* Dresden-Radebeul: Bilz, 1921.

Birlinger, Anton. *Volksthümliches aus Schwaben. Sagen, Märchen, Volksaberglauben,* vol. 1. Freiburg: Herder, 1861.

Bodens, Wilhelm. *Sage, Märchen und Schwank am Niederrhein.* Bonn: Bouvieu Verlag, 1937.

Boncœur, Jean Louis. *Le diable aux champs.* Paris: Fayard, 1981.

Bouvier, Jean-Baptiste. *Légendes valaisannes d'après les Wallisersagen de la Société d'Histoire du Haut-Valais.* Paris: Neuchâtel, Editions Victor Attinger, 1931.

Bozzano, Ernesto. *Les Phénomènes de hantise.* Paris: Alcan, 1926.

Broughton, R. S. *Parapsychologie, une science controversée.* Monaco: Le Rocher, 1995.

Brückner, Wolfgang. *Volkserzählung und Reformation. Ein Handbuch zur Tradierung und Funktion von Erzählstoffen und Erzähllitteratur im Protestantismus.* Berlin: Erich Schmidt, 1974.

Brueyre, Loys. *Contes populaires de la Grande-Bretagne.* Paris: Librairie Hachette, 1875.

Capdecome, Marie. *La vie des morts. Enquête sur les fantômes d'hier et d'aujourd'hui.* Paris: Imago, 1997.

Carrington, Hereward. "Historic Poltergeists." *International Institute for Psychical Research, Bulletin* 1 (ca. 1935).

Carrington, Hereward, and Nandor Fodor. *The Story of the Poltergeist Down the Centuries*. London: Rider, 1953.

Cérésole, Alfred. *Légendes des Alpes vaudoises*. Re-edited from the 1885 Lausanne edition, 2 vols. Geneva: Slatkine, 1985, 2000.

Chapisseau, Félix. *Le folklore de la Beauce et du Perche*. Paris: Maisonneuve, 1896.

Chassande, E. "Monographie du Mandement d'Avallon and Bayard et de la commune de Saint-Maximin, canton de Goncelin (Isère)." *Bulletin de la Société dauphinoise d'Ethnologie et d'Anthropologie* 14 (1907).

Chervet, Maurice. *Contes du Tastevin*. Monaco: Rocher, 1955.

Cohen, Daniel. *Encyclopédie des fantômes*. Paris: Robert Laffont, 1984.

Coulton, George Gordon, ed. *Social Life in Britain from the Conquest to the Reformation*. Cambridge: Cambridge University Press, 1918.

Cousée, Bernard. *Les plus belles légendes du Nord*. Lille: La Voix du Nord, 2001.

Coxe, Anthony D. Hippidley. *Haunted Britain: A Guide to Supernatural Sites Frequented by Ghosts, Witches, Poltergeists and Other Mysterious Beings*. London: Hutchinson, 1973.

Crowe, Catherine. *The Night Side of Nature; or, Ghosts and Ghost Seers*. London: T. C. Newby, 1848.

———. *Die Nachtseite der Natur oder Geister und Geisterseher*. Translated by C. Kolb. Stuttgart: Scheible, 1849.

Dawes, Elizabeth, trans. *Three Byzantine Saints: Contemporary Biographies of St. Daniel the Stylite, St. Theodore of Sykeon and St. John the Almsgiver*. London: Blackwell, 1948.

De la Salle, Germaine Laisnel. *Croyances et Légendes du cœur de la France,* vol. 1. Paris: Misonneuve, 1875–1881.

De Lyon, Constance. *Vita Germani*. Edited and translated by R. Borius. Paris: Éditions du Cerf, 1965.

De Marliave, Olivier. *Trésor de la mythologie pyrénéenne*. Bordeaux: Editions Sud-Ouest, 1996.

De Nogent, Guibert. *De vita sua sive monodiae*. Edited and translated by E. R. Labande. CHFMA 34. Paris: Les Belles Lettres, 1981.

Des Gervasius von Tilbury Otia imperialia. Abridged and edited by F. Liebrecht. Hannover: Rümpler, 1856.

Doerflinger, Marguerite, and Gérald Leser. *Toute l'Alsace. A la quête de l'Alsace profonde. Rites, traditions, contes et legends*. Ingersheim and Colmar: SAEP, 1986.

Dvorakova, Marcela, and Rodolphe Meidinger. *Contes de Bohême.* Paris: Editions Dufourg-Iandrup, 2003.

Eclectic magazine of foreign literature, acience, and art, vol. 58. New York: Pelton, 1893.

Eisel, Robert. *Sagenbuch des Voigtlandes.* Gera: Griesbach, 1871.

Fabre, Daniel, and Jacques Lacroix. *Légendaire du Languedoc-Roussillon. Enquête ethnographique.* Montpellier: Université Paul Valéry, 1972.

Federspiel, Martin. *Spukgeschichten.* Frankfurt and Berlin: Ullstein, 1988.

Finucane, Ronald C. *Appearances of the Dead: A Cultural History of Ghosts.* New York: Prometheus Books, 1984.

Flammarion, Camille. *Les maisons hantées.* Paris: Ernest Flammarion, 1923. [Revised and abridged edition. Paris: Éditions J'ai lu, 1974. English edition: *Haunted Houses.* London: T. Fisher Unwin, 1924.

Fleury, Jean. *Littérature orale de la Basse-Normandie.* Paris: Maisonneuve, 1884.

Gauld, Alan, and A. D. Cornell. *Poltergeists.* London: Routledge and Kegan Paul, 1979.

Gaup, Ailo. *Trommereisen.* Oslo: Gyldendal, 1988. English edition: Gaup, Ailo. *In Search of the Drum.* Translated by Bente Kjos Sjordal. Fort Yates: Muse, 1993.

Gazette des Tribunaux. February 2–4, 1846.

Gazette des Tribunaux. December 20, 1849.

Gerald of Wales. *The Journey to Wales and the Description of Wales.* Translated by Lewis Thorpe. London: Penguin, 1978.

Grabinsky, Bruno. *Spuk- und Geistererscheinungen oder was sonst? Eine kritische Untersuchung.* Hildesheim: Borgmeyer, 1920.

Grässe, J. G. *Sagenbuch des Preußischen Staates,* vol. 1. Glogau: Verlag von Carl Flemming, 1867.

Greber, Johann. *Der Verkehr mit der Geisterwelt, seine Gesetze und sein zweck. Selbsterlebnisse eines katholischen Geistlichen.* New York: John Felsberg, 1937.

Grossier, Jean, and Guy-Jean Michel. *Légendes et fauves du pays des lacs.* Gérardmer: Société d'arts et traditions populaires Les Ménestrels de Gérardmer, 1963.

Gueriff, Fernand. *Brière de brume et de rêves: histoire, coutumes, mythes et légendes.* Nantes: Bellanger, 1979.

Guillaume, Alfred. *L'âme du Morvan.* Dijon: Société des Amis du vieux Saulieu, 1971.

Harper's Family Library XI (1830).

Heyl, Johann Adolf. *Volkssagen, Bräuche und Meinungen aus Tirol.* Brixen: Verlag Anst. Athesia, 1897.

Hertlé, Jean-Marc. *Sorciers, magiciens et enchanteurs de nos terroirs.* Paris: Jean de Bonnot, 1996.

Hervordia, Henricus de. *Liber de rebus memoriabilioribus sive chronicon Heinrici de Hervordia.* Edited by August Pottast Göttingen, 1859.

Hottinger, Marie. *Mehr Gespenster. Die besten Gespenstergeschichten aus England, Schottland und Irland.* Zurich: Diogenes, 1978.

Huertas, Monique de. *Contes et légendes de Savoie.* Rennes: Ouest-France, 2001.

Hupfauf, Erich. *Hifalan & Hafalan, Sagen aus dem Zillertal.* Hall in Tirol: Hupfauf, 2000.

Illig, Johannes. *Der Spuk in Großerlach.* Göppingen: Illig, 1916.

Journal of the American Society for Psychical Research. 1910–1911.

Jaffé, Aniela. *Geistererscheinungen und Vorzeichen. Eine psychologische Deutung.* Zurich and Stuttgart: Rascher-Verlag, 1958.

Jalby, Robert. *Le Folklore du Languedoc. Ariège, Aude, Lauraguais, Tarn.* Paris: Maisonneuve and Larose, 1971.

Joisten, Charles. *Récits et contes populaires de Savoie.* Paris: Gallimard, 1980.

———. *Êtres fantastiques du Dauphiné. Patrimoine narratif de l'Isère.* Grenoble: Musée dauphinois, 2005.

Jung, C. G. *Erinnerungen, Träume und Gedanken.* Edited by Aniela Jaffé. Zurich and Stuttgart: Rascher-Verlag, 1962.

Kaech, René. *Der Mesmerismus.* Basel: Ciba-Zeitschrift, 1947.

Kemmerich, Max. *Die Brücke zum Jenseits.* Munich: Langen, 1927.

Kervella, Divi. *Légendaire celtique.* Speied: Editions Coop Breizh, 1999.

Krappe, Alexander H. *La genèse des mythes.* Paris: Payot, 1952.

Kuoni, Jakob. *Sagen des Kantons St. Gallen.* Saint-Gall: Wiser & Frey, 1903.

Lambert, L. R. *Spuk, Gespenster und Apportphänomene.* Berlin: Schwarz, 1923.

Lang, Andrew. *Cock Lane and Common-Sense.* London: Longmans, Green, and Co., 1894.

Lascaux, Mikaël. *Contes et légendes de Bretagne recueillis dans le pays de Rennes.* Paris: France-Empire, 1994.

Latry, Marie-Claire. *Le fil du rêve. Des couturières entre les vivants et les morts.* Paris: L'Harmatton, 2002.

Lecanu, Abbé A. F. *Geschichte des Satans. Sein Fall, seine Anhänger, seine Offen-*

barungen, seine Werke, sein Kampf gegen Gott und die Menschen. Regensburg: G. J. Manz, 1863.

Lecouteux, Claude. *Au-delà du merveilleux: des croyances au Moyen Age.* Paris: P.U.P.S., 1996. 3rd revised and expanded edition.

——. *Culture et Civilisation médiévales,* XIII. Paris:, P.U.P.S., 1998.

——. *Démons et génies du terroir au Moyen Age.* Paris: Imago, 1995.

——. *Dictionnaire de mythologie germanique.* Paris: Imago, 2005.

——. *Eine Welt im Abseits. Studien zur niederen Mythologie und Glaubenswelt des Mittelalters.* Dettelbach: Quellen & Forschungen zur europäischen Ethnologie, 2001.

——. *Elle mangeait son linceul. Fantômes, revenants, vampires et esprits frappeurs, une anthologie.* Collection Merveilleux, 28. Paris: José Corti, 2006.

——. "Gespenster und Wiedergänger. Bemerkungen zu einem vernachlässigten Forschungsfeld der Altgermanistik." *Euphorion* 80 (1986): 219–31.

——. *La maison et ses génies: croyances d'hier et d'aujourd'hui.* Paris: Imago, 2000.

——. *Le Livre des amulettes et talismans.* Paris: Imago, 2005.

——. "Les bruits de l'au-delà." *Revue des Langues romanes* 101 (1997): 113–24.

——. *Les nains et les elfes au Moyen Age.* Paris: Imago, 1988. Third revised edition. Paris: Imago, 2004.

——. *The Return of the Dead.* Rochester, Vt.: Inner Traditions, 2009.

——. "Revenants." In P. Sbalchiero, ed. *Dictionnaire de l'extraordinaire chrétien.* Paris: Fayard, 2003.

——. *The Secret History of Vampires.* Rochester Vt.: Inner Traditions, 2010.

——. "Typologie de quelques morts malfaisants." *Cahiers slaves* 3 (2001): 227–44.

——. "Vom Schrat zum Schrättel. Dämonisierungs-, Mythologisierungs- und Euphemisierungsprozeß einer volkstümlichen Vorstellung." *Euphorion* 79 (1985): 95–108.

——. *Witches, Werewolves, and Fairies.* Rochester, Vt.: Inner Traditions, 2003.

——. "Zwerge und Verwandte." *Euphorion* 75 (1981): 366–78.

Lecouteux, Claude, and Philippe Marcq. *Les esprits et les morts. Croyances médiévales.* Essais 13. Paris: Champion, 1990.

Légendaire du Languedoc-Roussillon. Ethnographical investigation conducted by the students of the State Technical School of Montpellier, 1972.

Leser, Gérard. *La vallée de Munster. Des paysages, des légendes et des homes.* Strasbourg: Editions Oberlin, 1988.

Liebrecht, Felix. *Zur Volkskunde. Alte und neue Aufsätze.* Heilbronn: Henninger, 1879.

Lindig, Erika. *Hausgeister. Die Vorstellungen übernatürlicher Schützer und Helfer in der deutschen Sagenüberlieferung.* Artes Populares 14. Frankfurt and Bern: Peter Lang, 1987.

Locher, Theo, and Guido Lauper. *Schweizer Spuk und Psychokinese. Kommentierte Fälle aus jüngster und früherer Zeit.* Freiburg: Aurum, 1977.

Lombroso, Cesare. *Ricerche sui fenomeni ipnotici e spiritici. Turin: Unione Tipografico Editrice, 1909.*

Luther, Martin. *D. Martin Luthers Werke. Kritische Gesamtausgabe, Tischreden, Schriften.* Weimar: H. Bohlaus Nachfolger, 1912.

Maple, Eric, and Lynn Myring. *Fantômes et lieux hantés.* Paris: Hachette, 1980.

Markale, Jean. *Contes de la mort des pays de France.* Paris: Albin Michel, 1992.

Martin, Jean Baptiste, and Anne-Marie Vurpas. *Le Beaujolais, contes, légendes, récits, chansons.* Saint-Étienne: Le Hénaff, 1982.

Martine, Francois, trans. *Sources chrétiennes.* Paris: Les Editions du Cerf, 1968.

———, ed. and trans. *Vie des Pères du Jura.* Sources chrétiennes 142. Paris: Gallimard, 1968.

Massignon, Geneviève. *De bouche à oreille. Le conte populaire français.* Paris: Editions Territoires–Berger-Levrault, 1983.

Masson, René. *Fantômes, médiums et maisons hantées.* Paris: Hérissey, 1964.

Michel, Guy-Jean. *Légendes et fauves du pays des lacs.* Gérardmer: Harpers, 1963.

Michelet, Sylvain. *Lorsque la maison crie. Tensions familiales et phénomènes paranormaux.* Paris: Laffont, 1994.

Mirville, Jules-Eudes de. *Pneumatologie. Des esprits et de leurs manifestations diverses. Mémoires adressés aux Académies,* 5 vols. Paris: Vrayet de Surcy, 1863–1864.

Moser, Fanny. *Spuk. Irrglaube oder Wahrglaube? Eine Frage der Menschheit.* Baden: Gyr-Verlag, 1950.

Mozzani, Éloïse. *Le Livre des Superstitions: Mythes, Croyances et Legendes.* Paris: Robert Laffont, 1995.

Müller, E. *Der Spuk von Resau.* Berlin: Siegismund, 1889.

Ohlhaver, Heinrich. *Die toten Leben. Eigene Erlebnisse.* Hamburg: Tesmer, 1916.

Olaru, Ramona. "Strigoiul a fost dezopat. Necazurile familiei Grecu au fost provocate de fantoma Titinei." *Evenimentul Zilei.* March 14, 2005.

Orain, Adolphe. *Trésors des contes du Pays Gallo.* Collected by O. Eudes. Rennes: Terre de Brume, 2000.

Otto, Bernhard. *Die Sprache der Verstorbenen oder das Geisterklopfen. Stimmen aus dem Jenseits und enthüllter Geheimnisse des Grabes.* Leipzig: Schmitt, 1855.

Pabst, Karl Robert. *Über Gespenster in Sage und Dichtung.* Bern: Heuberger, 1867.

Peuckert, Will-Erich. *Die große Wende.* Hamburg: Verlag Claassen and Goverts, 1948.

Pfleger, Alfred. *Das Talbuch, Melkersagen und Bauerngeschichten.* Annuaire de la Société d'Histoire du Val et de la Ville de Munster 21 & 22 ,1966–1967.

Piniès, Jean-Pierre. *Croyances populaires des pays d'Oc.* Paris: Editions Rivages, 1984.

Piper, Otto. *Der Spuk. 250 Gespenstergeschichten aller Arten und Zeiten aus der Welt des Übersinnlichen.* Munich: Piper, 1922.

Pluquet, Frédéric. *Contes populaires, préjugés, patois, proverbes, noms de lieux, de l'arrondissement de Bayeux.* Rouen: E. Frère, 1834.

Podmore, Frank. *Modern Spiritualism.* London: Methuen, 1902.

Pons, Christoph. *Le spectre et le voyant. Les échanges entre morts et vivants en Islande.* Paris: P.U.P.S., 2002.

Poulain, Albert. *Sorcellerie, revenants et croyances en Haute-Bretagne.* Rennes: Editions Ouest-France, 1997.

Pourrat, Henri. *Légendes du pays vert.* Rodez: Subervie, 1974.

Proceedings of the American Society for Psychical Research. London: Kegan Paul, 1897.

Pugh, Jane. *Welsh ghosts, poltergeists and demons. A collection of stories, ancient and modern.* Denbigh: Pugh, 1978.

Puls, H. von. *Spukgeschichten. Der Spuk von Resau.* Berlin: self-published, n.d. [ca. 1900].

Rechenberg, F. W. *Die Geheimnisse des Tages. Geschichten und Wesen der klopfenden Geister und tanzenden Tische von der ersten Wahrnehmung ihrer Existenz an bis auf die neueste Zeit.* Leipzig: Otto Spamer, 1853.

Reiser, Karl. *Sagen, Gebräuche und Sprichwörter des Allgäus,* vol. 1. Kempten: J. Kosel, 1894.

Revue des Traditions populaires 13 (1898).

Robe, Stanley Linn. *Hispanic Legends from New Mexico: Narratives from the Rev. D. Jameson Collection.* Berkeley: University of California Press, 1980.

Roll, William G. "The Changing Perspective on Life after Death." *Advances in Parapsychlogical Research,* vol. 3. New York: Plenum Press, 1982.

Salter, William H. *The Society for Psychical Research: An Outline of Its History.* London: Society for Psychical Research, 1948.

Sand, George. *Légendes rustiques.* Edited by Christian Pirot. Paris: Alexandrine, 2000.

Sasso, Luisa. "Le phénomène des pierres frappantes d'Issime (Val d'Aoste) en 1909. Le témoignage du curé Grat Vesan." *Le Monde alpin et rhodanien* 1999/4 (1999): 39–54.

Sauvé, Léopold-François. *Le folk-lore des Hautes-Vosges.* Paris: Maisonneuve and Larose, 1967.

Schambach, George, and Wilheim Müller. *Niedersächsische Sagen und Märchen.* Göttingen: Vandenhoeck and Ruprecht, 1854.

Schenda, Rudolf. *Von Mund zu Ohr. Bausteine zu einer Kulturgeschichte volkstümlichen Erzählens in Europa.* Göttingen: Vandenhoeck and Ruprecht, 1993.

Schloempf, Felix, ed. *Das Gespensterbuch.* Munich: Müller, 1920.

Sébillot, Paul. *Le Folklore de France.* Paris: Imago, 1988.

———. *Littérature orale de l'Auvergne.* Paris: Maisonneuve, 1898.

———. *Traditions et superstitions de la Haute-Bretagne.* Paris: Maisonneuve, 1881.

Seignolles, Claude. *Le diable dans la tradition populaire.* Paris: Maisonneuve, 1959.

———. *Les Evangiles du diables. Le Grand et le Petit Albert.* Paris: Maisonneuve, 1998.

Sitwell, Sacheverell. *Poltergeists: An Introduction and Examination Followed by Chosen Instances.* New York: University Books, 1959.

Solymossy, Sándor. *Contes et légendes de Hongrie.* Paris: Les Editions Internationales, 1936.

Spencer, John, and Anne Spencer. *The Poltergeist Phenomenon.* London: 1997.

Stöber, August. *Die Sagen des Elsasses.* Saint-Gallen: Scheitlin and Zollikofer, 1858.

Thurston, Henry. *Ghosts and Poltergeists.* New York: Regnery, 1954.

Underwood, Peter. *The A–Z of British Ghosts: An Illustrated Guide to 236 Haunted Sites.* London: Bounty Books, 1993.

Valk, Ülo. *The Black Gentleman: Manifestations of the Devil in Estonian Folk Religion.* FFC 276. Helsinki: Suomalainen Tiedeakateia, 2001.

Vaugeois, M. E. "Légendes et curiosités de Nantes et du pays nantais." *Revue des Traditions populaires* 13 (1898): 129–50.

Vesan, Romain. "Les diables dans la Vallaise." *Messager Valdôtain* (1912): 84–87.

Virtanen, Leea. *"That Must Have Been ESP!" An Examination of Psychic Experiences.* Bloomington and Indianapolis: Indiana University Press, 1990.

Von der Hagen, Friedrich Heinrich. *Gesamtabenteuer, hundert altdeutsche Erzählungen,* 3 vols. Stuttgart and Tübingen: Cotta, 1850.

Von Görres, Johann Joseph. *Die christliche Mystik,* vol 3. Regensburg: Manz, 1879.

Waibl, Joseph, and Hermann Flamm. *Badisches Sagenbuch,* vol. 1. Freiburg: Waibl, 1898.

Wallon, Philippe. *Expliquer le paranormal. Les niveaux du mental.* Paris: Albin Michel, 1996.

———. *Le Paranormal.* Paris: PUF, 1999.

———. "Poltergeist." In Sbalchiero, Patrick. *Dictionnaire des miracles et de l'extraordinaire chrétien.* Paris: Fayard, 2002.

Warner, David. *Ottonian Germany: The Chronico of Thietmar of Merseberg.* Manchester: Manchester University Press, 2001.

Whitaker, Terence. *Ghosts of Old England.* London: Robert Hale, 1987.

Wilson, Colin. *Poltergeist: A Study in Destructive Haunting.* Sevenoaks: New English Library, 1982.

Winer, Richard, and Nancy Osborn. *Haunted Houses.* New York: Bantam Book, 1979.

Wossidlo, R. *Mecklenburgische Sagen,* vol. 2. Rostock: Christopher Schmidt, 1939.

Yuan Mei. *Chinesische Geistergeschichten.* Translated by R. Schwarz. Frankfurt and Leipzig: Insel, 1979.

DICTIONARIES

Collins English Dictionary. London: Collins, 2002.

Dictionnaire alphabétique et analogique de la langue française. Paris: Le Robert, 1993.

Harrap's Standard French and English Dictionary. London and Paris: Harrap, 1977

Kluge, Friedrich. *Etymologisches Wörterbuch der deutschen Sprache,* 22nd edition. Berlin and New York: Walter de Gruyter, 1989.

Nouveau Larousse illustré. Dictionnaire universal encyclopédique. Paris: Larousse, 1897.

Pfeifer, Wolfgang. *Etymologisches Wörterbuch des Deutschen.* Berlin: Akademie Verlag, 1989.

Thompson, Stith. *Motif-Index of Folk-Literature.* Revised edition. Bloomington: Indiana University Press, 1955–1958.

Trousset, Jules. *Nouveau Dictionnaire encyclopédie illustré.* Paris: Librarie Illustrée, 1891.

Wolman, Benjamin B. *Encyclopedia of Psychiatry, Psychology, and Psychoanalysis.* New York: Holt, 1996.

Index

Page numbers in *italics* indicate illustrations.